MOSELEY ROAD INC.
International Rights and Packaging
32 N. Dutcher St.,
Irvington, NY 10533
www.moseleyroad.com.

President **Sean Moore**
International Rights
Karen Prince: kprince@moseleyroad.com

Written by **Ariel Slick**
Series Management: **Oiloften.co.uk**
Editors: **Duncan Youel and Fiona Baile**
Book design: **Nicola Plumb**
Series art direction and covers: **Duncan Youel**
Picture research: **Sean Moore, Nicola Plumb**

Other titles in the series: **The Mythology of Ancient Greece** | **Norse Mythology**

Printed in China

ISBN 978-1-62669-223-7

10 9 8 7 6 5 4 3 2 1 21 22 23 24 25

THE DEFINITIVE GUIDE TO

EGYPTIAN MYTHOLOGY

ARIEL SLICK | FIONA BAILE

THE GODS, HEROES, MONSTERS, AND LEGENDS OF ANCIENT EGYPT

CONTENTS

Ancient Egypt was a Bronze Age civilization concentrated along the lower reaches of the Nile River. It is one of six civilizations that evolved independently of outside cultural influences.

EGYPT

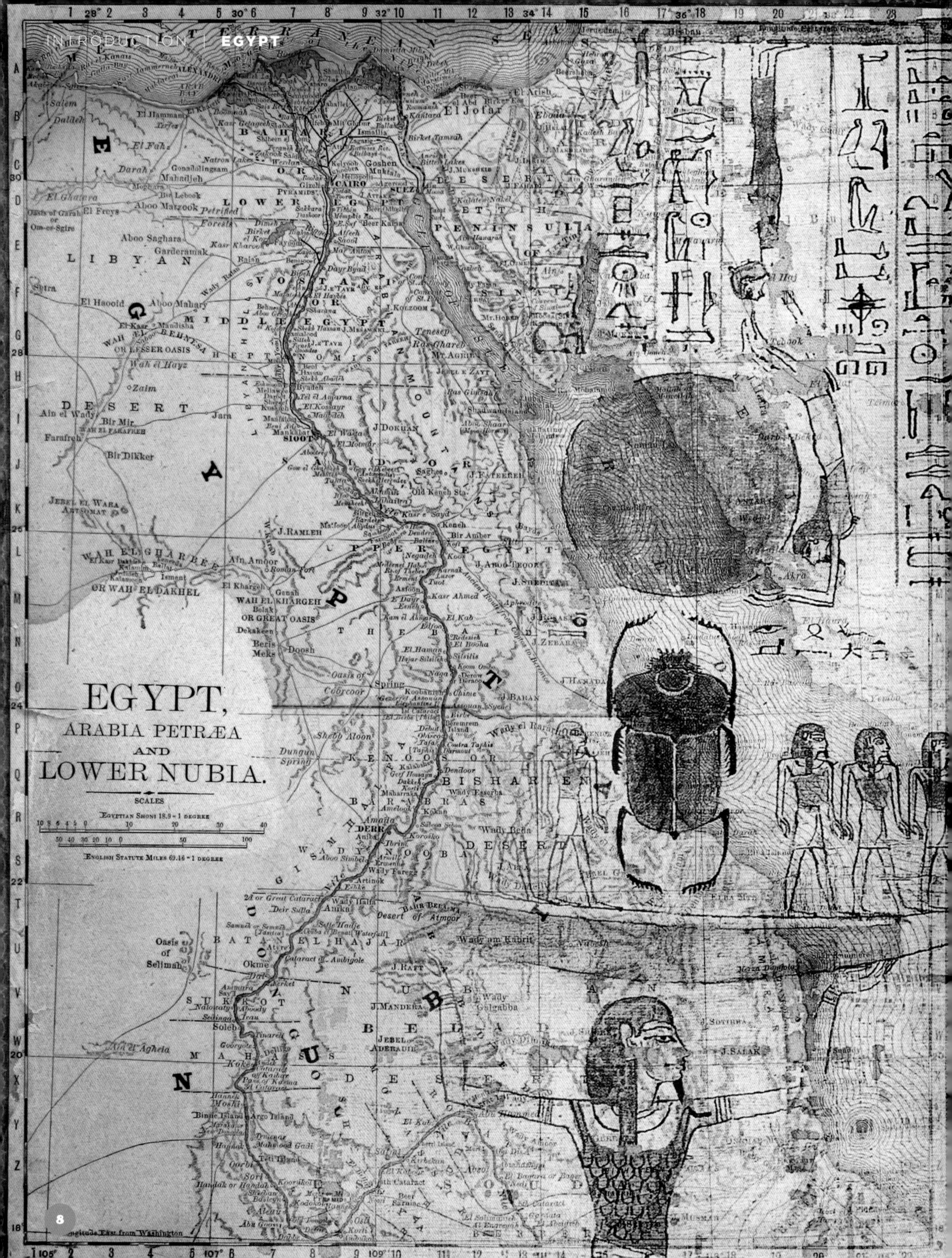
EGYPT,
ARABIA PETRÆA
AND
LOWER NUBIA.
SCALES
EGYPTIAN SHONI 18.9 = 1 DEGREE
ENGLISH STATUTE MILES 69.16 = 1 DEGREE
CAIRO
ALEXANDRIA
LIBYAN
DESERT
LOWER EGYPT
MIDDLE EGYPT
UPPER EGYPT
THEBAID
SUEZ
PENINSULA OF SINAI
WAH EL KHARGEH
OR GREAT OASIS
BISHARIEN
Longitude East from Washington

The ancient Egyptian civilization was complex and intricate, with a highly structured society and system of beliefs.

EGYPTIAN MYTHOLOGY

It was a monotheistic country, but because of the way it had evolved, a superficial polytheism also existed—a consequence of the union of various gods from individual cities, all under the aegis of the god-pharaohs who had unified the country.

Each pharaoh was not only the religious head chosen by god, he was god himself. When he died, his soul continued to live near his body, hence the care taken with mummification and preservation. Great emphasis was placed on the importance of funeral practices, particularly with regard to royalty: bodies were embalmed with rare and exotic oils and ointments, and ritual practices were observed before the body was placed in a sarcophagus. The dead pharaoh would join the god Osiris in paradise, and he would have need of many things for the journey. He was furnished with ushabti dolls—funerary figurines, and statuettes—servants who would do his bidding in the realm of the god.

The ancient Egyptians also venerated a host of different gods, many of which were animal figures, or a strange mixture of the real and imagined—like the Sphinx, with a feline body and human head.

Writing consisted of hieroglyphs—pictograms, which were carved into stone or painted on papyrus, and which covered every aspect of Egyptian life, from trade agreements written on tablets, to inscriptions on columns telling the history of pharaohs and gods. These were augmented by shallow-relief carvings showing various events in Egyptian life, or of victories over enemies. That ancient Egypt was so successful in the building of pyramids and other giant constructions, depended entirely on slave labour, and the difficulties of moving stone and other heavy materials were solved by merely increasing the size of their slave armies—taken as the primary spoil of war.

But fundamental to the entire Civilization and its continuing success was the river Nile—the life-blood of Egypt. The river not only provided transit between different settlements, but, essentially, it also watered the crops at the time of the annual flood, bringing silt to enrich the soil with vital minerals, and thereby sustaining the population.

TOP: A statuette of Anubis, the god of mummification, greeting the deceased into the afterlife; **ABOVE:** Anubis in jackal form. It is speculated that jackal statues like this would have originally stood in the pavilions used for embalming.

From the earliest times in the region which became Egypt, as elsewhere in the Paleolithic (Old Stone Age) era, humans were nomadic hunter-gatherers who survived from hunting, fishing and gathering plants.

PERIODS OF ANCIENT EGYPT

ABOVE: Naqada II jar decorated with gazelles.

PRE-DYNASTIC PERIOD

From the beginning of the Neolithic (New Stone Age) era, around 12,000 BC, to the early Bronze Age, around 3500 BC, fixed human settlements had appeared with the discovery of crop-growing and primitive farming. People collected around the Nile because it was an easy source of food and water—and provided optimum conditions for agriculture. These settlements were composed of small, self-governing tribes, which culturally, and politically, developed at different rates.

Crafts began to be discernible, notably stone masonry, early metal-working, jewelry-making, and pottery. As people and tribes began to specialize, trade emerged and settlements grew into small cities. What was to become the ancient nation of Egypt began to form around two main areas, both centered on the Nile: Upper and Lower Egypt, the former referring to the south of Egypt and the latter to the northern Nile Delta area.

EGYPT IN THE OLD KINGDOM c.2649–2130 BC

ABOVE: The Narmer Palette depicts the unification of the Two Lands and some of the earliest hieroglyphic inscriptions ever found; **ABOVE LEFT:** Ivory label depicting the pharaoh Den, found at his tomb in Abydos, circa 3000 BC. The side shown here depicts the pharaoh striking down an Asiatic tribesman along with the inscription "The first occasion of smiting the East."

EARLY DYNASTIC PERIOD
1ST & 2ND DYNASTIES
C.3150 TO 2686 BC

The first king to unite Upper and Lower Egypt was Menes (also confusingly known as Narmer), around 3150 BC, though each tribal region kept much of its original identity, and autonomy. During the First and Second Dynasties the capital was established at Memphis in Lower Egypt, just south of present-day Cairo. In Abydos and Saqqara bodies were interred in mastaba tombs, which were rock pits dug into the ground with a mud-brick structure above. During this period servants were sacrificed and buried with the dead king, although after the Second Dynasty, ushabti dolls representing servants began to be used instead. Kings were interred with everything they might need in the afterlife, including furniture, animal figures, and models of boats.

DYNASTY 5 c.2465–2323 BC

NEBKA II c.2494–2490 BC

SHEPSESKAF c.2472–2467 BC

THAMPHTHIS c.2467–2465 BC

USERKAF c.2465–2458 BC

SAHURE c.2458–2446 BC

NEFERIRKARE c.2446–2438 BC

SHEPSESKARE c.2438–2431 BC

NEFEREFRE c.2431–2420 BC

NIUSERRE c.2420–2389 BC

MENKAUHOR c.2389–2381 BC

ISESI c.2381–2353 BC

UNIS c.2353–2323 BC

TOP: A statue of Djoser of the 3rd Dynasty; **ABOVE:** This close up section of the funerary stele of Intef II was thought to be one of many small stela set up in the courtyard of his tomb at Thebes. The king is shown presenting a bowl of beer and a jug of milk to the god Re and the goddess Hathor.

OLD KINGDOM
3RD - 6TH DYNASTIES
2686 TO 2181 BC

This was the era of the great pyramids, built as royal tombs. During the Third Dynasty, Djoser commissioned Imhotep, his chief minister, (who was later elevated to god status) to build the step pyramid. During the Fourth and Fifth Dynasties, Sneferu had three pyramids built, and his son Khufu commanded the construction of the great Pyramid of Giza. Egyptian trade expanded to into Nubia, Libya and near Asia. Around this time, the priests became more powerful, concurrent with a shift of control away from the pharaoh and back to a more tribal level.

FIRST INTERMEDIATE PERIOD
7TH - 10TH DYNASTIES
2181 TO 2055 BC

The intermediate periods of ancient Egyptian history were characterized by instability and governmental chaos. For around 125 years, two competing factions vied for power in Upper Egypt—one based on the west bank of the Nile at Hierakonpolis and the other further north, on the eastern bank of the river, at Thebes. Political unrest arose from a period of poor harvests, low Nile flooding, and the steady decline of centralised power. Eventually the Theban ruler Mentuhotep gained control of the whole region, and Egypt was once again unified.

MIDDLE KINGDOM
11TH - 13TH DYNASTIES
2055 TO 1650 BC

As a consequence of the political instability of the Intermediate Period, there was a strong shift to centralized power—and the pharaohs once again ruled from Memphis. To enable a more controlled future transfer of power, the pharaohs introduced the concept of co-regency, in which their successor (most often a son), ruled alongside them. However, during the Thirteenth Dynasty, Egypt was invaded.

TETI
c.2323-2291 BC

PEPI I
c.2289-2255 BC

MERENRE I
c.2255-2246 BC

DYNASTY 6 c.2323-2150 BC

USERKARE
c.2291-2289 BC

PEPI II
c.2246-2152 BC

FIRST INTE

DYNASTY 7

MERENRE II
c.2152-2152 BC

NETJERKARE SIPTAH
c.2152-2150 BC

SECOND INTERMEDIATE PERIOD
14TH- 17TH DYNASTIES
1650 TO 1550 BC

Invaders known as the Hyksos, who may have come from Palestine, captured the Nile Delta region of Lower Egypt, and imposed their rule in the north of the nation, whilst the Egyptian kings continued to govern from Thebes. The Hyksos had invaded Egypt with horses and chariots—a technological advance which soon transformed Egyptian methods of warfare.

NEW KINGDOM
18TH - 20TH DYNASTIES
1550 TO 1069 BC

In the Eighteenth Dynasty, under Ahmose I, the Egyptians wrested power back from the invaders. During the New Kingdom Period, Egypt pushed into new territory in the south and east, and expanded its borders. Alliances were also made with kingdoms in Western Asia. The New Kingdom Period also saw a flourishing of the arts, literature, and architecture. Huge temples and other edifices were constructed, and this Period is known for its succession of great rulers: Queen Hatshepsut, Amenhotep, Akhenaten, and Tutankhamun, among others. However, Egypt once again experienced a decline in central authority, as more incursions by foreign armies weakened the pharaoh's authority. At the same time, the priesthood of the major Egyptian deity, Amun, had garnered power (and great wealth) from the popularity of their god, and eventually usurped the pharaoh's power.

TOP: Remnants of a sculpture of Queen Hatshepsut—a female pharaoh who reigned for nearly twenty years in the fifteenth century BC; **ABOVE:** Sandstone sculpture of Tutankhamun.

EDIATE PERIOD c.2150-2030 BC

MENTUHOTEP II
c.2051-2030 BC

DYNASTY 11 (FIRST HALF) c.2124-2030 BC

INTEF I
c.2120-2108 BC

INTEF II
c.2108-2059 BC

INTEF III
c.2059-2051 BC

MENTUHOTEP I
c.2124-2120 BC

THIRD INTERMEDIATE PERIOD
21ST - 24TH DYNASTIES
1069 TO 664 BC

During the Twenty-first Dynasty, power once again divided in two, with the Pharaoh Smendes ruling from the Nile Delta region, and the priests of Amun ruling Upper Egypt down in the south. The Twenty-second, Twenty-third, and Twenty-fourth Dynasties were ruled simultaneously in different parts of Egypt.

LATE DYNASTIC PERIOD
25TH - 30TH DYNASTIES
664 TO 332 BC

By the Twenty-fifth Dynasty, a ruler from the kingdom of Kush, to the south of Egypt, had gained control in Thebes. It was in this period that the Greeks began settling the Mediterranean coast of the African continent.

In the Late Dynastic, Egypt did not have an Egyptian king until the Twenty-eighth Dynasty. During this time Assyrians from the east took control of Egypt, and ruled until the Twenty-sixth Dynasty. Then, in 525 BC, armies of the Achaemenid, the first great Persian Empire, invaded the country and established power with the Twenty-seventh Dynasty. One hundred and twenty years later, in 404 BC, the Egyptian armies finally overthrew the Persians, and ruled the Twenty-eighth to the Thirtieth Dynasties—though the Persian Empire invaded once more, in 343 BC, and Darius III became pharaoh of Egypt. At this time also, all Egyptian Jews were expelled to Babylon, by the Euphrates River, in present-day Iraq.

MACEDONIAN AND PTOLEMAIC PERIODS
332 TO 30 BC

In 332 BC, the armies of Alexander the Great, the famous martial leader of the Greek kingdom of Macedon, overran the sitting Persian army in Egypt, as part of his grand plan to conquer all of the Persian Empire. In 331 BC he founded the Egyptian coastal city of Alexandria. After his death in 323 BC, control of Egypt passed to Ptolemy I Soter, who had been the Macedonian administrator under Alexander. The Ptolemies ruled for almost 300 years, until 30 BC, and as well as carrying out many successful irrigation and land reclamation projects, making Egypt one of the wealthiest countries in the Mediterranean, they shifted the capital to Alexandria—which only served to increase Greek Hellenistic influence on Egyptian art and culture. There was much assimilation and syncretization of religious ideas with the Greek religion during this time.

THE ROMAN PERIOD
BC-AD 337

For over a hundred years since the defeat of the Greeks by the Roman Empire at the Battle of Corinth in 146 BC, Rome's influence in the Mediterranean had been growing inexorably, and the definitive Roman occupation of the Greek world was established after the Battle of Actium in 31 BC, when Augustus defeated Cleopatra VII, the Greek Ptolemaic Queen of Egypt, and her lover, the Roman General Mark Antony, with Octavian later taking the

MIDDLE KINGDOM c.2030-1640 BC

DYNASTY 11 - (SECOND HALF) c.2030-1981 BC

MENTUHOTEP II c.2124-2120 BC

MENTUHOTEP III c.2000-1988 BC

QAKARE INTEF c.198 5BC

SEKHENTIBRE c.198 5BC

MENEKHKARE c.198 5BC

MENTUHOTEP IV c.1988-1981 BC

DYNASTY 12 c.1981-1802 BC

AMENEMHAT I c.1981-1952 BC

AMENEMHAT I c.1919-1885 BC

Egyptian Capital of Alexandria—by then the last great city of Hellenistic Greece—in 30 BC. Cleopatra VII and her brother were the last of the Ptolemies. Roman emperors took control of Egypt and it became part of the larger Roman Empire.

BYZANTINE EMPIRE AND BEYOND

During the fourth century AD, the Roman Emperor ordered all pagan temples to be closed—effectively the death knell for the old Egyptian religion. Some cults survived for a while, but then the Emperor Justinian ordered the last of the temples to be closed. When the Roman Empire was divided between Rome and Byzantium, Egypt became part of the Byzantine Empire. It developed a unique form of Christianity, which incorporated elements of Egyptian and Greek religion. Three hundred years later, during the seventh century AD, the Arabs invaded and established Islam as Egypt's state religion. Because Egyptian religion was effectively destroyed, the meaning of hieroglyphs was lost, until the discovery of the Rosetta Stone in July 1799 by French Officer Pierre-Francois Bouchard, during Napoleon's Egyptian Campaign. When the British took Alexandria from the French in 1801 the Rosetta Stone was seized and taken to London. It has been on display in the British Museum ever since, and is the Museum's most visited object.

TOP: Marble bust of Alexander the Great made in Alexandria (c. 200BC); **ABOVE:** Coins minted in Alexandria depicting the Lighthouse at Alexandria; **LEFT, MAIN IMAGE:** A detail of the Nile mosaic of Palestrina, depicting life in Ptolemaic Egypt (c. 100 BC); **LEFT, INSET:** The Rosetta Stone is inscribed with three versions of a decree issued in Memphis, Egypt during the Ptolemaic dynasty on behalf of King Ptolemy V Epiphanes. The top and middle texts are in Ancient Egyptian using hieroglyphic and Demotic scripts respectively, while the bottom is in Ancient Greek. The decree has only minor differences between the three versions, making the Rosetta Stone key to deciphering the Egyptian scripts.

SENWOSRET II
c.1887–1878 BC

SENWOSRET III
c.1878–1840 BC

AMENEMHAT III
c.1859–1813 BC

AMENEMHAT IV
c.1814–1805 BC

NEFRUSOBEK
c.1805–180 2 BC

DYNASTY 13 c.1802–1640 BC

The ancient Egyptians worshiped hundreds of gods and goddesses. They lived in a world rife with danger and needed a way to understand the natural and frequently hazardous phenomena around them.

EGYPTIAN RELIGION

ABOVE: Bastet was a goddess in the ancient Egyptian religion; **RIGHT:** Anubis attending a mummy of the deceased.

THE GODS

Much of what they encountered—storms, lightning, solar eclipses, famine, pregnancy and birth, and health problems, were challenging events which could be helped by appealing to deities. Where there was chaos, religion infused meaning and brought order and stability.

The gods and goddesses gave a meaning and explanation to the unknowable—the mystery of darkness and night, and of illness and death.

Religion was central to the lives of ancient Egyptians. They did not have one sole sacred book into which they consolidated their ideas. There was no single explanation of the divine origins of mankind and the universe, and many myths contradicted each other. Each cult center had its own version of events and it is impossible to say with any certainty which was the most popular at any given time during the 3000 year span of Ancient Egypt.

The gods and goddesses were often depicted in animal form for several reasons. One was that the gods embodied the attribute of a certain animal. For example, the lion was associated with strength and ferocity, the ram with fertility. Another reason was that there were many dangerous animals: crocodiles, hippos, lions, jackals, other desert felines, snakes, and scorpions. By worshiping the god in its animal form, it was thought that the god could be placated and the danger reduced.

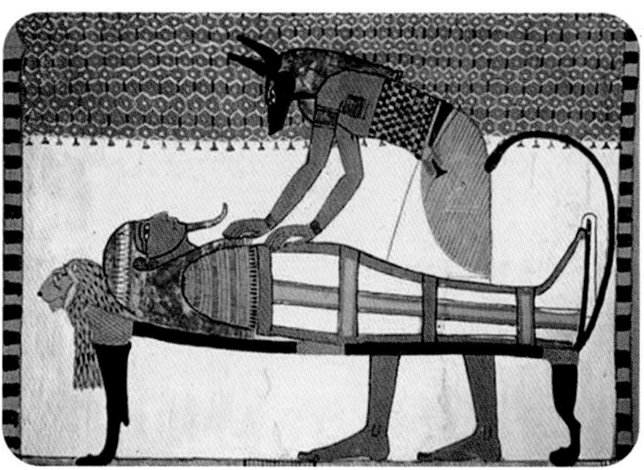

SECOND INTERMEDIATE PERIOD c.1640–1540 BC

DYNASTY 14–16 c.2030–1981 BC

DYNASTY 17 c.1635–1550 BC

TAO I c.1560 BC

TAO II c.1560 BC

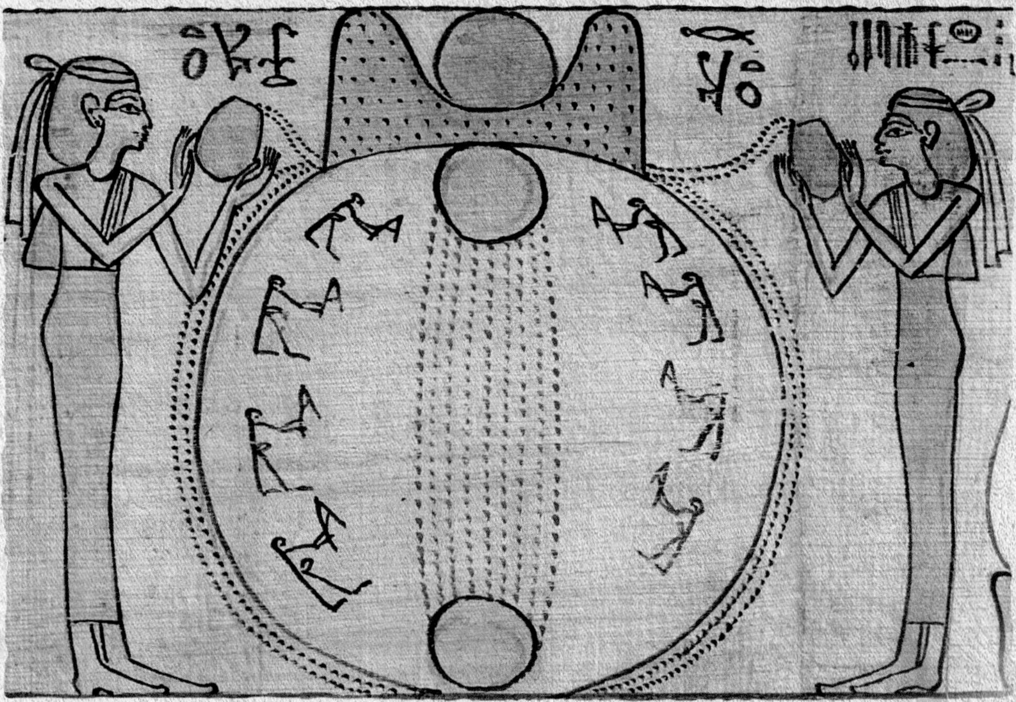

ABOVE: Statuette of Wadjet, in the name of Akanosh son of Pediamenopet; **TOP:** The human spirit is ready for its journey through the underworld. There, the person's heart will be judged by the person's good deeds on earth. If the heart is found to be pure he will be sent to live for all eternity in the beautiful 'Field of Reeds,' or possibly sent to Ammit; **LEFT:** The sun rises over the circular mound of creation as goddesses pour out the primeval waters around it.

KAMOSE
c.1552–1550 BC

NEW KINGDOM c.1550–1070 BC

DYNASTY 18 c.1550–1295 BC

AHMOSE
c.1550–1525 BC

AMENHOTEP I
c.1525–1504 BC

THUTMOSE I
c.1504–1492 BC

THUTMOSE II
c.1492–1479 BC

THUTMOSE III
c.1479–1425 BC

HATSHEPSUT (AS REGENT)
c.1479–1473 BC

HATSHEPSUT
c.1479–1473 BC

BELIEFS

TOP: Wall relief at Karnak Temple showing the Egyptian Ka Symbol; **ABOVE:** Maat wearing the feather of truth.

KA, BA AND AKH

There are three concepts which were used to describe the 'soul' of ancient Egyptians. Ka is usually translated as 'spirit' or 'creative life force'. The ka was tied to the physical body and it was not entirely without substance as it still needed physical nourishment after death. For this reason Egyptians buried food and drink with mummies in the coffin. The ka was said to come into existence at the time of birth.

Ba was the concept of the soul, although direct translation is difficult. It was the idea of a non-physical entity that made each human unique. It also implied the 'moral essence' of a person. It was through this that someone could move through the afterlife.

The akh is sometimes translated as 'transfigured spirit'. It was essentially the soul of a deceased person. It was said that when the ba and ka united at death, the spirit could pass on to paradise. If they did not, the person was doomed to eternal death.

MAAT

Maat was the principle woven into ancient Egyptian moral code and served as the basis for it. It is usually translated as 'truth', 'order', 'justice', and 'balance'. The ancient Egyptians personified maat with the goddess Maat, and she was the one whose feather decided the fate of those who had died. Maat was the concept that there should be order and harmony in the universe, a balance ahat defined everything. When someone did something morally wrong, the balance of maat was off, and so disharmony ensued. It defined the fundamental role of the pharaoh, who was supposed to uphold maat by worshiping the gods and making the appropriate sacrifices. Its opposite was the concept of isfet, which was chaos, disharmony, disunity and evil.

People in ancient Egypt were expected to lead a life that was in accordance with maat; that is, to behave in a socially responsible and ethical way. It was important to live a just life overall, so that when the time came for one's heart to be weighed on the scale, the heart would be lighter than Maat's feather.

By observing maat, people could maintain the balance between the gods and humans. Living with maat meant being respectful, hardworking, unselfish, quiet, modest, trustworthy, and humble. Only by living in accordance with maat could the entire society survive and thrive. If there was an imbalance, Egyptians believed that the kingdom was susceptible to invasion, disease and drought.

CONCEPT OF DUALITY

Another vital concept in ancient Egyptian religious belief was duality. Everything had its dual opposite; in this way, maat was maintained.

DYNASTY 18 c.1550–1295 BC

AMENHOTEP II c.1427–1400 BC

THUTMOSE IV c.1400–1390 BC

AMENHOTEP III c.1390–1352 BC

AMENHOTEP IV c.1353–1349 BC

AKHENATEN c.1349–1336 BC

NEFERNEFERUATON c.1338–1336 BC

SMENKHKARE c.1336 BC

TUTANKHAMUN ca.1336–1327 BC

AYA c.1327–1323 BC

HAREMHAB c.1323–1295 BC

DYNASTY 19 c.1295–1186 BC

RAMESSES I c.1295–1294 BC

SETI I c.1294–1279 BC

RAMESSES II c.1279–1213 BC

Even maat itself had its opposite in isfet, chaos or disorder. A state of chaos must exist for equilibrium to be achieved. Hence, duality pervaded almost every aspect of religious belief. Many gods and goddesses came to have a counterpart. For example, Horus was associated with goodness, righteousness, and order, but Seth, his enemy, was associated with chaos and evil. Only by having both could a sense of completeness be achieved.

The sense of duality also applied to the world and in nature. For example, the Nile was a place of water, and it deposited rich, black soil that helped fertilize the crops every year. Life along the Nile flourished, and Egypt was known as "Kemet," to the Egyptians, meaning "Black Land," for the soil. On the other hand, the desert flanking the Nile to the east and west was known as the "Red Land," or "Deshret." Unlike the fertile land around the river, the desert was arid, barren, devoid of life, and a place of chaotic sandstorms.

Duality as part of Egyptian theological and social life is perhaps why the pharaoh was considered the "Lord of Two Lands." Egypt was not considered one single kingdom but rather the unification of Upper and Lower Egypt. The hieroglyphs used to represent the unification of Egypt reflect the duality. They contain two Nile gods, one with papyrus and the other with the lotus flower. The papyrus was associated with Lower Egypt (in the north) and the lotus was a symbol of Upper Egypt (in the South).

The pharaoh himself reflected the concept of duality, both in his titles and in his royal regalia. One of his titles was "Nsw Bity," which translates to "He of the Sedge and the Bee." The bee was a symbol of the Delta region in the north, and the sedge represented the Nile valley. He was also called "He of the Two Ladies," referring to Nekhbet and Wadjet, who it was said protected him. In addition, many depictions of pharaohs show him wearing both the White Crown of Upper Egypt and the Red Crown of Lower Egypt. In short, everything had its equal and opposite concept, and both needed to exist for the universe to have harmony.

MAGIC

The word for "magic" in ancient Egypt was "heka," which was a concept of energy or the catalyst that made all things possible. Belief in magic pervaded every stratum of society, and it wasn't considered counterculture at all. Rather, everyone believed in magic. Magic was not thought to be good or bad; it was neutral, but it could be channeled according to the wielder's intention and purpose. Heka was associated with "sia," or "divine knowledge," and "hu," which was "divine utterance." A similar concept was akhu, which is usually translated as "sorcery." There were some people who were considered intrinsically infused with heka, such as pharaohs, deities, the dead, and dwarves. Sometimes, people could gain heka during special periods of their life; for instance, women who breast-fed were thought to have an increased amount of heka at that time.

TOP: Relief of the god Horus in the Temple of Edfu; **ABOVE:** The ba is an aspect of a person's non-physical being. After death, the ba was able to travel out from the tomb, but it had to periodically return to be reunited with the mummy. The ba was usually represented as a bird with a human head, and sometimes with human arms. It's shown here as an amulet.

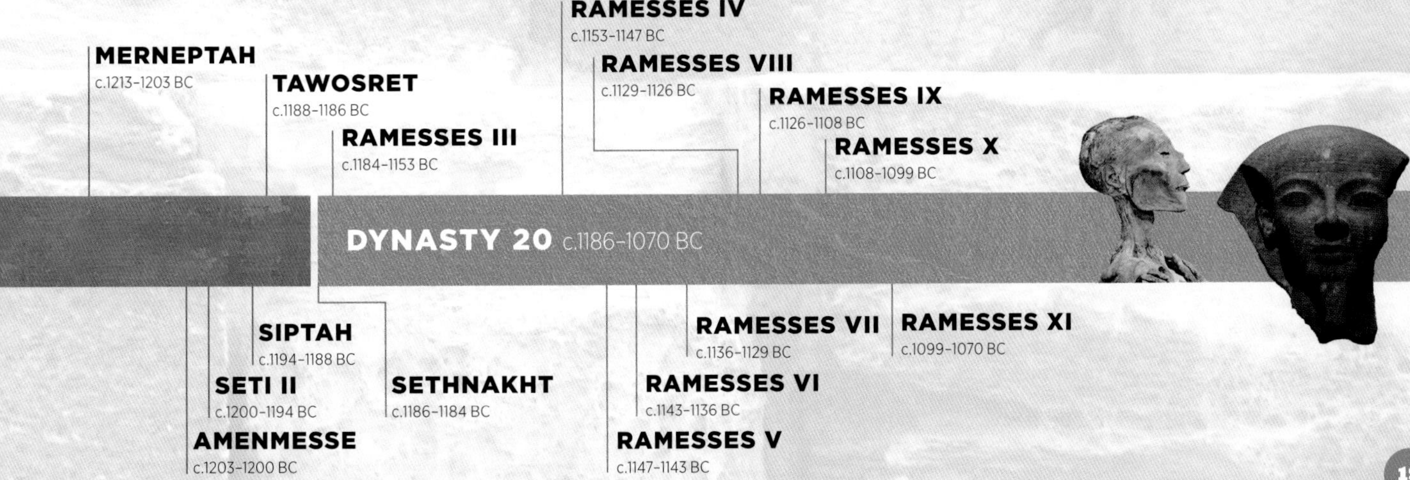

INFLUENCE OF THE DEAD

TOP: Pendant of Tutankhamun; **ABOVE:** The ancient Egyptians put green stone scarab beetles into the coffins of important people alongside their mummified bodies.

POSITIVE INFLUENCE

The ancient Egyptians believed that the deceased (especially relatives) had supernatural powers and could solve different problems for the living. They were called on for help with infertility issues, illnesses, and even legal trouble. Special "letters to the dead," have survived, and these were letters written to specific deceased persons on pottery, linen and were likely written on papyrus as well. For letters written on pottery dishes, it is presumed that the bowl would be filled with food as an offering, and then when the spirit "ate" the food, the writing would appear. Some of the letters beseech ancestors, and the living invoke the link between themselves and their ancestors.

In the case of fertility issues, ancient Egyptians would inscribe a request for a woman to become pregnant on a small figurine. The figurines would have exaggerated pubic areas, symbolizing sexuality and fertility. These figurines were offered to the dead. A typical inscription might read something like, "May a birth be granted." The ancient Egyptians strongly believed in the power of the written word, so inscribing a request was meant to promote the potency of the spell.

The dead were believed to be able to give help both in the divine court, in the case of legal justice, or be able to influence magical forces, in the case of illnesses and infertility.

NEGATIVE INFLUENCE

Just as the dead could positively influence a person's life, so, too could troubled spirits cause difficulties. If someone had died violently, too young, or without a proper burial, it was believed that their soul was disturbed and could wreak havoc on the living. If livestock suddenly died, a severe disease struck a family, or other (minor) disasters, then the unsettled spirit of the dead could be to blame. Perhaps reflecting the patriarchal nature of the Egyptian society, dead women tended to be blamed more often as troublesome spirits. Female ghosts were considered especial threats against pregnant and nursing women.

THIRD INTERMEDIATE PERIOD c.1070-713 BC

HIGH PRIESTS OF AMUN c.1080-1070 BC

HIGH P HERIHOR c.1080-1074 BC

HP PAIANKH c.1074-1070 BC

DYNASTY 21 c.1070-945 BC

SMENDES c.1070-1044 BC

HP PAINEDJEM I c.1070-1032 BC

HP MASAHARTA c.1054-1046 BC

HP DJEDKHONSEFANKH c.1046-1045 BC

HP MENKHEPERRE c.1045-992 BC

AMENEMNISU c.1044-1040 BC

PSUSENNES c.1040-992 BC

In ancient Egyptian belief, a mut was thought to be a ghost who could not pass on to the land of the dead, and so continued to wander on Earth, disrupting the lives of the living. "Mut" is usually translated as "dangerous dead." The ancient Egyptians used spells to protect themselves against the malignant ghosts and wore amulets to ward off their negative influence. They also carved special figures to keep evil at bay and protect their families. Just as the dead could bring healing, evil ghosts were blamed if a person became sick. Moreover, even a relatively benign spirit was thought to attack the living if their wrath was incurred (usually by tomb robbery).

Ancient Egyptians practiced exorcism to rid the influence of malignant ghosts. In exorcism rituals, the name of the spirit was defaced, and this symbolized the destruction of the spirit, and it was believed that the spirit's power and influence would break.

ABOVE: Fragment of coffin of Muthetepi c.747-656 BC. Book of the Dead, spell 79, attaching the soul to the body; and spell 80, Preventing incoherent speech.

AMENEMOPE
c.993–984 BC

OSOCHOR
c.984–978 BC

PSUSENNES II
c.959–945 BC

OSORKON I
c.924–889 BC

SHESHONQ II
c.890 BC

DYNASTY 22 (LIBYAN) c.945–712 BC

SIAMUN
c.978–959 BC

HP PAINEDJEM II
c.990–969 BC

HP PSUSENNES
c.969–959 BC

SHESHONQ I
.945–924 BC

HP SMENDES
c.992–990 BC

FUNERARY RELIGION

TOP, CENTER: The model represents a funerary barque transporting the deceased Djehuty. The mummified body lies on a bier under a canopy and is tended by two women who play the roles of the goddesses Isis and Nephthys, sisters of the funerary god Osiris; **ABOVE, LEFT:** Cat Statuette intended to contain a mummified cat; **ABOVE, RIGHT:** Mummified cat.

BELIEFS ABOUT THE AFTERLIFE

The ancient Egyptians believed in an afterlife even in pre-dynastic times, although it is difficult to say with any certainty when exactly these beliefs arose. Still, even before the rise of social stratification, there is archaeological evidence for burials with funerary goods. The early practice of burying the body in a fetal position may reflect the belief in rebirth. In any case, it was believed that the body was required to be intact for the Afterlife.

They believed that the dead could rise to heaven on the back of a falcon or other bird, along the air with incense, climbing up a ladder formed by the arms of a god, or traveling on a reed boat, which reflected the belief that Ra sailed through the underworld on a boat. The entire journey to the afterlife was replete with hazards—demons, spirits, and other obstacles needed to be overcome, which is why there were so many magical spells to aid the deceased individual make it to paradise. Egyptian paradise was known as the Field of Satisfaction. It was a beautiful, lush place with an abundance of food, water, and fruit trees. Although some depictions of paradise show people working in fields, no one really expected to do any hard work. By dying, and passing into the afterlife, it was thought that the soul became closer to the gods and that the souls of the deceased could influence the land of the living.

The afterlife was personified as the god Aker, who was an earth divinity often shown as a tract of land. He sometimes has a human or lion head. Because Egyptians held duality to be of great importance, they believed in interdependent aspects of the afterlife. The Field of Satisfaction was associated with the western horizon, and this was balanced by the Field of Reeds, which was a place of purification, associated with the eastern horizon. There is also some evidence of a concept of an underworld were demons resided upside-down and that their mouths were where their anuses should have been.

DYNASTY 22 (LIBYAN) c.945–712 BC

TAKELOT I c.889–874 BC

OSORKON II c.874–850 BC

HARSIESE c.865 BC

TAKELOT II c.850–825 BC

SHESHONQ III c.825–773 BC

PAMI c.773–767 BC

SHESHONQ V c.767–730 BC

OSORKON IV c.730–712 BC

THE WEIGHING OF THE HEART RITUAL

The Ancient Egyptians believed that in order to pass on to paradise, the human soul had to be in balance with ma'at. Thus, a person's soul had to be weighed against all the evil deeds they had committed. The heart was said to be the seat of thought because strong emotions could be felt at the center of the chest. If a person was excited, the heart beat rapidly; love was a warm feeling, and jealousy seemed to make the heart heavy. It was thought that the heart held a record of every deed the person ever did in their lives.

When a person died, it was thought that Anubis led the soul of the deceased to a throne room to stand before Osiris. The goddess Ma'at was there with her feather to weigh against the heart on a golden scale; Thoth recorded the events and whether the person passed on; Ammit stood beside the scale, ready to eat the heart if it was not light enough to pass into paradise. There were also Forty-Two Judges who would confer with the gods on the fate of the person's soul.

The soul would then, according to the Book of the Dead, recite the "Negative Confessions," a series of statements that told the gods that the person had not committed certain (major) sins and tried to live according to the principles of ma'at during their lifetime. Then, Osiris took the heart of the soul and placed it on the golden scale. If the heart was light (free from sin) and lighter than Ma'at's feather, then the soul could pass into paradise—the Field of Reeds. However, if the heart was heavy with sin, it was thrown onto the floor where Ammit would eat it. The soul would then disappear from existence, which, to the ancient Egyptians, was the worst fate possible.

TOP: The weighing of the heart ritual from the Book of the Dead for the Chantress of Amun, Nauny, ca. 1050 BC; **ABOVE:** This scene from the Papyrus of Hunefer (c. 1275 BC), shows the scribe Hunefer's heart being weighed on the scale of Maat, against the feather of truth. If his heart equals exactly the weight of the feather, Hunefer is allowed to pass into the afterlife. If not, he is eaten by the waiting chimeric devouring creature Ammit, composed of the deadly crocodile, lion, and hippopotamus.

DYNASTY 23 c.818–713 BC

- **PEDUBASTE I** c.818–793 BC
- **IUPUT I** c.800 BC
- **SHESHONQ IV** c.793–787 BC
- **OSORKON III** c.787–759 BC
- **TAKELOT III** c.764–757 BC
- **RUDAMUN** c.757–754 BC
- **IUPUT II** c.754–712 BC
- **NAMLOT** c.740 BC
- **PEFTJAUBAST** c.740–725 BC
- **THUTEMHAT** c.720 BC

DYNASTY 24 c.724–712 BC

- **TEFNAKHT** c.724–717 BC
- **BAKENRENEF** c.717–712 BC

ABOVE: In the Roman era, mummies might be kept above ground for periods of some months, up to several years, before final burial. They were thought to have been deposited in chapels within cemeteries, where they were visited by relatives for ritual meals.

MUMMIFICATION

It is thought by some scholars that mummification came about because of bodies being preserved by the hot, dry sands of the desert. During the pre-dynastic times, resin was used to both preserve the body and make it smell better. As Egyptian religious belief became more complex, it was believed that preserving the body was vital to surviving in the afterlife. Moreover, it was thought that when Osiris came back to rule on Earth once more, there would be a great "awakening," and that people would need their bodies to be revived. Embalming the body took about forty days, but the entire ritual of purifying, preparing, and burying took seventy. The Egyptians noted that a group of stars (called the "decan") dipped below the horizon, only to emerge seventy days later. It was their hope that the body would be "reborn" after seventy days, and the soul would live on in the afterlife. It's important to note that only the very wealthy could afford to have the body mummified with all the trappings of the rituals.

PURIFYING THE BODY

When someone died, the body first had to be "purified" in a ritual sense. First, it was transported to an "ibu" ("place of purification,") which was a temporary structure made of reeds located on the west bank of the Nile. The west bank was associated with the setting sun and thus, death. It was strategically located near the Nile for easy access to water. Then, it was washed with palm wine and sweet-smelling herbs and spices. The solution also contained natron, which is a natural salt compound of sodium carbonate and bicarbonate. This was not only a natural antiseptic but also a dehydrating agent, which was a useful first step to preserving the body.

PREPARING THE BODY

Then, the body was moved to a "wabet" ("pure place"), which was a red tent or stone building, but the first embalming houses were made of mudbrick. The Chief Embalmer was known as "He who Controls the Mysteries," and it is thought that they wore a jackal mask to represent Anubis, the god of embalming.

The body was stretched out on a wooden board, and they embalmers first preserved the face by coating it with molten resin. From the Eighteenth Dynasty onward, the embalmer used a hook tool to break the nose bone then scoop out the brain, which was thrown out, as it was considered useless. Then, they stuffed resin-soaked linen or sawdust into the head to preserve its shape. The internal organs, except the heart, were removed, desiccated with natron, preserved in resins and oils, wrapped in linen, and placed into canopic jars (or, in later dynasties, back into the body).

EMBALMING

The body, now without its internal organs, was packed with temporary stuffing then covered in natron and left to dry for forty days. Then, once forty or so days had passed, the temporary stuffing was taken out, and the whole body was rinsed out, washed, and dried. After, the embalmers stuffed resin-soaked linen, natron,

LATE PERIOD c.712–332 BC

DYNASTY 25 (NUBIAN) c.712–664 BC

PIYE c.743–712 BC

SHABAQO c.712–698 B

SHEBITQO c.698–690 BC

TAHARQO c.690–664 BC

TANUTAMANI c.664–653 BC

DYNASTY 26 (SAITE) 688–525 BC

NIKAUBA 688–672 BC

NECHO I 672–664 BC

PSAMTIK I 664–610 BC

sawdust, and other materials into the body to help it retain its shape. During the Late Period, bodies were often filled with only resin. The embalmer anointed the body with juniper oil, beeswax, natron, other spices, milk, and wine. All incisions to remove the organs were stitched up and covered with wax or gold foil.

The nostrils, ears, and mouth were plugged with linen, wax, or sometimes onion skins. False eyes were placed under the eyelids, sometimes made of quartz or stone, but sometimes whole onion bulbs were used.

Finally, the body and face were painted, and makeup was applied. The soles of the feet and palms of the hands might be decorated with henna. Rouge was applied to cheeks, and lips and eyebrows were painted. Sometimes the skin was painted red, for men, and yellow, for women. Often, the body was dressed in clothes, sandals, and even a wig. Wealthy deceased were decorated with jewelry.

WRAPPING THE BODY

Finally, the body was wrapped in a yellow shroud before being bound with linen. The linen was ritually anointed with oils, resins, and the embalmer spoke spells. The whole process took fifteen days, starting with fingers and toes. It took a very long time because an enormous quantity of linen was used—approximately 450 square yards for just one body. To save money, recycled linen was sometimes used from old towels or clothes, and the most sought-after cloth was from discarded clothes of priests and others connected to divinity. The wrapping of the body was accompanied by recitation of magical spells by a "Lector Priest." Sometimes, spells were written on the linen itself. An amulet was often placed on the mummy's chest as magical protection.

Great emphasis was put on the perfect preservation of the body. So, for instance, if someone had lost a limb in life, it was replaced with an artificial one. Men were usually buried with their hands crossed over their groin and women with their arms on their thighs. During the New Kingdom onward, pharaohs were wrapped with their arms crossed over their chest, to reflect the manner of Osiris. The wrapped body was then placed in a red shroud, which was knotted at the top. Finally, a mummy mask was placed over the head and shoulders. The mask was usually made of linen or papyrus stiffened with plaster, but royalty and the very wealthy wore masks of solid gold. Those of the upper elite who could not quite afford solid gold used the plaster mask gilded with gold. The body was now ready for the funeral.

TOP: The mummy of the Chief Treasurer Ukhhotep. The head of the mummy is covered by a wooden mask; **TOP, LEFT:** Egyptian mummy, Ptolemaic period; **TOP, RIGHT:** Tutankhamun's golden death mask is one of the most familiar of all Egyptian works of art; **ABOVE:** Wooden funerary Mask of the Overseeer of Builders Amenhotep.

NECHO II 610–595 BC

PSAMTIK II 595–589 BC

APRIES 589–570 BC

AMASIS 570–526 BC

PSAMTIK III 526–525 BC

CAMBYSES 525–522 BC

DARIUS I 521–486 BC

XERXES I 486–466 BC

ARTAXERXES I 465–424 BC

DARIUS II 424–404 BC

DYNASTY 27 (PERSIAN) 525–404 BC

FUNERARY EQUIPMENT

TOP RIGHT: Shabti box, and shabtis of members of the Sennedjem tomb (Dynasty 19); **TOP:** Scarab beetle; **ABOVE:** This beetle scarab was found in the coffins of Amenemhab and Huwebenef, alongside their statuettes.

SCARAB BEETLE

One of the most popular amulets in ancient Egypt was of the scarab beetle. They were used as pieces of jewelry, seals, and funerary amulets. It was the protective amulet for heart, and by the Middle Kingdom, it was the most important amulet in funerary practices. It was seen as a manifestation of the creator and solar deity. It was a symbol of rebirth and resurrection because the scarab beetle pushed a ball of dung along the ground, and equated with the sun being "pushed" along the sky. The scarab was also linked to mummification because the pupae resembled a wrapped mummy. The heart amulet was inscribed with spells from the Book of the Dead, which would ensure the person's heart would not speak against them and confess any wrongdoings the person may have committed in life. The amulet was carved from green or black stones, including steatite, schist, feldspar, hematite, and obsidian. However, sometimes the scarab could be of different stones or metals, such as the green jasper and gold scarab of Hatnofer of the New Kingdom. Sometimes, the scarab had a human head or the head of another animal. From the New Kingdom onward, the scarab was often depicted with outstretched wings, signifying the protection it offered to the wearer.

SHABTIS

Shabtis were figurines of wood, stone, pottery, bronze, wax, or glass, and they accompanied the dead so that the deceased would not have to do any work in the afterlife. It was thought that with the right spells, the shabti would become alive, and so the magical inscription was written on their body in hieroglyphs. They emerged in the Middle Kingdom, and were meant to do all the labor of food production, irrigation, clearing sand, etc. These model humans were between 3-10 inches tall and made to look like the person they were buried with. They became so popular that a person might be buried with 365 shabtis, one for every day of the year, along with overseers. Sometimes, there were so many that they had to be buried in a box separate from the coffin.

DYNASTY 28 522–399 BC

PEDUBASTE III
522–520 BC

PSAMTIK IV
c.470 BC

INAROS
c.460 BC

AMYRTAIOS I
c.460 BC

THANNYROS
c.445 BC

PAUSIRIS
c.445 BC

PSAMTIK V
c.445 BC

PSAMTIK VI
c.400 BC

AMYRTAIOS II
404–399 BC

CANOPIC JARS

Canopic jars were sacred containers used to hold the internal organs of the deceased before mummification. They were embalmed separately after removal. The jars were placed in a wooden chest, then placed in a stone chest, and buried with the sarcophagus. There were four jars that each kept a particular organ: the stomach, intestines, lungs, and liver. The heart— the seat of the soul—was left inside the body. The brain was considered worthless, and discarded. The ancient Egyptians believed the body was needed for existence in the afterlife, and so went to great lengths to preserve it. The jars were usually carved from limestone or pottery, although they changed over time. During the Old Kingdom, the jars were stone with flat lids. During the Intermediate Period, they became decorated with human heads. From the Eighteenth Dynasty onward, they became associated with funerary deities, who together were the "Four Sons of Horus." They were: Hapi, with a baboon head, whose jar contained the lungs; Duamutef, with a jackal head, whose jar contained the stomach; Imsety, with a human head, whose jar contained the liver; Qebehsenuef, with a falcon head, whose jar contained the intestines. Each jar represented one of the four cardinal points, North, East, South, and West respectively, of the aforementioned gods. The role of the gods was to protect the internal organs, and the jars themselves were protected by other gods: Nephthys guarded the jar of the lungs; Isis the jar of the liver; Neith the jar of the stomach; and Selket the jar containing the intestines. As time went on and embalming practices improved, the Egyptians no longer needed to store the organs separately. Rather, they were removed for embalming, then placed back inside the body. Therefore, around the late Middle Kingdom, the four canopic jars were buried empty and were kept only symbolically.

COFFINS AND SARCOPHAGI

The ancient Egyptians buried their dead in a fetal position. If they were poor, they buried the bodies in contact with the sand, or they used baskets. During the Old Kingdom, food was placed in the coffin because it was believed that the ka needed physical nourishment to survive. Two eyes were painted on the coffin so the deceased could look through them once their sense of sight was restored with the "Opening of the Mouth" ritual. Coffins were placed so that the eyes faced east, associated with Horus, the rising sun, and the realm of the living. Royalty were buried in sarcophagi. The coffins were made of imported cedar from Lebanon—a status symbol. Locals who could not afford expensive wood had to make do with the flimsier sycamore. The first use of sarcophagi in Egypt was in the Third Dynasty, c.2860–2813 BC. They were made of granite, basalt or limestone, and protected the bodies and served as their dwelling place for all time. Around the Middle Kingdom, coffins were painted inside and out.

The first use of sarcophagi in Egypt was during the Third Dynasty, from approximately 2860-2813 BC. It was meant to protect the body and serve as its dwelling place for all time. The sarcophagi were made of granite, basalt, limestone, or calcite. As time went on, coffins were painted, including the interior walls of coffins, especially around the beginning of the Middle Kingdom. During later periods, coffins were often made in the shape of the Per-Nu, or Lower Egyptian shrine.

TOP: Coffin of Irtirutja, Ptolemaic Period; **ABOVE:** Canopic jar of pharaoh Smendes, founder of the 21st Dynasty. This particular jar was intended to contain the king's liver, since it is inscribed for Qebehsenuef, the falcon-headed deity deputed to the protection of this organ.

NEPHERITES I
399-393 BC

NECTANEBO I
380-362 BC

NECTANEBO II
360-343 BC

DYNASTY 29 399-380 BC

DYNASTY 30 380-343 BC

TEOS
365-360 BC

NEPHERITES I
399-393 BC

NEPHERITES II
380 BC

PSAMMUTHIS
393 BC

ACHORIS
393-380 BC

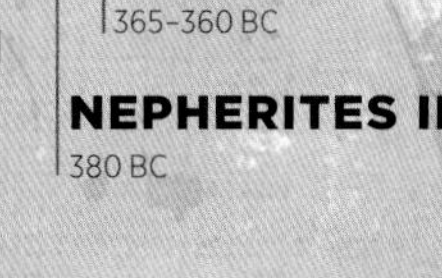

FUNERALS AND TOMBS

TOP: The entrance of the mastaba of Seshemnufer IV; **ABOVE:** The Mastabat al-Fir'aun at Saqqara.

Ancient Egyptian funerals were all accompanied by rituals and mourning. After the body was mummified, it was carried in procession from embalming house to tomb. The body was laid on an open booth decorated with bouquets. The booth was placed on a boat-shaped bier, then placed on a sled pulled by oxen. A priest walked in front, sprinkling milk, and burning incense. Food offerings were also carried in the procession, to be buried with the body. Accompanying the body were professional female mourners dressed in pale blue. They tore their hair, beat their breasts, wept, wailed, and threw dirt over themselves. They symbolized Isis and Nephthys, who had mourned Osiris. In addition, dancers and priests were part of the procession (depending on the wealth of the deceased). The final act was the purifying of the mummified body with water and incense, anointing the mummy with sacred oil, and the Opening of the Mouth ceremony, which was thought to restore the sensory powers of perception. Every stage of the funeral was accompanied by spells spoken aloud by a priest. The spells ensured the person passed safely into the afterlife and had a successful rebirth. Final offerings were made of incense, eye makeup, food, drink, and the leg and heart of a bull. The mummy was then placed inside a coffin or nest of coffins, then placed in the burial chamber with the offerings, amulets, and other funerary equipment essential for the deceased to be comfortable in the afterlife. Magic bricks were placed around the coffin, and finally, the tomb was sealed. The family then sat down to an elaborate feast.

MASTABAS

The mastaba was a tomb made from mudbricks. It consisted of a pit dug in the desert or carved out of bedrock then covered by a flat-roofed structure. The word "mastaba" comes from the Arabic word for "bench." The first kings of Egypt during the First and Second Dynasties were buried in mastabas, along with their families and some important elite. They are the first stage of building on a monumental scale. The tombs were marked with stone stelae, with the name of the king in hieroglyphs with the serekh design. Although kings shifted toward being buried in pyramids, nonroyals were buried in mastabas for over a thousand years.

Above ground, there was a small chapel with

KHABEBESH
343–332 BC

ARSES
338–336 BC

DARIUS III CODOMAN
335–332 BC

PERSIANS 343–332 BC

ARTAXERXES III OCHUS
343–338 BC

a false door, where priests and family members would bring food, drink, and other offerings for the ba, or soul of the deceased, so that they could continue existing in the afterlife. The burial chamber was dug deep in the earth and lined with wood. A hidden chamber was stocked with anything of comfort that the deceased might want in the afterlife—food, beer, clothes, jewelry, and furniture.

In early designs, the mastaba was accompanied by a mortuary temple, referred to as a funerary palace, where the ka of the deceased was said to reside. By the end of the First Dynasty, architects had fused the tomb and funerary palace into a single structure.

Alongside the mastabas of royalty were the simple graves of the members of the royal staff—craftsmen, court dwarves, even favorite pets—who had been sacrificed in order to accompany the pharaoh into the afterlife. By the Old Kingdom, this aspect had been replaced by shabti figures representing the king's entourage.

PYRAMIDS

The pyramids emerged as monumental structures to function as tombs for the pharaoh and as a monument to the gods. They symbolized the sheer might and power of the pharaoh who built them. To build a pyramid signified great success as a ruler.

It's thought that the pyramids began as a ladder for the souls to reach heaven. They may have also symbolized the "primordial mound" of Geb that Amun-Ra created at the beginning of time. The smooth, straight sides may have symbolized the rays of the sun. They became symbols of the solar god Ra. Pyramids were built to last through eternity, so that whoever spoke the name of the pharaoh who built it would continue his legacy.

The word "pyramid" comes from the Greek "pyramis," meaning "wheat cake." The foundation for the architectural engineering was laid with the development of mastabas, then gradually into "bent" pyramids, and finally, with the Pyramids of Giza, the first true pyramids came into existence. Eventually, pharaohs were interred in less conspicuous caves in the Valley of the Kings, in the hope of evading tomb robbers.

STEP PYRAMID

The earliest structure that we might call a "pyramid" is the Step Pyramid, commissioned by Djoser in the Third Dynasty and designed by master architect Imhotep. The Step Pyramid began as a mastaba, then six "steps" or levels were gradually added. It was built out of limestone at Saqqara.

MEIDUM PYRAMID

The next phase of architectural development can be seen with the Meidum Pyramid, first built as a seven-step pyramid, then filled in with limestone. Later, an eighth step was added and filled-in with limestone to create the smooth sides of a geometric pyramid.

GREAT PYRAMID

The Great Pyramid is the largest of all the pyramids. Originally, it would have been 480 ft tall, although wind erosion has led to it lessening over time. It was built from over two million blocks of stone, each weighing two tons. The blocks were perfectly carved

TOP: The Pyramid of Sahure at Abusir; **CENTER:** Djoser's step pyramid at Saqqara; **ABOVE:** The great pyramid at Giza.

MACEDONIAN PERIOD 332–304 BC

ALEXANDER IV
316–304 BC

PHILIP ARRHIDAEUS
323–316 BC

ALEXANDER THE GREAT
332–323 BC

TOP: Great sphinx of Giza; **TOP, RIGHT:** Sphinx of Amenhotep III; **ABOVE:** The Obelisk of Hatshepsut is the tallest obelisk still standing in Egypt and one of two still standing at Karnak.

and needed no mortar. Some have suggested that it was built with a series of ramps, with hundreds of people toting each block with ropes. It remains one of the great examples of architectural engineering in the world.

BENBEN STONES AND OBELISKS

The benben stone was a mini pyramid ("pyramidion") at the top of the pyramid. It would originally have been gilded in gold, so that it gleamed in the sunlight—and a significant solar symbol. The benben stone importantly symbolized the original sacred mound that arose from the waters of Nun. The obelisk was essentially a form of the benben stone in a needle-like design. Obelisks were called "tekhen," and originally also had gilded tips, making them too an important solar symbol.

THE GREAT SPHINX

The Great Sphinx was the earliest colossal statue to be built in Egypt, around 2500 BC. It was carved out of a natural outcrop of limestone and was probably meant to be a guardian of Pharaoh Khafre's tomb. It is thought that the Sphinx bears Khafre's face. The word "sphinx" is most likely a distortion of the words "shesep ankh," meaning "living image." Through its lion's body, the Sphinx is connected to solar imagery. The lion was associated with kingship, as well as the sun. During the Eighteenth Dynasty, Pharaoh Thuthmosis IV restored the temple. According to the "Dream Stela," which was erected between the paws of the Sphinx, King Thutmosis dreamed of the Sphinx, who promised him the throne of Egypt if he repaired his statue.

PTOLEMY I SOTER I
304–284 BC

PTOLEMY II PHILADELPHOS
285–246 BC

ARSINOE II
278–270 BC

PTOLEMY III EUERGETES I
246–221 BC

BERENIKE II
246–221 BC

PTOLEMY IV PHILOPATOR
222–205 BC

PTOLEMY V EPIPHANES
205–180 BC

HARWENNEFER
205–199 BC

ANKHWENNEFER
199–186 BC

CLEOPATRA
194–176 BC

PTOLEMAIC PERIOD 304–30 BC

PYRAMID TEXTS

The Pyramid Texts were a collection of magical spells that protected the Pharaoh in the afterlife and were most likely read at his funeral. They are the oldest surviving funerary texts, and they are called the Pyramid Texts because they were inscriptions on the inner walls of various pyramids. The oldest inscription was found on the pyramid of Unas, (approximately 2350 BC). No one pyramid contained all the spells but taken together they total over 800 spells. The language used is very archaic (even for ancient Egyptian), and they are thought to have emerged even before the Old Kingdom.

The Pyramid Texts dealt solely with the life, death, and rebirth of the pharaoh. Some scholars think that the spells were written in sequences to be spoken at his funeral, then the procession to the tomb. They describe his afterlife, and that he lives with Ra among the "imperishable stars." Some texts say that the pharaoh travels with Ra on his royal boat in the afterlife. The ancient Egyptians believed that the king joined the stars, and so they linked the dead king with the god Osiris. The spells are to help the pharaoh reach the afterlife by invoking several helper deities. The texts focus on the cult of the sun god, Ra, and so were most likely written by the priests at Heliopolis. The spells are known as "utterances," because each section begins, "words to be spoken."

COFFIN TEXTS

The Pyramid Texts were the foundation for the Coffin Texts. By the Middle Kingdom, the idea that magical assistance could be given to nonroyalty spread, and so the elite of Egypt began placing textual spells in their coffins and tombs. Although they are known as Coffin Texts, and most of the writing is found on coffins, they were also inscribed on stelae, canopic chests, and even mummy masks. They were widely used by the First Intermediate Period, although the earliest dates from around the end of the Old Kingdom.

THE BOOK OF TWO WAYS

The Book of Two Ways is a detailed guide to the afterlife for the common Egyptian. The deceased could pass on and enjoy the afterlife only if they recited the correct spells. The Coffin Texts promised that, like the pharaoh, the deceased could be reborn into the Afterlife, and they would become one with Osiris and the sun god, Ra. Although the spells were written in the coffin, it was expected that the person know them by heart.

THE BOOK OF THE DEAD

The Book of the Dead is a collection of spells for anyone who could afford to have them copied, and placed into their coffin. The spells were known as "The Book of Going Forth by Day." They were available to everyone. There are approximately 200 spells, but no one copy contains all of them. They were a set of funerary texts that were written on papyrus but were also recorded on coffins, amulets, tomb walls, and heart scarabs. The text itself was usually accompanied with illustrations and vignettes. The main purpose of the Book of the Dead was to give the deceased a chance at passing into the afterlife and become one with Osiris. The earliest versions are known to be from at least the Second Intermediate Period. Much of the religious framework is based on the earlier Pyramid and Coffin texts.

TOP: The Benben Stone from the Pyramid of Amenemhat III; **ABOVE:** Map of the netherworld from the coffin of Gua.

CLEOPATRA II
175–115 BC

PTOLEMY VI PHILOMETOR
180–145 BC

PTOLEMY VII NEOS PHILOPATOR
145–144 BC

HARSIESE
c.130 BC

PTOLEMY IX SOTER II
116–80 BC

PTOLEMY VIII EUERGETES II
170–116 BC

1

ORIGINS

Every culture has its own version of how the world, life, and creation began, and the ancient Egyptians were no different. They wove their beliefs of the gods into their explanations of natural phenomena such as lightning, earthquakes, or sandstorms. Ancient Egypt differs from other cultures, however, in that it has no single "creation myth;" each region of Egypt had its own, although there were some similarities between them. The following is a collection of the most significant of those myths.

In the beginning, nothing but dark, infinite, and directionless water existed. This water was called Nun.

CREATION MYTH OF HELIOPOLIS

Even after the world was created, Nun would continue to exist and return to destroy creation and begin the cycle of rebirth again. Four pairs of deities personified the male and female aspects of Nun: invisibility, infinity, lack of direction, and darkness.

From this infinite void, Atum created himself by uttering his own name and willed himself into being. He emerged from the waters as a Bennu bird, then flew to Heliopolis and landed on the Benben, an obelisk representing the very first ray of light to strike the Earth.

Atum, then, was the source of all creation. Some texts say that he masturbated until his semen spilled forth and created Shu, the god of dry air, and Tefnut, the goddess of moist air. Other sources say that he sneezed or spat, which produced Shu and Tefnut (this explanation came from puns of their names). He also created a primeval mound of earth on which he could stand. This image of a primeval mound emerging from waters is clearly linked to the flooding of the Nile every year. The river flooded and when the waters receded, rich, deposits of mud were left. In addition, ancient Egyptians would build their homes on the highest possible ground to avoid the inundation.

According to the myth, Shu and Tefnut produced two other deities—Nut, the sky goddess, and Geb, the dry land. Geb and Nut coupled and produced children of their own: Osiris, Seth, Isis, and Nephthys. Altogether with Atum, the gods and goddess represented the Ennead, the sacred nine divinities, called the Ennead.

ABOVE: A *menat* (a musical instrument similar to the sistrum), depicting the deities Tefnut and Shu; **OPPOSITE PAGE:** Tefnut and Shu.

In the glorious days of Ra, before old age had begun to creep up on him, a prophesy foretold that if he coupled with the goddess Nut and if she bore children with him, one of them would end his reign among men.

HOW THE MOON LOST ITS LIGHT

Ra spoke a curse over Nut so that she would not be able to bear any children on any day in the year. This made Nut very sad, and so, full of sorrow, she sought out Thoth, the god of wisdom and magic, who loved her.

"Tell me," she said, "is there any way that I can break this curse?"

Thoth shook his head, for he knew that a curse of Ra, once uttered, could never be broken. However, he was the wisest of the gods, and he devised a plan for the poor goddess who wished to bear children. So, he went to Khonsu, the god of the Moon and challenged him to a game of draughts, which Khonsu particularly enjoyed. Their wager was light and if Khonsu lost, he would give some of his light to Thoth.

Thoth made sure to win but he also made sure to keep Khonsu playing. The stakes grew higher, and Khonsu could not refuse because he loved the game so much. They played many rounds, with Thoth always winning and gaining more light from the Moon god.

ABOVE: The blue faience inlays of this game box and the gaming pieces were discovered in a tomb at Abydos; **OPPOSITE PAGE:** Queen Nefertari Playing Senet.

Finally, Khonsu gave up, having lost so much light. So, Thoth gathered up all the light that he had won and crafted five extra days, which he placed at the end of the old year. Where once there had been three hundred and sixty days, there were now three hundred and sixty-five, which were not days of the old year and would always be festival days.

Khonsu therefore, having lost some of his light, did not have enough to shine continually through the month. He had to dwindle in brightness, then grow again to his full glory, and he continues to do this even today. So Nut was able to bear children on these new days. On the first day, Osiris was born, and on the second came Horus. On the third day, the dark and evil god Seth was born. Isis was born on the fourth day, and Nepthys came on the fifth. In this way, the curse of Ra was avoided, and the gods came into being.

Now it came to pass that Ra grew old with age. As he walked along the land of Egypt, it was evident in every part of his body that he was old–his hands trembled, his skin was mottled, and he even dribbled spittle at the corner of his mouth.

ISIS TRICKS RA

One day, some of his spittle fell onto the ground where it mixed with the dirt and made mud. Isis took some of this mud into her hands and kneaded it as carefully as bread dough and crafted it into the shape of a serpent, creating the very first cobra. This would become the uraeus, the holy serpent that protects the kings and queens of Egypt, worn on their royal crowns. Isis placed this cobra on the ground on the road that Ra walked along every day as he surveyed his two kingdoms of Upper and Lower Egypt. So, as he passed by the cobra, it struck as quick as lightning and bit Ra, vanishing into the grass with barely a whisper.

Ra cried out in pain and this cry was so loud that it echoed across the earth, reaching even to the western horizon. The venom coursed through his limbs and felt as though he were burning with fire. All the gods were alerted by his cry of pain and rushed to him. They asked what the matter was, but the pain from the poison was so great that Ra could not speak. His lips trembled with effort but nary a word passed his lips. The poison continued to flow through his veins. Finally, he found the strength to speak. He said, "Help me, all of you, whom I created with my own will. Something has struck me, but I do not know what it is or from whence it came. I created everything before you, but this I did not make. I am in such pain as I have never felt before, and no pain is its equal. Yet I do not understand who could possibly have hurt me, for none know my Secret Name, that Name which is guarded deeply in my heart, which gives me power and guards me against the magic of others."

"What is this pain?" the other gods asked. They wept and lamented for the fate of their ruler.

"It burns like fire, but it is not fire. It courses through me like water, yet it is not water. I shiver and my limbs tremble, and I know that I will perish unless something is done. Call every god who has the skill of healing and the wisdom of magic."

ABOVE: Uraeus with the Red Crown of Lower Egypt; **OPPOSITE PAGE:** Ra, from the tomb of Nefertari, 13th century BC.

So all the gods gathered around Ra, including Isis, the healer and the queen of all magic. She knew powerful words to revive the dying and could save Ra.

She said, "What happened, my father?"

Ra replied, "O daughter, something terrible has befallen me. I was walking my usual path through Egypt to make sure that all was well when I was bitten by a snake—a snake that I did not create. Now my veins burn with the venom and my body feels full of ice. I sweat as mortal men sweat on the hottest of days. I fear that I will perish."

"I will drive out the poison with the magic that is mine by rights; I will make the serpent who bit you tremble and fall down before you."

"How will you do this daughter?" asked Ra.

"Only tell me your Secret Name, and all will be well," said Isis, her voice dripping with honey. "Only by speaking your Secret Name in my spells can I cure you."

With what little remaining strength that he had, Ra lifted his head and said, "I am Maker of Heaven and Earth. I am Builder of Mountains and Source of Waters. I am Light. I am Darkness. I am Creator of the Nile. I am the Fire that burns in the sky, Khepera in the morning, Ra at noon, and Tum in the evening. I am all these and more."

Isis recited her magic spells with these names, but she knew that it would be in vain. The poison continued to work its way through Ra's body, and he was at death's door.

So, she said, "You know that the magic will not work unless I have your Secret Name. Tell me, before you perish, and once you do, the poison will immediately leave your body, and you will be free from pain."

The poison burned with the strength of a bonfire in Ra, and he was at the point where he would no longer be able to speak. So, with the last of his strength, he said, "I will give you my Secret Name. But before I do, swear to me that you will tell no one else, except the son that you will bear, whose name shall be Horus. Bind him, too, with this oath that he will never tell another

ABOVE: Faience amulet of Ra Horakthy; **RIGHT:** The goddess Isis kneels and raises a hand before her face in a gesture of mourning.

ABOVE: Egyptian Cobra; **LEFT:** Egyptian wall relief depicting snakes, Komombo, Egypt.

soul, neither god nor man, my Name of Power."

Isis swore the oath and bent her ear to Ra's lips to hear the name. He whispered the Name of Power to her, and she gained power over Ra for eternity. She said, "By the Secret Name that I now know, be banished, poison, from Ra's body."

At once, the venom left Ra's body, and he felt no more pain. But the poison had left its eternal mark on Ra, and he no longer ruled the Earth. It was his time to rule in the heavens, and so he travelled there and took his rightful place. But he still wanted to pass over his two kingdoms every day, and so he took on the likeness of the sun, passing over the earth every day, and cross the underworld by night in his boat. So, every day he goes through Amenti and the twelve regions of Duat, where he must face many perils and dangers. Still, he always comes through safely, and he carries the souls of the dead who know the correct prayers and words that must be said. Thus, every Egyptian prepared for this journey by boat into the underworld with Ra.

There has never been anyone to visit the Land of the Dead, Duat, except for Se-Osiris, the wonderful child-magician, who read the sealed letter, the grandson of Pharaoh Rameses the Great.

THE LAND OF THE DEAD

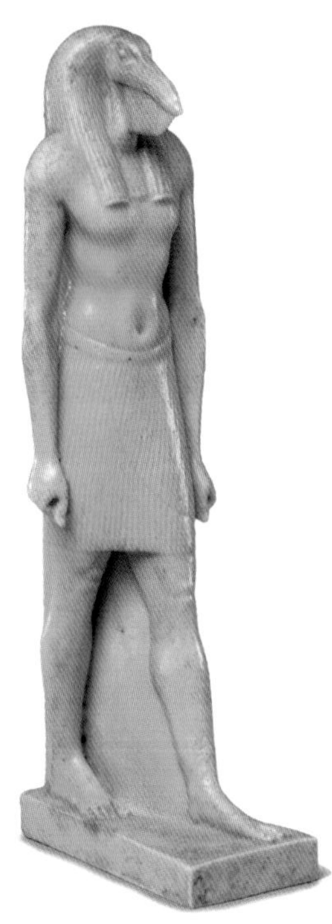

ABOVE: Striding Thoth; **OPPOSITE PAGE:** False door in the tomb of the vizier Mereruka, 24th century BC, depicting his ka returning to the tomb.

One day, Se-Osiris and his father stood by a window in the palace at Thebes watching two funeral processions. The first to go by was that of a rich man. His body had been properly embalmed, wrapped in linens, and it was carried in an expensive, cedar case inlaid with gold and painted with beautiful inscriptions. Many servants and attendants followed after him, mourning and holding gifts for his tomb. Priests stood in front and behind, singing hymns and reciting proper incantations to help him on his way to the afterlife. The second funeral was for a poor laborer. His coffin was a simple wooden box. Only his widow and daughters mourned him.

As they watched both processions go by, Setna, Se-Orisis' father, said, "I hope that my fate will be as grand as that of the rich man's and not like the poor laborers."

"On the contrary, Father," replied Se-Orisis. "I hope that the poor man's fate will be yours and not the rich man's."

He said this as the two funerals made their way to the Nile, where boats stood read to carry the bodies across the river. Se-Osiris's words grieved Setna greatly. When asked to explain what he meant, Se-Osiris replied, "Don't be fooled by the grandiosity of the rich man's funeral. He did nothing but wicked in his life, while the poor man acted with honor and righteousness. If you will trust me, I can prove it to you. I know the words of power that open all gates, even the gate to the Land of the Dead. If you come with me, I can release the Ba, our souls so that we may fly into Duat and discover the fate of the rich man and the fate of the poor man."

Although such an expedition was rife with danger, Setna had come to believe in his son and trusted him. He agreed to follow Se-Osiris into the Land of the Dead, even though if they embarked on such a perilous journey, they might never return. That night, they went to the Temple of Osiris, where they were allowed to pass, since they were royalty. They entered the dark sanctuary and lit lamps and torches so that they could see better. Se-Osiris barred the doors, so that no one would disturb them while

TOP: Amulet of ba bird wearing a sun disk; **ABOVE:** Ba hovering over the dead. Illustration from the Tehenena Book of the Dead.

they were on their journey. Then, he drew three magic circles: one around the statue of Osiris, one around the altar where a fire burned, and one around himself and his father. Se-Osiris took out a magic powder from a small leather pouch and threw the powder on the flames three times. On the third time, a huge ball of flame rose into the air and floated away. Finally, Se-Osiris spoke a word of power, and when he spoke the word, the whole temple shook with the power of it, and the fire in the altar rose ever higher, then quickly extinguished itself. But although there was no fire, the temple was still illuminated. Setna turned this way and that to see where the light came from, and when he saw what had happened, he nearly shrieked in horror, but he was too astonished to make a sound. Setna saw his body and the body of his son near the altar. In addition, he saw the double of their forms, their Ka, and above their Kas' like a small flame hung their Khou, or spirit. The light came from the Khou, and it illuminated their bodies. The silence in the temple was holy as Setna realized that they were out of their bodies. But Se-Osiris spoke in a voice as soft as a feather: "Follow me, Father, for we must return before the morning light breaks over the horizon if we wish to live to see the sun of Ra again, and time is already short."

Setna turned to see not his son but his Ba, which was in the shape of a golden bird with the head of his son. "I will follow," he forced himself to say. Then he stretched his arms out and found feathers, for he, too, was in the shape of a golden gird. They rose to the roof of the temple which seemed to melt before them and soon they were flying on the wind toward the west, as swift as arrows. They flew toward the setting sun, which shone with red light at the end of the western horizon. They passed over mountains and slipped into the Gap in the Western Desert and into the First Region of the Night. Below them was the sacred Mesektet Boat that Ra rowed every night in his voyage across the Underworld. The boat was splendid with carvings and glorious to behold. It was made of the finest wood and inlaid with gold and silver, with precious stones of amethyst, emerald, jasper, turquoise, and lapis lazuli. The boat stood at the ready for the last rays of the sun to fade from the horizon; only then would it begin its journey through Duat. The doors of the portal were shut, and on either side were six serpents, guarding the doors. Osiris gathered the souls, the Kas, of all the people who had died that day and who would face judgment in the Hall of Osiris.

When the last rays of the sun had faded, the doors of the great portal of Duat opened, and the boat of Ra entered the First Region. Gods pulled the boat with golden ropes, and it passed gently along the River of Death and through the portal. The boat continued on the ghostly waters until it came to the portal of the Second Region. At this portal, too, mighty serpents who breathed fire and poison guarded the gate. The portal was immense in height, and the walls of the gate were pointed with sharp spears, so that none could climb over. Those who were on the boat were buried with the proper rites, and they knew the words of power to speak. When they spoke the magic words, the portal opened, and they passed safely through.

The Second Region was a heavenly kingdom of Ra, and all the gods and heroes of old lived there in peace and happiness. This region was guarded by the Spirits of Plants, who made the whole region verdant and lush. However, no one in the boat was allowed to stay there or even set foot on the land. They had to pass into Amenti, the Third Region of Duat where the judgement Hall of Osiris waited to receive them.

The boat then passed on and came to the third portal. Everyone in the boat spoke words of power, and the wooden doors screamed on their hinges, but not as loudly as the man who screamed when one of the pivots turned in his eye as punishment for the evil acts he committed during his life.

Once the boat entered the Third Region, the dead disembarked and stood in the outer court of the Hall of Osiris and awaited judgment.

Once everyone had left the boat, Ra continued along his voyage, into the other nine Regions of Night until Ra was re-birthed from the mouth of the Dragon of the East and brought the sun to the Earth. Every night, Ra had to fight the great serpent-dragon Apep, who fought savagely and sought to devour Ra in the Tenth Region. The Bas of Setna and Se-Osiris did not follow Ra but stayed with the Kas of the dead. One by one, they each came to the gate of the inner court in the Hall of Osiris, and one by one, the Gatekeeper challenged them.

"You cannot pass unless I announce you, and I will not announce you unless you know my name." The Gatekeeper was fierce and wielded a great sword in his hands.

"Your name is The One Who Understands Hearts," replied each of the dead when it was his turn. "And Searcher of Bodies."

"Very good," replied the Gatekeeper. "But to whom shall I announce you?"

"Announce me to the one who is called the Interpreter of the Two Lands," the dead Kas said. They knew the ritual words to speak for they had been buried with all the proper rites.

"And who is that exactly?"

"It is Thoth, the god of wisdom."

The Gatekeeper nodded deeply when they had spoken the correct ritual words and let them pass through the doorway into the Hall. Thoth waited for them until they approached. When they did, Thoth asked, "Why have you come here?"

The dead replied, "I have come to be announced."

"And what is your condition?" asked Thoth with a kind voice.

"I am pure of all sin."

"And so, to whom will I announce you?"

"Announce me to him who is named the Temple of Fire, whose walls are writhing serpents and whose floor is water."

"And who is that exactly?" asked Thoth.

"Osiris."

So, Thoth bent his ibis head and led them to where Osiris sat on his throne in all his glory, wrapped in mummy linens and wearing the crown with the sacred uraeus and holding a crook and scourge in his hand. In front of him was a huge balance with two scales. Next to the scale was Ammit the Devourer, who had the head of a crocodile, the front legs of a lion, and the back legs of a hippo. He was terrifying to behold, and he licked his lips in anticipation. He waited for the judgement and ate the hearts of

TOP: Weighing of the heart scene, with Ammit sitting, from the book of the dead of Hunefer; **ABOVE:** The Weighing of the Heart ritual, shown in the Book of the Dead of Sesostris.

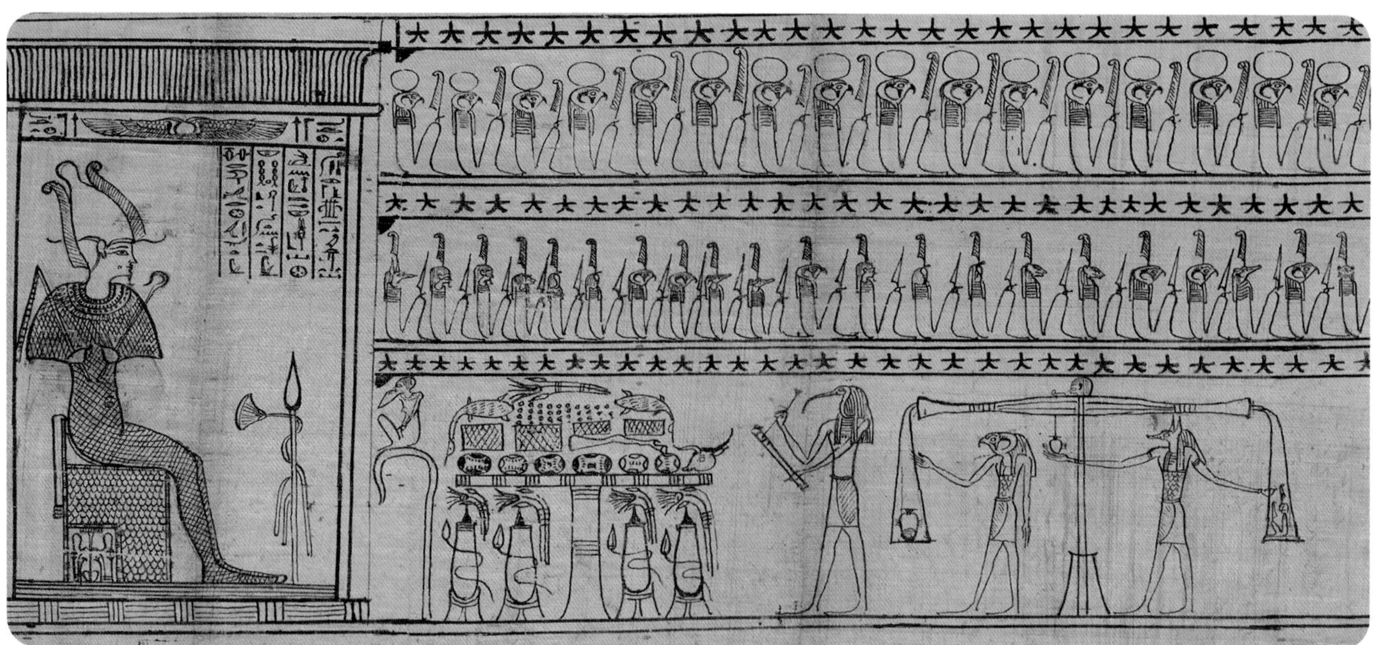

those who were not pure. Se-Osiris and Setna watched in awe as the dead proclaimed their innocence to Osiris, saying, "I am pure! I am pure! I am pure! I am as pure as the Bennu bird. I have come without sin, without guilt, and without evil. I lived in truth, and I have satisfied the justice of the gods. I gave to the poor, I lived in love, and I honored my ancestors. I provided sacrifices to the gods. Preserve me from Apep, the Devourer of Souls, great god Osiris."

When the time came, Anubis with his jackal-headed form led the Ka of the dead to one scale. From the Ka Anubis took the heart and placed it on a scale. On the other scale was placed a Feather of Truth. If the heart of the Ka was heavy with evil, it weighed down the scale. If it sank so low that Ammit could catch it in his jaws, he would gobble it and the evil Ka was cast into the Pits of Fire to live in torment with Apep. However, if the Ka had lived a good life on Earth and dedicated themselves to good deeds, the heart would be light and the Feather of Truth would be heavier, and so the heart would rise up. When the heart rose, Thoth cried to Osiris, "True are the words of him who spoke! He has not sinned, and he lived in goodness. Apep shall have no power over him. The eternal bread of Osiris shall be given to him, and he has earned a place in the Fields of Peace with Horus forever."

So Se-Osiris and Setna watched as the heart of the rich man was weighed in the scale. In life, he had been evil and committed all sorts of acts of wickedness, and so his heart was heavy. It sank so low that Ammit snatched it in his jaws and ate it straightaway. But the poor man had lived a good life, humble and true. So, his heart was light, free from the weight of sin. The scale rose, and he was led to the Fields of Peace to dwell forever, until Osiris returned to the Earth. So Se-Osiris turned to his father and said, "Now you know why I wanted you to have the fate of the poor man and not the rich man. The rich man now lives in agony with Apep, but the poor man lives in happiness and plenty." He paused for a moment and said, "But we must now take our leave, for Ra has almost completed his journey through the Underworld and will soon emerge in the East. We must go now."

So, the father and son spread their golden wings and flew in haste through all the portals of the Regions of Night. Their Bas returned to the Land of the Living, and they were undisturbed. Their Kas had guarded them faithfully through the night. When they had fully returned to their bodies, Setna was astonished at all he had seen. They emerged from the temple in time to see the golden sun rising in the east, spreading its fiery rays across the sky, turning the desert rock pink and purple and eventually gold as dawn came once more to Egypt.

TOP: Book of the Dead of the Priest of Horus, Imhotep (Imuthes); **ABOVE:** wall relief of pharaoh Seti I offering to the god Osiris at Abydos temple. Egypt; **OPPOSITE:** Nun, the embodiment of the primordial waters, lifts the barque of the sun god Ra into the sky at the moment of creation.

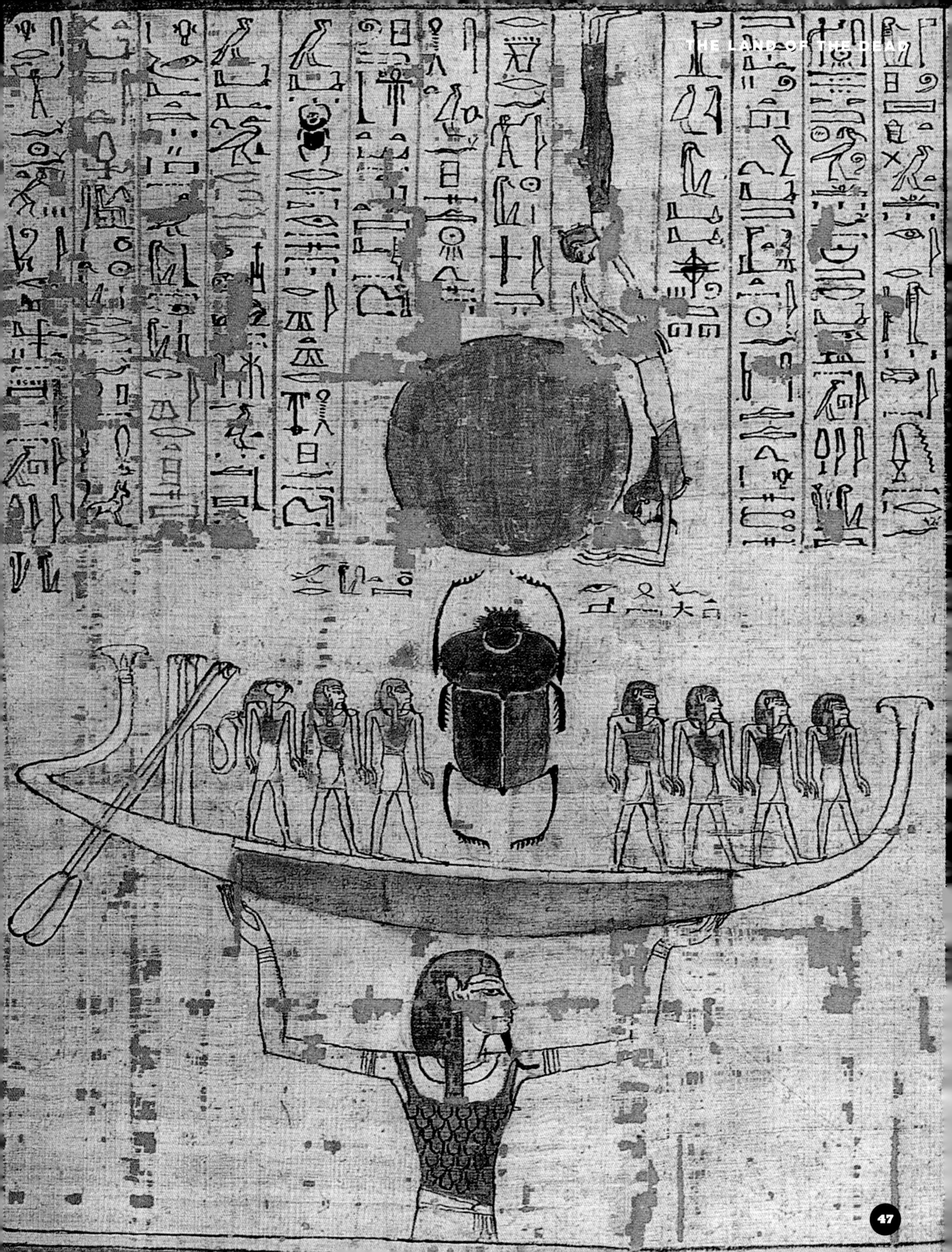

On the first day of the newly made days of Thoth, Osiris was born. The men in Egypt and throughout the world saw many wonders and signs that astounded them, and they knew that a god was born.

THE OSIRIS MYTH

When Osiris was fully grown, he married his sister Isis, and the ancient Pharaohs followed this custom thereafter, for a god could only marry a goddess. After Isis learned the Secret Name of Ra, Osiris ascended to power and reigned on Earth along with his queen. Now, at the time, mankind was savage and knew little more than beasts, and they constantly fought one another, killing, and fighting among themselves and eating each other. Osiris and Isis wanted to help the pitiful mortals. Isis discovered the power of wheat which grew wild in the land, and along with Osiris, taught mortals how to plant the seeds, how to irrigate the land with the Nile, how to tend the crops, and how to reap the produce when it was time. They showed humans how to make bread and how to make beer out of barley. They also showed them how to plant grapes and craft wine from them. Finally, the two deities showed man how to tend animals, raising them to kill and eat.

When the people of Egypt learned how to grow crops, make bread, and tend animals, they became more peaceful. Osiris went on to teach them laws and how to live in peace with one another. The mortals learned music and poetry, and soon Egypt was bountiful with prosperity and humans were no longer as savage as they had been. Osiris delighted in teaching humans, so he often left Egypt to teach other nations, and in his absence, Isis ruled in his stead. However, their brother, Seth, the evil god, envied and hated them both. The more that Osiris taught the humans, the more they loved and worshiped Osiris. The more they did, the more Seth hated his brother, and his jealousy grew stronger. He wanted to kill his brother and rule over Egypt. However, Isis was such a good and wise ruler, that Seth dared not attack while Osiris was away. In fact, whenever Osiris returned, Seth was always the first to bow before him and welcome him back. But all the while, Seth plotted and schemed to take the throne. He devised a wicked plan, aided by seventy-two of his friends. In secret, Seth measured the body of Osiris and made a chest with his exact measurements. He crafted the chest from the best wood, cedar from Lebanon and ebony from Punt. He inlaid it with gold and silver and set gemstones into it, so that the chest gleamed in the sunlight.

ABOVE: Head of Osiris, wearing Atef crown.

One day, Osiris returned from one of his travels, and Seth gave a great feast in honor of Osiris. The feast was the greatest that Egypt had ever known; the meat was the choicest game, the wine was strong, and all the dancing girls who entertained were each more beautiful than the last. However, all the guests of the feast were the seventy-two conspirators of Seth. When Osiris had drunk plenty of wine, and when his heart was light with gaiety, the beautiful chest was carried in, and all marvelled at its beauty. Osiris was amazed at the rare cedar, and even more so at the beautiful paintings of gods, birds, fish, and beasts that adorned the inside of the chest, and he desired it for himself.

"I will give this chest as a present to whoever fits inside exactly!" proclaimed Seth.

So, all the conspirators lined up to see if they could fit, which of course, they couldn't. Some were too tall, others too short; some too fat, others too thin.

"Let me see if I fit," said Osiris, getting up from his place at the table.

"Wait, husband," exclaimed Isis, clutching the arm of Osiris. "Perhaps it is a trick of Seth's."

But Osiris did not listen and went to inspect the chest and lay down to see if he fit. Of course, he did, having been measured by Seth. "I fit exactly, and the chest is mine!" he cried.

"It is indeed, and it shall be yours forever!" hissed Seth.

Immediately, he slammed the lid down, and the

ABOVE, MAIN IMAGE: Osiris and the Four Sons of Horus; **ABOVE, INSET:** A triad of Osiris, Isis, and Horus.

conspirators rushed to nail it shut and seal the lid with molten lead. Osiris could not lift the lid, and neither could Isis, and so he died. His spirit traveled west into Duat, but he could not pass beyond, into Amenti.

Seth ignored Isis' weeping and took the chest and threw it into the Nile. Hapi, the Nile god, bore it along his waters until it came to the Great Green Sea, where the waves tossed it about for many months, until finally it came to the shore of Phoenicia, near Byblos. The waves tossed the chest into a tamarisk tree that grew along the shoreline. The tree wrapped its branches around the chest and so took it into itself to make a resting place fit for a god. The flowers that bloomed were the most beautiful in the land, and soon the tree became famous for its beauty and its lovely fragrance. Soon, the king of Byblos heard of the famous tree, so he and his wife came to the seashore to gaze at it in wonder. By that time, the branches had completely grown over the chest, so that they did not know that the body of a god lay inside the tree. The king ordered that the tree be cut down and made into a pillar for his palace.

Meanwhile, in Egypt, Isis lived in great fear of Seth's wrath. Although she had tried to warn Osiris about Seth's evil, he had not listened, and so she was alone and defenceless. She was trapped her in her house, but the god Thoth came to help her. He freed her and gave her seven scorpions as companions, and she fled into the marshes with her baby, Horus. She finally found shelter on an island where the Goddess Buto lived, and she gave Horus to Buto for a time so that she could help Osiris and restore him. To guard the child and Buto from Seth, Isis lifted the island up into the air, so that it floated. No one could then scale the island and harm her child. Next, she sought the body of Osiris because he could not pass on to Amenti unless he was buried with the proper rites and spells. Isis wandered and searched all over Egypt, but she could not find his body, and she grieved greatly. She asked anyone she passed if they had seen it, but no one had, and not even her magic powers could help her. Finally, one day she came to rest by the riverside where some children were playing. She asked them if they had ever seen a beautiful cedar chest, inlaid with gold and silver, and they replied that they had, and that it had floated downstream into the Great Green Sea. Isis blessed the children and said that they should become great magicians, speaking words of power and could prophesy of things to come. So Isis traveled to the Great Green Sea and crossed it and arrived at Byblos. She was very weary, so she sat down by the seashore, and very soon some maidens of the Queen of Byblos passed by her. Isis looked kindly on them and taught them how to braid their hair, which they had never done before. They left and returned to the palace where they attended the queen. Because they had been so close to Isis, a strange and wonderful perfume clung to their skin, and the Queen marveled at how wonderful they smelled. She asked them how their hair came to be braided in such a lovely fashion and why they smelled so good. They told their queen of the beautiful woman who sat by the seashore, and the queen immediately sent them to look for her. The maidens brought Isis to the palace, and the queen asked her to serve in the palace, but she did not know that she spoke to a goddess. Isis agreed, and she tended the queen's sons, Maneros and Dictys, who was very sickly and weak. Isis, by her magic, cured Dictys, and she became very fond of the little baby, and wanted to make him immortal. She transformed herself into a swallow and flew around him, creating a powerful spell and burned away all his mortal parts with magic fire. The Queen watched her in secret, and when she saw that her baby seemed to be on fire, she rushed into the room with a loud shout. Isis then took on her true form, and the queen quivered and shrank in terror when she saw the goddess resplendent in all her glory. The king and queen immediately offered her gifts of their most precious treasures, the best offerings, and the choicest of animal sacrifices, but Isis only asked for the sturdy pillar of the tamarisk tree which held up the roof of the palace. The king

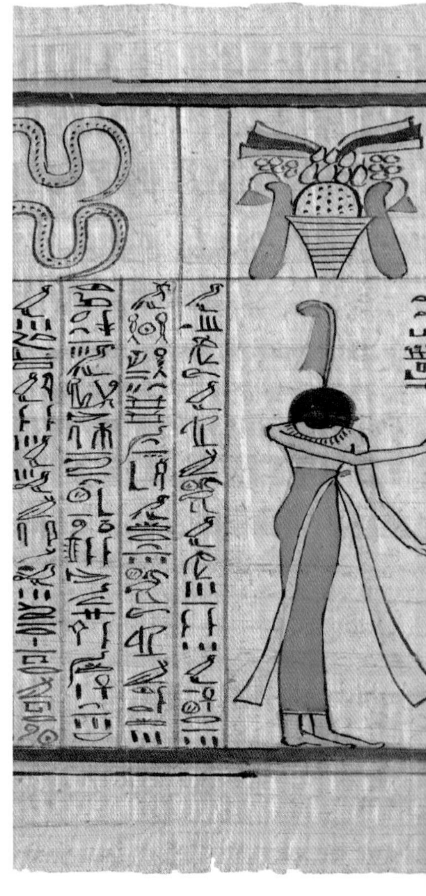

ABOVE & CENTER: Book of the Dead for the Chantress of Amun, Nauny.

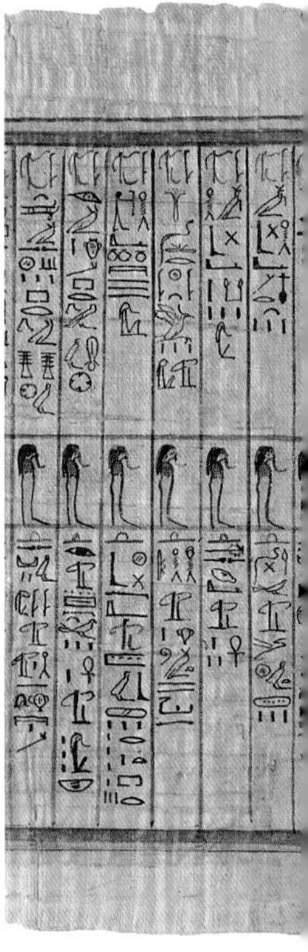

and the queen did not understand this strange request but immediately granted it. When Isis received the pillar, she opened it and took out the chest which held her husband's body. She gave the pillar back to the king and queen, and it became the most sacred object in Byblos, because it had held the body of a god. When Isis received the chest, she was despondent with sorrow. Still, she placed it on a ship which the king and queen of Byblos provided for her and left for Egypt. She returned safely to Egypt and hid the chest in the marshes of the delta while she returned for her son, Horus, on the floating island where Buto had cared for him and nurtured him.

Unfortunately, it came to pass that Seth happened upon the chest while he was hunting at night. He loved the darkness which made evil deeds easier to do and easier to hide, and by the light of the moon he recognized his infamous chest. He immediately knew that Isis was trying to recover Osiris' body, and he became filled with rage and hatred. He tore open the chest, took out the body of Osiris and tore it into fourteen pieces, which he scattered up and down the Nile, so that the crocodiles would gobble them up. When he had completed his wicked task, he cackled with laughter, for he thought that he had destroyed the body of Osiris forever. When Isis came back to the chest, she saw that it had been opened, and knew what Seth had done. She wept for Osiris but not for long, for determination filled her bones and she swore that she would recover the body no matter what befell her. So, Isis beseeched the other gods to help her, and this time, Nephthys joined in the search, for she did not like her wicked husband, Seth. Anubis, the son of Osiris and Nephthys, took on the form of a jackal and sniffed the riverside for clues. Isis crafted a boat of papyrus and scoured the Nile for Osiris' body. The crocodiles, in reverence for the goddess, did not eat the pieces of Osiris' body nor attack Isis in her boat. Ever after, it was said that whoever traveled in a boat made of papyrus would be safe from crocodiles, for they thought it was still Isis searching for pieces of her husband.

Slowly, Isis recovered Osiris, piece by piece. Whenever she found a piece of his body, she made the priests of that region build a shrine to Osiris and perform the sacred funeral rites. In that way, she made it harder for Seth to ever disturb Osiris again. However, Isis could only recover thirteen pieces; the fourteenth was Osiris' male organ, and the fishes of the Nile had eaten it. She cursed those fish, and never did any Egyptian eat or touch them. So, Isis crafted with her magic a replica of the missing member and joined all the other pieces of Osiris' body together with magic. Finally, she could embalm the body and bury it with all the sacred funeral rites and words of power. She hid the body well from Seth so that he could not disturb it anymore. The spirit of Osiris passed into Amenti to rule over the dead, until the last battle between Seth and Horus would occur. Only then would Osiris return to Earth to rule once more.

As Horus grew, the spirit of his father visited him frequently and taught him all the skills and knowledge that a good warrior should know.

HORUS AND SETH

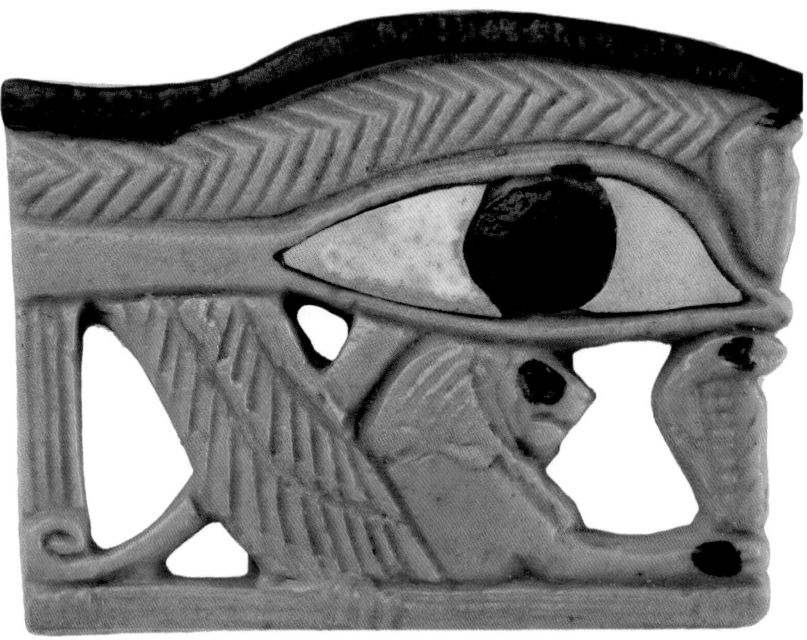

ABOVE: Wedjat eye amulets were among the most poular amulets of ancient Egypt. The wedjat eye represents the healed eye of the god Horus and embodies healing power, as well as regeneration, and protection in general; **OPPOSITE PAGE:** Horus spears Set, who appears in the form of a hippopotamus, as Isis looks on.

One day, Osiris said to Horus, "What is the noblest thing that a man can do?"

Horus replied, "To avenge his father and mother for all the evil done to them."

Osiris was very pleased with this answer and asked another question. "What animal is best to take into battle?" This was actually a test of Horus' knowledge.

"A horse," responded Horus.

"What about a lion?" suggested Osiris. "Surely a lion is more ferocious than a horse and has greater strength?"

"A lion is good for a man who is weak and needs help. But a horse is best for pursuing enemies and cutting them off from any escape."

When Horus answered thusly, Osiris clapped and exclaimed that it was time for him to declare war on Seth. Horus then gathered a large army and sailed up the Nile to attack evil Seth in the deserts in Upper Egypt.

The great god Ra knew that Horus was right to seek revenge against Seth for his mother and father, so he came to his aid. He sailed across the heavens and through the underworld, until at last he arrived in front of Horus. He took the warrior aside and told him to stare deeply into his blue eyes, for whoever looked into them, god or human, could see the future. But Seth was watching in the shadows, as he usually did. He transformed himself into a fierce, black pig, as black as soot, and his tusks were enormous and sharp.

TOP: The goddess Isis, breastfeeding her son, Horus; **ABOVE:** The god Horus Protecting King Nectanebo II; **OPPOSITE:** Photograph c.1920s, when much excavation of the tombs of ancient Egypt was conducted.

So, when Ra said to Horus, "Gaze into my eyes, and you will see what will come to pass in this war." Horus gazed into Ra's eyes, which were the deepest blue of the Great Sea to the north. But as he gazed, Seth in his disguise as a pig passed by and distracted him, so that he said, "Look! I have never seen such a huge and ugly pig before."

Then the pig attacked, but Horus was unprepared, and he did not have a sword with him, nor words of power to cast a spell.

Seth created an arc of fire and aimed it at Horus' eyes, and it struck with all of Seth's fury behind it. Horus howled in pain, and he now knew that the pig was really Seth. But Seth had disappeared in the blink of an eye and so escaped once again.

Ra took Horus to a dark room, where he was allowed to heal. Soon, his eyes could see even better than they could originally. When Horus was fully recovered, Ra returned to the sky. Horus was filled with joy that he could see, and so he set out at the head of his army. The country rejoiced that he was going off to fight Seth, and even the flowers seemed to be happy, for they bloomed whenever Horus passed.

Although there were many battles in the war, the last and largest was at Edfu. It was so great that a temple of Horus was erected in memory of it. When the time came, the forces of Seth and Horus clashed among the islands and rapids of the First Cataract of the Nile. Seth, in a form of a gigantic, red hippopotamus, uttered a curse against Horus and Isis. He said, "Let a raging tempest come and flood my enemies!" His voice rolled like thunder across the land, and nearly tore the sky in two. Immediately, a great and terrible tempest swept over Egypt, and the storm came upon Horus and his army. The wind howled fiercely, and the waves tossed the boats that held Horus and his soldiers. But Horus guided his boat safely through the spraying surf and foam, and he was able to navigate the storm. On the opposite side of the river, Seth still stood as a ferocious hippopotamus. He was so large that he could straddle the river on either side. So, Horus turned himself into a giant of a man, so tall that he could wield a harpoon thirty feet long with a blade six feet wide. Seth and Horus turned to each other to fight.

Seth opened his mouth as wide as it could go, to destroy Horus and all his men. But Horus threw his harpoon with such force that it struck the hippo deep into his head, even into its brain. With that single blow, Horus smote Seth. The hippo fell dead beside the Nile, and the storm faded away. The sky once again became clear and blue, and the clouds changed from churning gray to fluffy white. Then the people of Egypt came out to celebrate Horus and his victory and shouted in triumph. They erected a shrine to him to commemorate his vengeance against Seth, where the great temple now stands. They sang praises and held festivals in his honor. They continued to hold festivals every year thereafter.

Eventually, Horus passed from the Earth and did not reign anymore as the Pharaoh of Egypt. He appeared before the gods. Unfortunately, Seth was also there in spirit, and in this heavenly realm, they fought for the right to rule. They argued and so sought out Thoth to decide. But not even Thoth in all his wisdom could give judgement as to who should rule. Thus, Horus and Seth still fight over the souls of men and for the right to rule the world. They will continue to fight until the Last Battle of All Time, but it is fated that Horus will ultimately defeat Seth. When Seth is finally destroyed, Osiris will rise from the dead and return to Earth, bringing all his faithful followers, who were properly buried with all the sacred rites and words of power. It is said that this is why the Egyptians embalm their dead, so that their souls can pass into Amanti and rest until Osiris comes once again to bring peace to the Earth forever.

There are more than 1500 named gods and goddesses of Egypt. Ancient Egyptian religion was highly localized, and there could be (and often were) many gods of the same aspect. Often, older deities were "taken over" by other, more popular deities and so became linked in the minds of the Egyptians over time in a process called "syncretization." This chapter highlights some of the most well-known and significant gods and goddesses, such as Osiris, Isis, and Seth, as well as many of the lesser-known gods and goddesses.

2

THE GODS AND GODDESSES

AMUN

Amun became one of the most popular deities in Egypt. He is the god of sun, air, and an "invisible" aspect.

His name means "the hidden one," or "invisible," and he was considered, along with Ra, the Lord of All Creation, and he represented every aspect of creation.

He is first mentioned in the Pyramid Texts. Amun started off as a simple local god of Thebes. Initially, Atun was the supreme deity, and the god Montu was the tutelary god of Thebes. Amun represented protection and fertility but wasn't as important as the other gods, at first. Because he represented the "mysterious" aspect of life, he could be whatever people wanted or needed him to be. Because he represented nothing specific, people could pray to him for whatever aspect of their lives they needed and so Amun came to represent many roles in the daily lives of ancient Egyptians.

Over time, Amun grew in popularity, and during the Middle Kingdom, he became part of a triad of gods with Mut and Khonsu, their son and Moon god. Perhaps the most important point in the history of Amun was when he became linked with Ra, the sun god. This occurred when Ahmose I defeated the mysterious Hyksos (or "Sea Peoples") who attacked Egypt. Ahmose I credited Amun with the victory and linked him with Ra. Because Amun was not linked to a single, definable attribute, it was easy for him to mesh with another god in the minds of the Egyptians.

Amun rose to prominence during the New Kingdom, and he became known as the "Self-Created One," and the "King of the Gods." He became linked with Ra, who was also himself associated with Atum of Heliopolis. Therefore, Amun took on many of Atum's characteristics, and even though they remained distinct deities, Amun came to replace Atum in many ways. So under Amun, the most important parts of Atum and Ra were combined to create an all-encompassing deity who represented not only all of creation but Creation itself.

As such, Amun became wildly popular. His cult center was at Thebes, and he almost became a monotheistic deity. He was so popular that the priests of his cult at one time held more land and wealth than even the Pharaoh.

ROLES

Amun had many roles for the ancient Egyptians, and they developed over the millennia.

Concealed god—the Greek Plutarch gives us a hint as to what Amun's name originally meant. He quoted an earlier Egyptian historian, Manetho, who said that Amun signified "that which is concealed," or "invisible." In his

GOD Man with double-plumed headdress; ram or ram-headed; goose; frog-headed.

ASSOCIATION/ROLE "King of gods," primeval; hidden power; consort of Amaunet; father of Khonsu.

MAIN CULT CENTER Thebes; Hermopolis Magna.

ABOVE: Statuette of Amun; **OPPOSITE PAGE:** The Barque of Amun arriving at Thebes

earliest form, Amun was something ethereal and concealed from the eyes of mankind.

Creator god—Plutarch also referred to Amun as "Kneph," which was an eternal, self-generating god. As Amun-Ra, Amun was said to be a creator god in the form of a snake. It was said that Amun generated himself, along with the other gods. In the 18th dynasty, the Temple of Karnak, Amun's primary temple, was said to hold the "mound" of earth that Amun first created and stepped on out of the primordial waters.

Solar god—The Book of the Dead refers to Amun as "the oldest of the gods of the eastern sky," which reflects his connection with the sun rising every morning. This association became stronger when he was syncretized with Ra, and so took on many of the sun god's aspects. Still, his most important form was that of the "hidden" or mysterious god.

Fertility god—Amun is sometimes referred to Amun-Min, and Min was the god of male sexual procreativity. In this syncretization, Amun symbolized strength and fertility. In addition, because Amun was self-generating, he carried the sexual potency to create himself. Finally, scenes painted on temple walls show Amun mating with a cow as a bull, and bulls for ancient Egyptians were the living embodiment of male sexual fertility.

Warrior god—Amun began as a local deity in the region of Thebes, along with Montu, a local god of war. However, as Amun gained popularity, he displaced Montu and so absorbed many of his warlike characteristics. This was especially true after the invasion of the Hyksos in c. 1550 BC when he received credit for defeating Egypt's enemies. This association with a warlike god strengthened in the New Kingdom, when Amun was credited for protecting and expanding Egyptian borders. He was called "the lord of victory," and "lover of strength."

King of the gods—The Pyramid Text refers to Amun as "king, son of Geb," and from the Middle Kingdom onward, he was referred to as "Lord of the Thrones of the Two lands." He is first referenced as "king of the gods" in the 12th

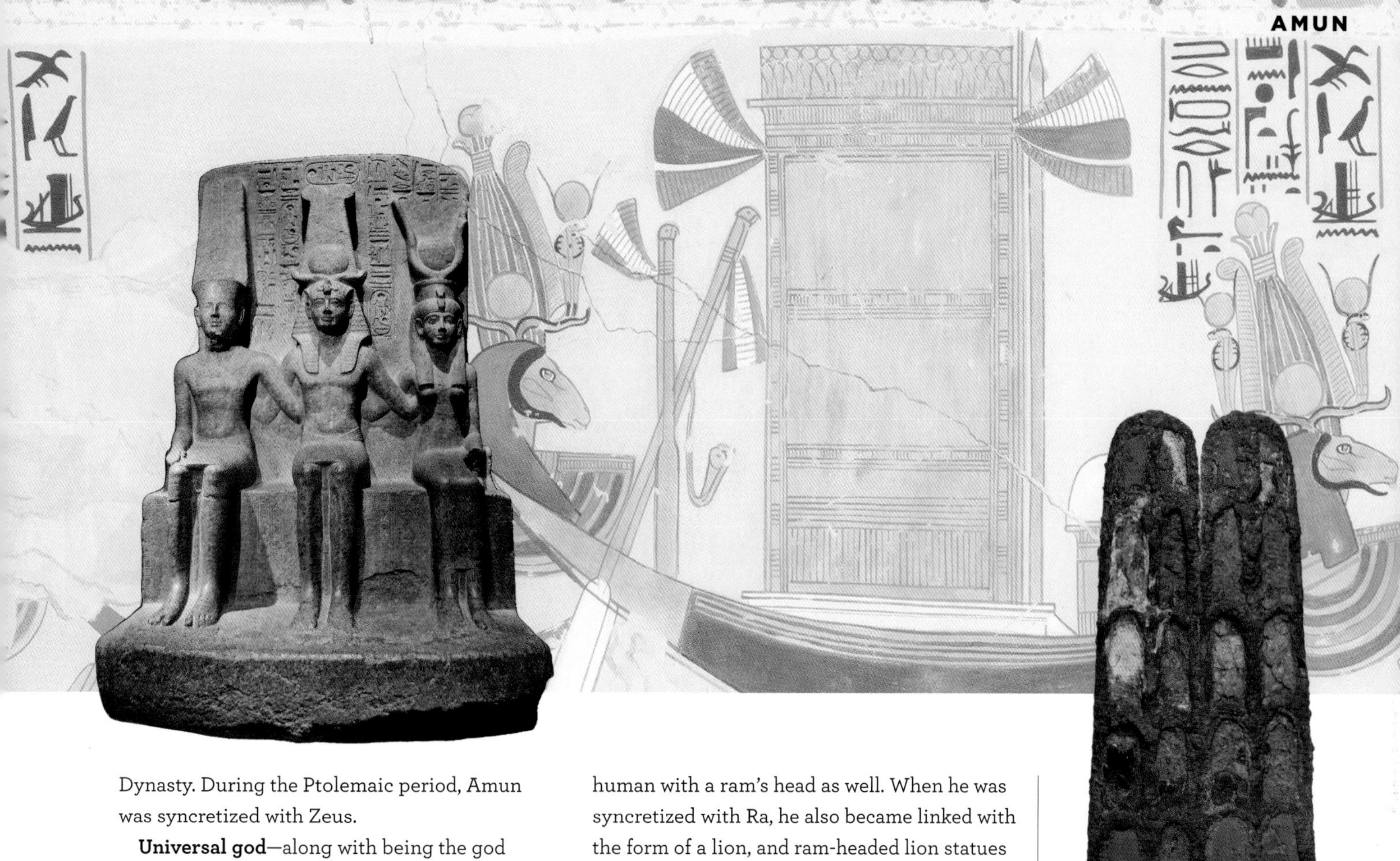

Dynasty. During the Ptolemaic period, Amun was syncretized with Zeus.

Universal god—along with being the god of creation, the king of all gods, and the "mysterious" god who permeated all things, Amun was said to be "universal" in nature. This meant that he existed in all things; every living being, or inert object had some aspect of Amun in it. It was also said that he was the Ba (or soul) of all nature.

ICONOGRAPHY

Amun was usually depicted as a human man wearing a short kilt, a tunic, and a double-plumed crown. The double plumes may stand for the duality that ancient Egyptians held in reverence. As the king of the gods, he is often shown sitting on a throne. As a warrior god, he is shown in a dynamic, striding pose. Finally, as the king of the gods, he is sometimes shown standing, with his legs together. In his human form, Amun was depicted with either red or blue skin. The red -skinned Amun is the oldest depiction, but he later was painted in scenes with blue skin, possibly linking him to his role as a sky god.

Amun was also shown as several animals. One was the ram, which symbolized his sexual potency. He was sometimes painted as a human with a ram's head as well. When he was syncretized with Ra, he also became linked with the form of a lion, and ram-headed lion statues are thought by scholars to be symbols of Amun. Finally, and more rarely, Amun was sometimes depicted as a serpent or goose, which had an association with the primordial world.

WORSHIP

The original locality of Amun was at Thebes, and the Temple of Karnak shows his immense popularity. It is the largest temple ever created by the Egyptians, and the entire complex consisted of a huge enclosure with various smaller temples of other gods. He also had cult centers in Deir el-Bahri and Medinet Habu. The Egyptians held an important festival, with Amun at the center of attention in which they celebrated his divine union with Mut.

During the New Kingdom, monetary gifts and sacrifices flowed into Amun's temples and filled the coffers of the priests there. As a result, the priests held considerable power during that time. However, Amun suffered a drop in worship when Akhenaten attempted to establish monotheism in Egypt. However, once Akhenaten died, Amun's popularity quickly rebounded, and he remained a very influential god.

ABOVE: Double feather crown of Amun; **TOP, LEFT:** Statue of Ramesses II with Amun and Mut at the Museo Egizio of Turin, Italy; **OPPOSITE PAGE, ABOVE:** Stela of the God's-father of Amun Pakeshi; **OPPOSITE PAGE, BELOW:** Head of the god Amun

ANUBIS

Anubis is one of the most important gods of ancient Egyptian mythology because of his connection with funerary practices.

Most ancient tombs had carvings with prayers to Anubis on them. Anubis was the god of death, embalming, cemeteries, the Underworld, and funerals. He was also the protector of tombs and mummified corpses. He is often depicted as a jackal or jackal-headed man. This may be because jackals were common scavengers in ancient Egypt and by praying to the jackal-headed god, the dead could avoid scavenging. It is likely that the original Anubis was a hybrid form of a dog, jackal, and possibly wolf or fox, as early representations show the long muzzle of a dog but the wide, club-shaped tail of a jackal or fox. The black color of the jackal was also symbolic, as it was connected to the discoloration of the corpse after death, as well as the black, fertile earth, which for the Egyptians was symbolic of regeneration and rebirth. During funeral and burial ceremonies, priests may have worn jackal masks and impersonated the god in this way.

One tale depicts Anubis as a protector of tombs. Anubis protected the body of Osiris when Seth tried to attack it. He is listed as the son of the cow goddess Hestat and also the son of Bastet, the feline goddess. In one account by Plutarch, he was the son of Osiris and Nephthys but also adopted by Isis when she discovered him as a baby. Nephthys abandoned Anubis because of her fear of Seth. He later became known as a protector of Isis from Seth when she gave birth to Horus. Later, this protective role was emphasized by the Greeks and Romans in the form of a leopard. Anubis branded Seth with a hot iron (and thus the legend was used to explain how leopards got their spots), flayed Seth, and wore his skin as a warning to others who would desecrate tombs.

Anubis in his jackal form is often depicted lying on a shrine or lying with his paws outstretched before him, with his tail hanging down behind him. He often wears a collar and ceremonial tie around his neck. Very rarely is he ever depicted in pure human form.

There are many myths about Anubis' parents. In one, he is the son of Seth or Ra with Nephthys or possibly Osiris. In some myths, Anubis first practiced embalming on the body

GOD Jackal or jackal-headed.

ASSOCIATION/ROLE Cemeteries, embalming; often depicted with a flail; son of Seth and Nephthys; daughter is the goddess Kebechet, who was the personification of embalming fluid. His name means "cooling water."

ABOVE: Anubis Statue; **OPPOSITE:** The King with Anubis, Tomb of Haremhab.

of Osiris after he was murdered by Seth. He embalmed Osiris, then carried out funeral rites for him. In the Book of the Dead, Anubis is the god who supervises the embalming and mummification ritual, protects the mummy, oversees the ceremony of the Opening of the Mouth, and who performs the Weighing of the Heart. The Opening of the Mouth was an important part of the funeral ritual, as the ancient Egyptians believed that a deceased person could not hear, speak, or see until this ceremony. Priests dressed as Anubis would hold the person's coffin upright, while another priest would touch the person's mouth with ceremonial objects, and once the ritual was completed, the person could now engage all five senses, and eat and drink in the afterlife.

During the Old Kingdom, Egyptians prayed to Anubis to protect their dead, before Osiris became the main god associated with death. He originally was only concerned with the burial and afterlife of the king but this was later extended to include commoners as well. After Osiris rose to prominence during the Middle Kingdom, Anubis had a place in Egyptian funerary practices by assisting in the judgement of the dead and the accompaniment of the deceased to the ritual of the Weighing of the Heart.

His name is also connected with death. One text shows that his name comes from a verb meaning "putrefy," although the exact origin is unknown. He has several epithets, including "Foremost of the westerners," alluding to the dead being buried on the west bank of the Nile, as well as the symbolic nature of the sun setting in the west and the direction of the Underworld. Thus, the deceased were known as "westerners." In addition, the title was syncretized from an earlier, similar canine deity that Anubis eventually superseded. "He who is Upon His Mountain," does not mean any one specific mountain, but rather to the desert cliffs overlooking the cemeteries.

"Lord of the Sacred Land," refers to the desert where burials were located, but Anubis also bore many titles that referred to specific parts of Egypt. "The one presiding over the god's pavilion," refers to the burial chamber or place of embalmment. "He who is in the place of embalming," places Anubis squarely in the center of the importance of the embalming

LEFT: Stela of Siamun and Taruy worshiping Anubis.

TOP: Lintel of Amenemhat I and Deities; **ABOVE, CENTER:** Anubis Weighing the Heart, Tomb of Nakhtamun.

process and the ritual tent (or pavilion) where the embalming ritual was carried out. The embalming ritual has been traced to at least the beginning of the Fourth Dynasty.

"The Ruler of the Bows," comes from the Pyramid Texts, which denotes Anubis as the ruler of nine, bound figures, which represented the enemies of Egypt. Anubis is often depicted as crouching over the nine, distinct men, which may symbolize the god's control over evildoers or the underworld enemies of the dead.

During the Old Kingdom, prayers to Anubis were carved on funerary stelae and on walls of the mastaba tombs. Eventually, during the Greco-Roman period, Anubis became syncretized with the Greek god Hekate and with Hermes, who escorted the souls of the dead across the River Styx.

Anubis is also commonly represented with an Imiut fetish, which is a headless, stuffed animal skin hanging from a pole connected to a pot. The skin was of a cat or bull, and the fetish often had a lotus flower attached at the end. The fetish can be traced to the First Dynasty, and images of it often appears on stelae, papyri, royal seals, and temples. Its exact origin is unknown, as well as its exact purpose, but later it was so frequently associated with the god of death and embalmment, around the Fourth Dynasty, that it became known as the Anubis fetish. Amulets of the god were also common among Egyptians throughout the pharaonic period.

Interestingly, Anubis had a female counterpart, Input. Although she did not reach the levels of importance that Anubis did, she nevertheless had her own cult in ancient Egypt.

Anubis' chief center was the 17th Upper Egyptian Nome, which is the modern-day el-Qeis Halt, which the Greeks called "Cynopolis," or "city of the dogs." However, Anubis was so important to the ancient Egyptians, even after Osiris rose in prominence to take the primary role of a god of the dead, that he was worshiped throughout the region. This continued until the very end of the pharaonic period, in the 22nd dynasty.

BASTET

Bastet was a cat goddess and the daughter of the sun god. She was one of the most popular deities in ancient Egypt, as she was the protector of the house and family.

GODDESS Also known as B'sst, Baast, Ubaste, and Baset; Cat or cat-headed.

ASSOCIATION/ROLE Daughter; 'Eye of Re'; daughter of Ra and Isis. Consort of Ptah, with whom she had a son, Maahes. Maahes was the god of war, protection, and weather, as well as that of knives, lotuses, and devouring captives. Goddess of protection, cats, perfume/ ointments, women's secrets, fertility, pregnancy, children, music, the arts, and warfare.

MAIN CULT CENTER Bubastis.

RIGHT: Bastet, in cat form; **OPPOSITE:** Bastet, in lion form.

In early depictions, she was associated with the lioness, but later Egyptians emphasized her domesticity and loving, caring aspects.

As the daughter of the sun god, she personified the sun's beneficial power and acted as a foil to the more ferocious Sekhmet. In the Pyramid Texts, she appears as a mild-mannered mother and nurse of the king. As the daughter of the sun god, she is identified with the "Eye of Ra," but also is associated with the "Eye of the Moon." She eventually became known as "The Cat of Ra," and who was responsible for destroying Apophis, the evil serpent enemy, and she is sometimes depicted decapitating Apophis in statues with a sharp knife.

Her name is unknown in origin and exact meaning, although Egyptologists have many theories. Some have traced her name beginning with B'sst, which became Ubaste, then Bast, then Bastet, but the exact meaning is unknown. Another theory is that her name means "She of the ointment jar," and the Greek word for alabaster may derive from her name. Since her son Nefertum was linked to sweet smells as the god of perfume, Bastet also was linked to ointments and perfumes in this way.

TOP: Bastet in cat form; **ABOVE:** Menat of Taharqo: the King Being nursed by the lion-headed goddess Bastet; **OPPOSITE:** Coffin for an animal mummy, surmounted by a cat.

ICONOGRAPHY

Bastet was often depicted as a lion in the early periods, but then after the Middle Kingdom, she was shown as a woman with a cat's head. The earliest form shows her as a woman with the head of a lioness. However, after her character changed, and her nature was viewed as a milder form of leonine energy, she became associated with cats and thus depicted. She is associated with being a mother-goddess and is often accompanied by kittens. Sometimes she is shown carrying a sistrum, a percussion musical instrument, which has connotations with Isis and Hathor. The sistrum was often decorated with images of cats. She was also often shown with the ritual menat necklace, which was associated with Hathor, and used by priestesses as a rattle. The necklace symbolized good luck, protection against evil spirits, and protection in the Underworld. Men also wore the necklace to symbolize virility. Finally, Bastet sometimes is shown holding a papyrus scepter or Wedjat eye symbol.

SYMBOLISM

Bastet is frequently association with motherhood and protector of mothers during childbirth. Eventually, the Greeks would associate her with Artemis, the goddess of the hunt, chastity, and childbirth. As cats were hugely important to ancient Egyptians, this particular goddess was widely renowned throughout the land.

ROLES

Bastet had many protective roles in ancient Egypt; she was the protector of Lower Egypt, (while her counterpart was Wadjet) defender of the king and the sun god Ra. She was also seen as a protective mother, a goddess of pregnancy and childbirth. As such, she was depicted as a loving, kind mother. She was also invoked as protection against evil spirits and diseases. In the Book of the Dead and the Coffin Texts, magic spells advise the practitioner to pretend to be the "son of Bastet" to avoid the plague.

Some of her names hint at the history of her ferocious nature, "The Lady of Dread," and the "Lady of Slaughter." While Bastet was seen as a loving mother, the other side was that she could be fiercely protective.

Bastet came to be associated with Mau, the divine cat, (the word "mau" is the Egyptian word for "meow," the sound a cat makes), as well as Mafdet, the goddess of justice and the first feline deity in Egyptian history.

WORSHIP

Bubastis was the main cult center of Bastet in the eastern Delta region. Ancient Egyptians made pilgrimages to Bubastis for the festival of the cat goddess, which was a festival of unrestrained revelry and fertility. Women would stand on the banks of the Nile River and women traveling on boats would shout abuse, dance, hitch up their skirts, and expose their genitals to the women on the banks. This was probably meant to symbolize passing fertility onto the women on the land (or vice versa). During other rituals, women would expose themselves before fertility statues, such as that of Hathor, hoping to benefit from its power. Herodotus wrote that approximately 700,000 people attended the festival of Bastet. Whether this figure is accurate or not is less important than the significance of attendance itself. People sang, played musical instruments such as the flute and castanets, made sacrifices, and drank wine in abundance. Herodotus claimed that this was the most elaborate of all religious festivals in Egypt, and he praised the magnificence of the temple in Bubastis. According to ancient Egyptian tradition, lioness goddesses were appeased with large feasts of drunkenness, and this can be seen in the myth of Sekhmet.

Although Bastet was popular from early times and continued throughout Egyptian history, her heyday was during the Greco-Roman period, when she held great status and importance. People made amulets of cats, and they were popular as New Year's gifts. In addition, her name was often inscribed on New Year's flasks because of her role as a protective deity, as she countered the dark forces of the "Demon Days," which arose at the end of the Egyptian year.

Cemeteries of cats mummified and buried

have been found at Bubastis and at other sites, in honor of Bastet, numbering approximately 300,000. She held importance in both Lower and Upper Egypt, where she was equated with Mut, a mother goddess of ancient Egypt. Mut's name means "mother," in the ancient form of Egyptian.

HISTORY

Bastet's popularity is linked to the veneration of cats in ancient Egyptian culture. This goddess even made her mark in recorded history when the Persians invaded Egypt. In 525 BC, Cambyses II, the king of Persia made his soldiers paint the image of Bastet on their shields, so that the Egyptian soldiers would not attack and deface her image. Not only that, but he also gathered all the animals he could and placed them before his army, as a sort of animal shield, knowing that the Egyptians would not want to harm the animals. His gamble paid off; the Egyptians refused to fight so as not to offend Bastet and so surrendered. To add insult to injury, Cambyses II hurled the cats in the Egyptians' faces in mockery of their willingness to surrender. However, this did not deter the Egyptians from continuing to worship Bastet.

THE TALE OF SETNA & TABOUBU

This tale indirectly links Bastet with justice and protection, showing the importance of Bastet in everyday life of ancient Egyptians.
One day, a young prince named Setna stole a book from a tomb, despite the inhabitants begging him not to. As tomb robbery was a great crime, the gods could not look past this dishonor. When Prince Setna traveled to Memphis, he came upon a beautiful woman, surrounded by her servants. She was the most beautiful woman he had ever seen and immediately lusted after her. As a prince, he had no trouble in introducing himself to her and learned that her name was Taboubu and that she was the daughter of a priest of Bastet.
After they parted ways, Prince Setna decided to send her a note, asking her to sleep with him for ten gold pieces. She offered him a counterproposal: to meet her at the Temple of Bastet in Saqqara, where she lived, and he could have all that he desired from her.
Gladly accepting her offer, Prince Setna eagerly traveled to Saqqara and met her at the designated temple. However, Taboubu came ready with stipulations. First, he had to sign over all his property and possessions. Setna readily agreed and attempted to seduce her. Taboubu reproached him and said that his children must also sign the documents, to legally protect herself in the exchange.
He immediately compiled and sent for his children. While the documents were being signed, Taboubu changed garments and returned wearing a linen dress so sheer that the prince could see every part of her body through it. His desire for her thus became nearly uncontrollable. Again, Prince Setna attempted to seduce Taboubu, but once again, she held him off with a third and final demand: he must kill his children, so that they could never renege on the contract and attempt to take back her property in the courts.
Setna agreed, murdered his children, and threw their bodies in the street. Once this was done, he took Taboubu into the bedroom, where he removed his clothes, and hers as well. As he lay with her, she suddenly screamed and vanished without a trace. Immediately, the room and villa surrounding the prince disappeared as well.
Setna was left standing naked in the street with his member thrust in a clay pot. The prince was completely humiliated. The pharaoh then arrived and informed him that his children were still alive and that everything that he had experienced was an illusion. The prince realized that he had been punished for his crime of stealing the book from the tomb and vowed to make amends. He returned the book so that there was restitution to the inhabitants of the tomb.

Bes is an interesting god of Egyptian mythology because he was a dwarf-like figure with leonine properties.

BES

GOD Leonine dwarf; Consort of Beset; His name perhaps comes from the word "besa," or "to protect".

ASSOCIATION/ROLE Household; childbirth.

TOP, RIGHT: Stela of the God Bes; **ABOVE:** Stela of the God Bes; **OPPOSITE:** Fresco from the Temple of Isis in Pompeii depicting the Egyptian god Bes; **OPPOSITE, INSET:** Relief of the god Bes by the Roman northern gate of the temple complex, Dendera, Egypt.

Bes usually had a beard, and unlike many other Egyptian gods and goddesses, he is usually shown full-face, rather than in profile. Because of this, some scholars think that he may have originated outside of Egypt in Sudan. However, others place him squarely within the realm of Egyptian mythology.

In addition, Bes is actually an amalgamation of several different gods—as many as ten—so this is a rather complex god. Aha, Amam, Bes, Hayet, Ihty, Mefdget, Menew, Segeb, Sopdu, and Tetetenu all share characteristics of Bes, so all these gods may refer to the same spiritual being. In short, he is a composite deity, eventually subsuming various minor gods and demons, and he also came to share elements of Amun, Min, Horus, and Reshef, among others. The complexity and variance of the different gods shows his enormous popularity among the common people of Egypt.

He is usually shown with a lion's tail, ears, and mane, although this does not necessarily mean he was a lion deity, as Bastet or Sekhmet was. He may be wearing a lion skin as protection, and some rituals have Bes wearing a leopard skin. He was also usually portrayed with shortened legs, an enlarged head, large, staring eyes, and a protruding tongue. Although some scholars have drawn comparisons to African pygmies and Libyan images, his distinct iconography may stem from that of a male lion rearing up on its hind legs.

Bes was a protective god who warded off evil spirits, and kept snakes away from houses. He is often shown holding or biting serpents, which may reflect a syncretization with the demon Aha, who was known to strangle serpents.

Egyptians usually depicted him as present at births, and he was a god of festivity, with singing, dancing, playing the tambourine or drum to frighten away evil. He is often shown alongside Taweret in protecting pregnant women or those giving birth. Because of his association with pregnant women, he is often shown with large, sagging breasts and a big, round belly.

He was also considered a protector of the dead, and his image often appears on the headdresses of mummies. Bes was considered a benevolent god, despite his sometimes-fierce appearance, and he rose to popularity among all classes of Egyptians. He was a powerful apotropaic deity, meaning he was powerful in deflecting evil.

Although he appears in Egyptian mythology as early as the Old Kingdom, it was only during the later periods of ancient Egyptian history, he became more popular. Many decorative and household items bore his image, such as mirrors, beds, headrests (where he would protect the sleeper), perfume jars, and other toiletry items, such as cosmetic jars. Cosmetics were used for protection not only from the strong desert sun, but also used to divert malevolent spirits. As such, it is no surprise that his image would be on anything that may have helped the ancient Egyptians protect themselves from the elements and evil spirits. He was also made into amulets for protective purposes and jewelry. His image appears on birth houses in the Greco-Roman period, as well as paintings in both royal and common houses. Finally, people may have dressed in Bes-themed masks and costumes to promote protection in a more ritualized context.

Eventually, the Greeks and Romans transformed his image further, frequently depicting him with a sword and shield, emphasizing his protective nature, and he was eventually adopted as a military deity.

Bes did not have an official cult center, but he was widely popular among the Egyptian people.

Geb was a god of the Earth, vegetation, and fertility. After Atum-Ra and Shu, he was the third divine pharaoh, and pharaohs sometimes referred to themselves as "Heir of Geb."

GEB (SEB, KEB, KEBB OR GEBB)

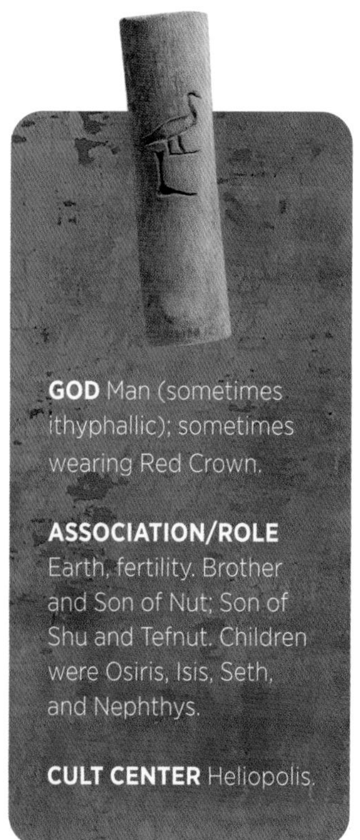

GOD Man (sometimes ithyphallic); sometimes wearing Red Crown.

ASSOCIATION/ROLE Earth, fertility. Brother and Son of Nut; Son of Shu and Tefnut. Children were Osiris, Isis, Seth, and Nephthys.

CULT CENTER Heliopolis.

ABOVE: Hieroglyphs of Geb; **OPPOSITE:** Sky goddess Nut and Geb with the head of a snake, and composite depiction of Geb.

He was the divine personification of the Earth and appears in the Creation Myth of Heliopolis (told below) and thus was one of the most important primeval gods. It is interesting that the ancient Egyptians associated a male figure with the Earth, as many other ancient cultures linked the Earth with feminine energy. Grain was said to sprout from his ribs and all vegetation from his back.

In depictions of Geb, he is almost always represented in strictly human form, a rarity for ancient Egyptians. However, during the pre-dynastic era, Geb appears as a sacred goose. According to some creation myths, Geb laid an egg from which Atum-Ra emerged and thus was sometimes called "The Great Crackler," referring to the sound an egg makes when broken.

As a god of fertility, he is sometimes shown with an erect phallus; he was also colored green at times and surrounded by plants or with plants growing out of him. (One must wonder if the Green Knight of Arthurian legend takes a page out of Geb's book.) As a fertility god, the hieroglyph used for his name became linked with vegetation and growth. He was also a god of mines and caves and all the precious stones that came out of them.

In images of creation, he is shown reclining beneath the arched body of his sister and consort, Nut, the sky goddess. Geb was also considered to be the husband of Renenutet, a cobra goddess. He is often depicted with headdresses, such as a white goose and occasionally wears the Red Crown of Lower Egypt.

Although Geb was generally seen as a benevolent god, he also could be malevolent. Earthquakes were known as "the laughter of Geb." He was also considered to be the god of fresh waters and therefore whatever the Earth produced came from him. If there were droughts, Egyptians traced them back to Geb withholding his blessing. (Hapy, the god of Nile inundation, was called "Friend of Geb.")

He had a dark side in funerary practices. He was considered to be able to imprison buried bodies within his own, trapping the dead.

Geb was known as "the heir of the Gods," and in mythology, he was the father of Osiris, which

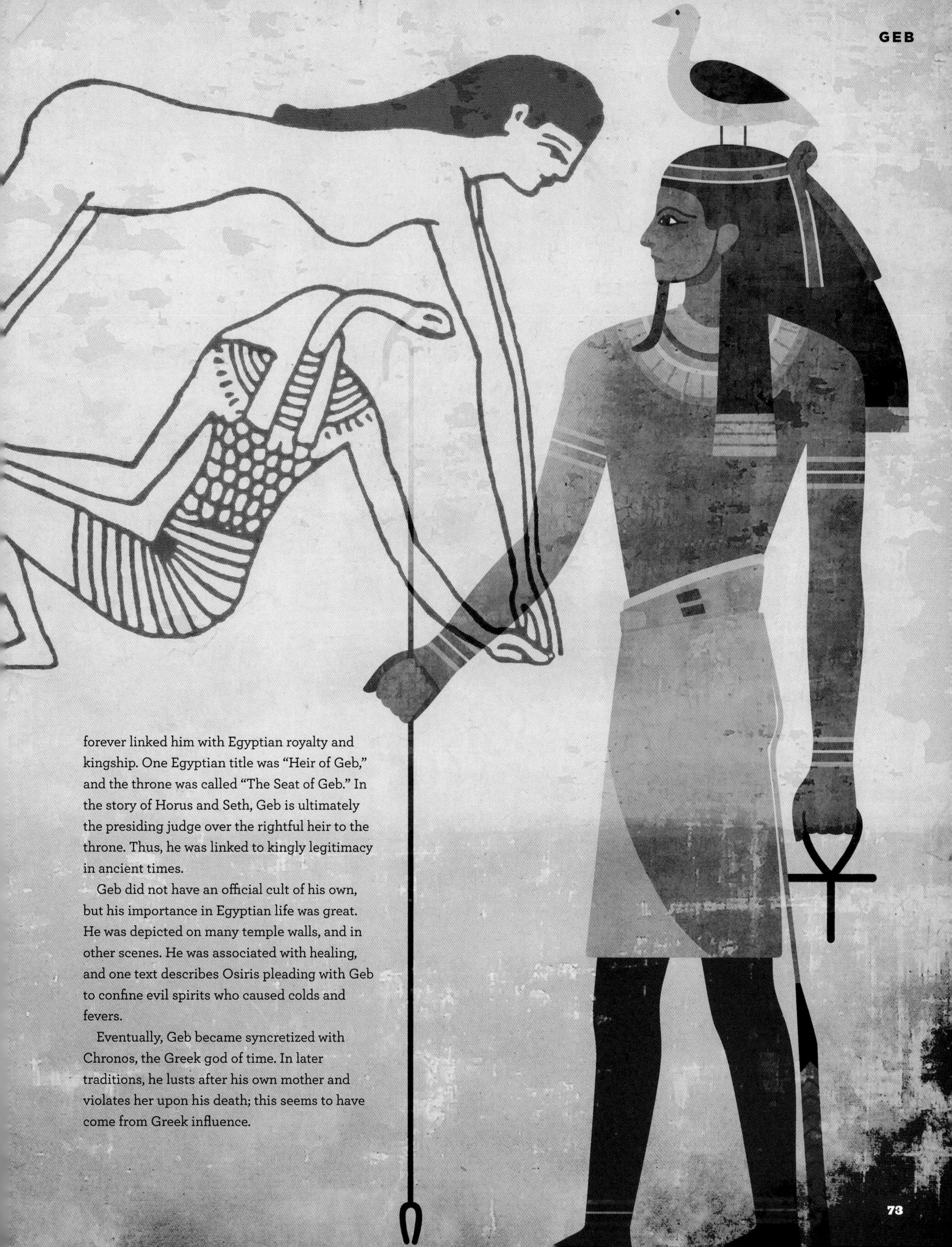

forever linked him with Egyptian royalty and kingship. One Egyptian title was "Heir of Geb," and the throne was called "The Seat of Geb." In the story of Horus and Seth, Geb is ultimately the presiding judge over the rightful heir to the throne. Thus, he was linked to kingly legitimacy in ancient times.

Geb did not have an official cult of his own, but his importance in Egyptian life was great. He was depicted on many temple walls, and in other scenes. He was associated with healing, and one text describes Osiris pleading with Geb to confine evil spirits who caused colds and fevers.

Eventually, Geb became syncretized with Chronos, the Greek god of time. In later traditions, he lusts after his own mother and violates her upon his death; this seems to have come from Greek influence.

HATHOR

Hathor was the goddess of the sky, women, fertility, and love.

In Egyptian mythology, she is the mother of Horus and wife of Ra, and because of their connection to kingship and pharaohs, she was seen as the symbolic mother of pharaohs. She is a relatively old deity, worshiped since the early dynastic periods, around 3000 BC. Hathor was the divine personification of represented music, dance, joy, love, sexuality, and maternal care. Because of her connection with maternal care, she was often depicted as a cow, or woman figure with long cow horns and a sun disk. She was one of the most important goddesses in Egyptian mythology and one of the most depicted. More temples were dedicated to Hathor than any other goddess. Eventually, she became equated to the Greek goddess Aphrodite.

ORIGIN

Cows were venerated in ancient Egypt because of their ability to give milk, meat, and hides to humans. They related to motherhood because of the way they nurse their young. Depictions of Hathor may stretch back to the earliest Egyptian artefacts, including the Narmer palette. On this stone palette, there are two figures of cows on either upper corner. However, this might be an earlier deity called Bat. Hathor is specifically described during the Fourth Dynasty, still relatively early in ancient Egyptian history. She eventually subsumed Bat, as they fused into one deity, and also that of an earlier crocodile deity. Because she was such an ancient goddess, who eventually fused with other goddesses, she had many roles associated with her.

ROLES

Some of Hathor's roles included a sky goddess, solar goddess, the goddess of music, dance, and joy; sexuality, beauty, and love; motherhood and queenship; and fate. Not only that, but she had a role in assisting ancient Egyptians, it was believed, into the afterlife.

ICONOGRAPHY

Hathor was most often shown as a woman wearing a headdress of horns and the sun disk, with a red or turquoise dress. Other times, she was depicted as a cow with the sun disk between her horns or as a cow-headed woman. Because she was associated with foreign lands, she was also known for the precious stones and minerals found elsewhere. For example, in Sinai, where turquoise abounds, she was known as "The Lady of Turquoise," and therefore is often shown wearing this particular color.

Because she was associated with the Eye of

GODDESS Cow; woman with cow ears or horns and sun disc on head, or falcon on perch on head.

ASSOCIATION/ROLE Mother (esp. of king); love; fertility; sexuality; music; dance; alcohol; sky; Byblos; turquoise; faience.

CULT CENTER Dendera; Deir el-Bahir.

MAIN IMAGE: Ramesses III and Prince Amenherkhepeshef before Hathor; **BELOW:** Votive Stela with Three Hathor Cows; **OPPOSITE, TOP:** Mirror, with a handle in the form of an Hathor emblem; **OPPOSITE:** The Head of a Cow Goddess.

Ra, she was also commonly depicted as the uraeus, or the rearing serpent on the pharaoh's crown. Because of her protective nature, she sometimes appeared as a lioness in Egyptian art or a domestic cat, which emphasized her loving, gentle nature.

Finally, Hathor is sometimes shown as a sycamore tree. The sycamore tree was very important in Egyptian religion because it was one of the few useful trees that was able to grow in the desert. Representations of Hathor sometimes show her offering fruit from this tree to the deceased, in her capacity of caring for them.

WORSHIP

Hathor's most important cult center was at Dendera, but she appeared at other important centers at Cusae, Deir el-Medina, and Atfih. Hathor had an important religious festival that lasted for weeks, beginning in the summer. Approximately two weeks before the first new moon of the summer, her statue was taken from her temple shrine at Dendera and ritualistically driven in a procession to the temple of Horus approximately 33 miles south in Edfu. Once there, the ancient Egyptians used the statues of Hathor and Horus in various rituals before placing them together to "spend the night," which represented their divine marriage.

HEKA

Heka was the Egyptian god of magic and medicine.

To the ancient Egyptians, heka was a divine force that permeated the universe and was believed to have existed since the beginning of time. Therefore, Heka was the personification of magic and was said to have empowered Ra in the creation event. The word heka literally means "Using the Ka." His name in the 20th Dynasty began to be used as the hieroglyph for "power." In the Coffin Texts, he is called "the Lord of the Kas." In the Pyramid Texts, he is a formidable god who the other gods feared. It was said that he protected Osiris in the underworld and accompanied Ra in his royal boat.

Heka was usually depicted as a man with a kilt and curved beard. During the Late Period, he began to be represented as a child and accompanied other deities as their son. According to myth, he defeated twin serpents and so two intertwined snakes became one of his symbols. We still have this symbol to represent medicine today.

Although Heka was important to the ancient Egyptians, he did not have his own cult center. Still, he was often invoked in magical rituals in both the common Egyptian household as well as temples. His statue during the Roman occupation of Egypt was used in a fertility ritual of the crops to make sure that they had a bountiful harvest. His name was often used in spells, and it was said that he was a very powerful god because of his link with magic.

The Coffin Texts name him as "The Lord of Miracles," and "The Lord of Oracles, who predicts what will happen."

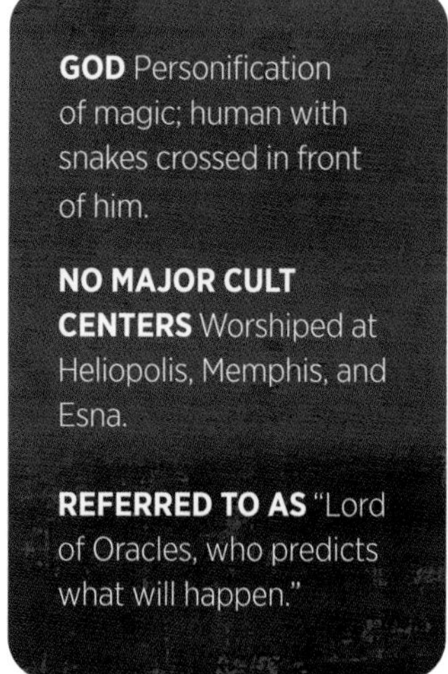

GOD Personification of magic; human with snakes crossed in front of him.

NO MAJOR CULT CENTERS Worshiped at Heliopolis, Memphis, and Esna.

REFERRED TO AS "Lord of Oracles, who predicts what will happen."

LEFT, BELOW: Detail of the temple wall, Esna, Egypt. The temple was dedicated to the triad of Latopolis; **OPPOSITE:** The child god Heka perched on a pedestal on the facade of the Khnum Temple in Esna, Egypt

HORUS

Horus was one of the earliest and most important Egyptian gods. It was said that his right eye was the sun or morning star, and his left eye was the moon.

He symbolized power and healing. His common form was a falcon, and there is evidence of widespread falcon cults in Egypt from the predynastic period.

Over time, Horus became linked with the Pharaoh, and it was said that the Pharaoh was a human manifestation of Horus. The Egyptian pharaohs had a series of names (originally three in the early dynasties but later increased to five), and the most important of their names was the one that identified them with Horus. In addition, Pharaohs were usually shown in paintings and wall scenes with Horus hovering above their heads.

Starting in the 1st Dynasty, it was said that Horus and Seth were perpetual enemies. Horus was said to be the son of Osiris, who Seth murdered to take the throne of Egypt. When Horus grew up to get revenge on Seth, they became irreconcilable enemies and went to war against each other. In their many years of fighting, Seth damaged Horus' eye, which Thoth healed. This eye became known as the wedjat and became a powerful amulet to the ancient Egyptians. Horus eventually defeated Seth to take the throne of Egypt.

During the Ptolemaic period, the myth of Osiris became an important ritual to enact, and the defeat of Seth became a symbol of Egypt defeating its enemies. At Idfu, a ritual drama took place in which Horus threw a spear at Seth in the form of a hippo, and killed him. Later, the Greeks equated Horus with Apollo, and Idfu became known as Apollinopolis, or "Apollo's Town."

The mythology of Horus was used as justification of the right of pharaohs to rule and to establish their legitimacy as kings. As Horus was the son of Osiris and Isis, who themselves were the sons of Geb and Nut, from Tefnut and Shu, going all the way back to Ra, Horus embodied divine kingship. The divine forces that produced Horus were venerated by ancient Egyptians. Then, because the Pharaoh became linked with Horus, and because Horus ruled over the whole world, the Pharaoh (theologically) had the right to rule the world as his human manifestation.

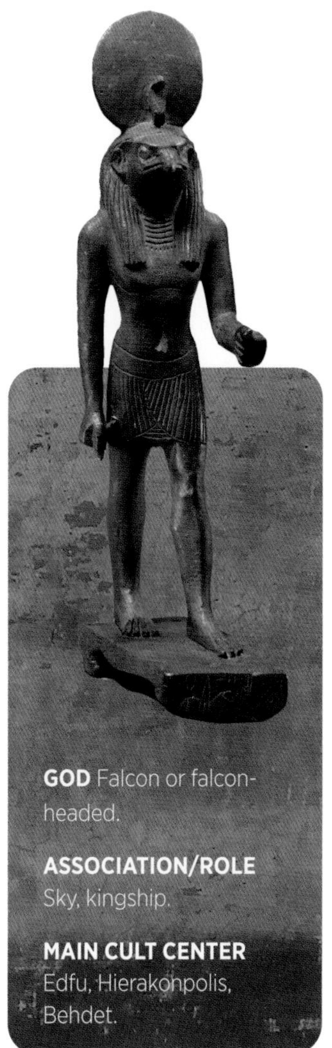

GOD Falcon or falcon-headed.

ASSOCIATION/ROLE Sky, kingship.

MAIN CULT CENTER Edfu, Hierakonpolis, Behdet.

ABOVE: Statuette of Horus; **OPPOSITE:** Temple of Horus at Edfu, Egypt.

TOP: Painted relief of the sacred eye of horus at the ancient Egyptian temple of the goddess Hathor at Dendera, Egypt; **ABOVE:** Relief of Horus in the temple of Seti I in Abydos; **OPPOSITE, TOP RIGHT:** Depiction of Horus; **OPPOSITE, INSET:** Inlay depicting "Horus of Gold."; **OPPOSITE, BELOW:** Horus and the Pharoahs.

ROLES

Sky god—Horus was known as the "lord of the sky," and his Egyptian name means "the one on high," or "the distant one," and this is connected to the image of a falcon by the soaring nature of falcons upon the wind. In addition, "the one on high" may also reference his solar aspect. As a falcon, Horus was said to have the right eye as the sun, left eye as the moon, and his speckled feathers were said to be stars. When he flapped his wings, wind was produced. The early Egyptians had many local sky gods, but Horus became the most important one and assimilated many lesser sky gods over time. The falcon also came to be associated with kingship from the earliest dynasties onward.

Sun god—Because of his association with the sky, Horus was also worshiped as a sun god. The Pyramid Texts mention Horus as "the god of the east," which refers to the rising sun. Horus became fused with many gods, and one of his names was Horakhty, which meant "Horus of the two horizons." Thus, Horus was associated with both the rising and setting sun, but over time, he became strongly linked with the rising sun and rebirth in the east. The Pyramid Texts state that the deceased pharaoh would be reborn as Horakhty. Eventually, this form of Horus was fused with Ra and became known as Ra-Horakhty. He also became Hor-em-akhet (or Harmarchis, "Horus in the horizon"). In this form, he took on the leonine aspect of the solar deity and was depicted as a lion. Eventually, the Great Sphinx of Giza became known as Harmarchis.

Son of Isis—One of the most important roles Horus had was as the son of Isis and Osiris. After Seth murdered Osiris, it was said that Isis reconstructed his body and created the missing male organ and fused Osiris' body together with magic. Then, they coupled, and Isis became pregnant with Horus.

God of kingship—Because Isis was said to be the divine mother of the pharaohs, and because Horus eventually defeated Seth in the myth to earn his rightful place as the king of

Egypt, Horus profoundly symbolized kingship in ancient Egypt. From the early dynasties, the pharaoh's name was written in a rectangle called a "serekh," which also showed Horus as a falcon perched on a palace. This suggested that Horus was a mediator between the earthly and heavenly realms. The pharaoh was called the "golden Hours," ***(is this a typo and should Hours be Horus?) ***and the hieroglyphs were the sign for gold and the divine falcon. There are other examples of Horus linked with kingship in Egyptian art. For example, a famous statue of Khafre has Horus the falcon behind Khafre's head with its wings outstretched, as though protecting the king.

ICONOGRAPHY

In his original form, Horus was depicted as a falcon. He is usually shown in profile this way, although the tail feathers were stretched out in full view. Early paintings of Horus show him leaning forward, but as time progressed, ancient Egyptians usually defaulted to showing him completely upright. Sometimes Horus is shown sinking its talons into an oryx (a large antelope), which was a common symbol of Seth. As Horakhty, he is sometimes depicted as a falcon-headed crocodile, which embodies several aspects of other lesser gods.

As a human, Horus is usually shown as an adult man but sometimes is depicted as a child, which references him as the son of Isis. In other forms, he is a falcon-headed man wearing the Double Crown of Egypt, which emphasizes his lordship over both Upper and Lower Egypt.

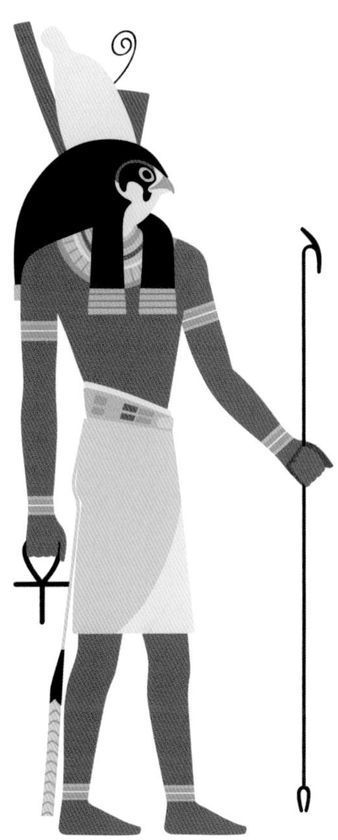

Isis is the goddess of magic, wisdom, healing, kingship, and protection of the kingdom, and sometimes a sky goddess or universal goddess.

ISIS

She was one of the most important and popular deities of Egypt, and she is part of the "Ennead of Heliopolis," which was made up of nine gods and goddesses (along with Atum, Shu, Tefnut, Geb, Nut, Osiris, Seth, and Nephthys).

She first appeared in the Fifth Dynasty in the Pyramid Texts, and was most famous for her role in the myth of Osiris. Because she was associated with the resurrection of Osiris in the myth, she became linked with helping the dead into the afterlife. In the myth of Osiris, she helped restore him to life and gave birth to their son Horus, so she became known as the protector of the dead and who provided nourishment to them in the afterlife. Ancient Egyptian beliefs posited that just as Isis restored Osiris in the afterlife, so too, could she help restore the souls of humans in the afterlife as well. The role of Isis in the myth of Osiris was also important because she essentially established the template of mummification and proper burial for ancient Egyptians.

In addition, because she was the royal wife (and sister) of Osiris and gave birth to Horus, the rightful heir of Egypt, she became known as the divine mother of the Pharaohs.

GODDESS Woman with throne headdress.

ASSOCIATION/ROLE
Mother (of king), magic. Child of Geb and Nut. Sibling of Osiris, Set, Nephthys, and Horus the Elder. Consort of Osiris, Min, Serapis, and Horus the Elder. Consort of Osiris, Min, Serapis, and Horus the Elder. Mother of Horus, Min, Four Sons of Horus, Bastet.

MAIN CULT CENTER
Philae.

ABOVE: Isis, breastfeeding Horus; **RIGHT:** Queen Nefertari being led by Isis.

ORIGIN

The meaning of Isis' name remains obscure, although scholars have many theories. The hieroglyphs for her name include the sign for a throne, and therefore, she may have started out as the personification of thrones.

ROLES

Goddess of Magic and Wisdom—Isis was known as the goddess of magic, and her magic was said to be more powerful than any other god's, even Ra. Because she was so powerful, she was said to protect Egypt from its enemies, protect and nurture creation, and even have power over fate. She often used her magic to protect Horus against Seth. She gained much of her power by making a snake from Ra's spit by mixing it with mud and having it bite him. He told her his true name and so gained unparalleled magical knowledge.

Sister-wife of Osiris—according to the mythology, Isis and Osiris were children of Geb and Nut, but Isis became Osiris' wife. This may have laid the foundation of rationale for the kings and queens of ancient Egypt to marry each other to protect the "purity" of the bloodline.

Mother and protector of Horus—Her role as the mother of Horus is one of the most important. According to the mythology, she protected Horus from various dangers, and there are thousands of amulets and statuettes showing Isis nursing the baby Horus. In one myth, Isis healed Horus from a scorpion sting, and through his lineage with Isis, Horus gained healing power as well.

Mother of the king—As the wife of Osiris and mother of Horus, the rightful king, Isis was the symbolic mother of all pharaohs. The Pyramid Texts state that Isis nursed the pharaoh, and he drank milk from her breast. Her name was also linked to the word "throne," as early hieroglyphs use the sign for throne in part for her name.

Mourner, sustainer, and protector of the deceased. Because she mourned Osiris after he was murdered by Seth, Isis became the archetype for Egyptian mourning. In addition, Isis was associated with the kite, which has a shrill, piercing cry, which may have suggested the sound of wailing. It was said that because she knew what mourning felt like, she was able to take care of the souls of the deceased better than any other god or goddess.

ICONOGRAPHY

Isis has many depictions in ancient Egyptian art and sculpture. Anthropomorphically, she is usually shown as a woman wearing a long sheath dress and wearing a crown. After the 18th Dynasty, she was commonly depicted having horns and a solar disk between them, most likely from her associations with Hathor. In the crown, there is usually a hieroglyph in the sign of a throne that also represents her name. Hathor's influence is also shown in depictions of Isis when she holds the sistrum rattle and menat necklace. She also often holds the ankh and papyrus staff. Most often, Isis is shown standing, but there are instances when she kneels. In this position, she may be in a posture of mourning, as she is often accompanied by the sign for eternity. If accompanied by Osiris, her arms are often outstretched to him or embracing him, representing her protective nature.

As an animal, Isis is sometimes represented as a scorpion, which harkens back to the myth of Isis and the Seven Scorpions. With her association as the mother of Horus, Isis is also depicted as a kite. Equally, she can be shown as a sow or cow, which came from her fusion with Hathor as a mother-goddess.

Finally, Isis is also depicted in the form of a tree, which symbolizes her association with life and nourishment.

Amulets of Isis were enormously popular, and they were often placed on mummies from the New Kingdom onward to protect them in their journey to the afterlife.

WORSHIP

Perhaps surprisingly, Isis did not have any main cult centers for much of Egyptian history. She was usually incorporated into other gods' or goddesses' temples. Her first temple in her own right started its construction in the 30th Dynasty, at Behbeit el-Hagar. Later, a temple was also dedicated to her at Deir el-Shelwit, south of Thebes. Her most famous temple was on the island of Philae, which was constructed during the Ptolemaic period. Songs found at this temple identify her with other goddesses, and by the time of Roman rule, had successfully absorbed many local deities.

Still, the lack of many major cult centers during ancient Egyptian history should not suggest that she did not have enormous influence, which she did. Isis also had a temple at Byblos, where she became syncretized with Astarte.

Once the Romans invaded Egypt, she became linked with the Greek goddess Aphrodite, and her association with love became stronger. As she was the goddess of magic, many spells invoke her name in love charms, either to attract a man and make him love a woman (as Isis had so loved Osiris) or repel a man (as Isis hated Seth). When the Romans conquered other lands, they brought Isis-Aphrodite with them. Archaeological evidence of Isis worship has been found as far away as England. Temples were built to honor Isis in the more local Greek cities and even in Rome. Isis was so important to the Egyptians that she was worshiped at Philae until the 6th century AD, which was long after most other Egyptian gods had ceased to be worshiped with the rise of Christianity.

TOP: Isis and Wepwawet, god of Asyut, with the name of Siese, Overseer of the Two Granaries of Ramesses; **ABOVE:** Isis, left, and Nephthys stand by as Anubis embalms the deceased, thirteenth century BC. A winged Isis appears at top; **RIGHT:** The remains of the temple of Isis on Delos; **BELOW:** Thoth sent seven scorpions to protect Isis and her son Horus.

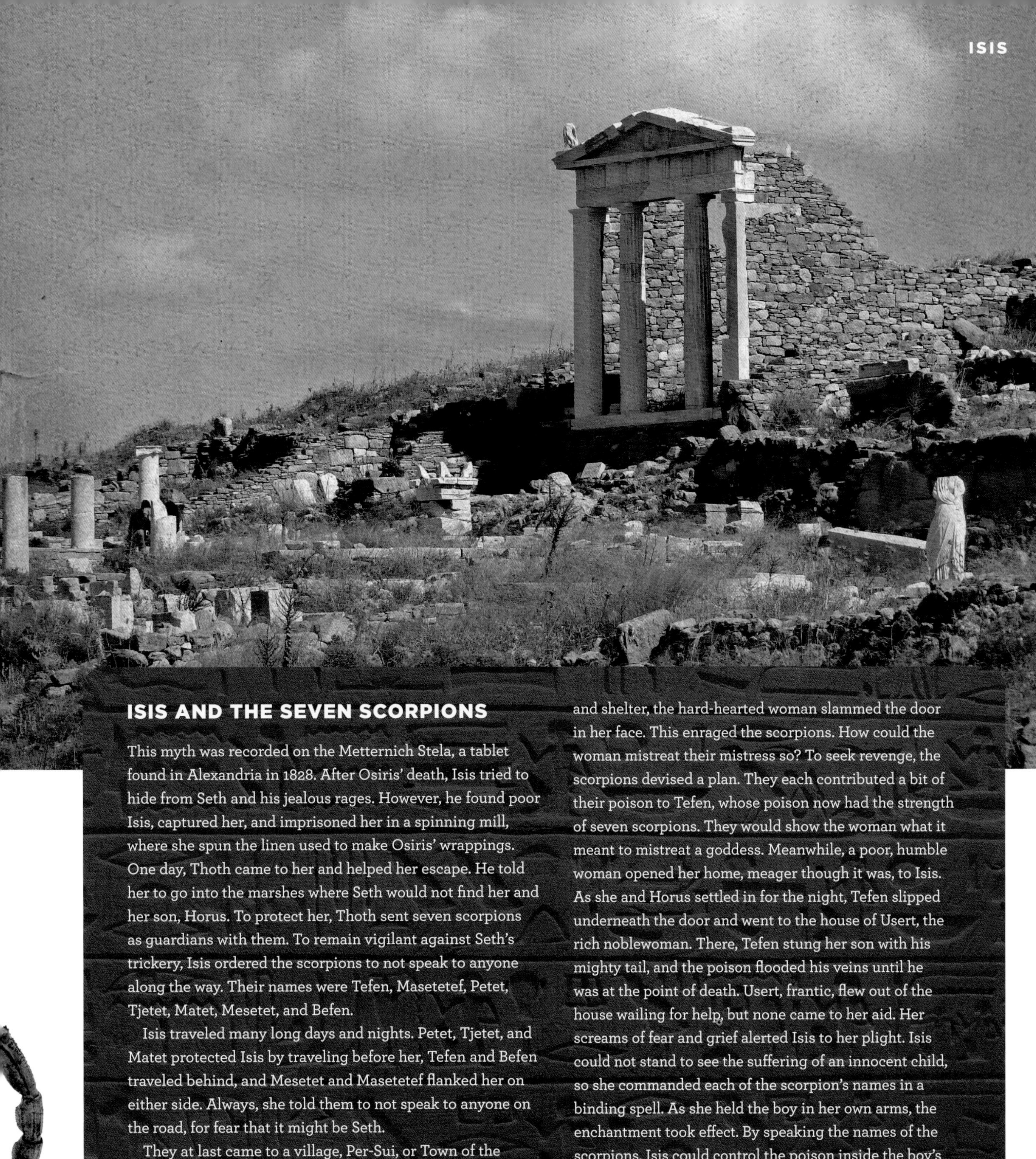

ISIS AND THE SEVEN SCORPIONS

This myth was recorded on the Metternich Stela, a tablet found in Alexandria in 1828. After Osiris' death, Isis tried to hide from Seth and his jealous rages. However, he found poor Isis, captured her, and imprisoned her in a spinning mill, where she spun the linen used to make Osiris' wrappings. One day, Thoth came to her and helped her escape. He told her to go into the marshes where Seth would not find her and her son, Horus. To protect her, Thoth sent seven scorpions as guardians with them. To remain vigilant against Seth's trickery, Isis ordered the scorpions to not speak to anyone along the way. Their names were Tefen, Masetetef, Petet, Tjetet, Matet, Mesetet, and Befen.

Isis traveled many long days and nights. Petet, Tjetet, and Matet protected Isis by traveling before her, Tefen and Befen traveled behind, and Mesetet and Masetetef flanked her on either side. Always, she told them to not speak to anyone on the road, for fear that it might be Seth.

They at last came to a village, Per-Sui, or Town of the Two Sisters, a village in the marshes of Egypt. The beautiful goddess disguised herself in the form of an old beggar woman and sought refuge for the night. In the town, a wealthy noblewoman named Usert saw Isis and her strange traveling companions. Although Isis beseeched Usert to give her food and shelter, the hard-hearted woman slammed the door in her face. This enraged the scorpions. How could the woman mistreat their mistress so? To seek revenge, the scorpions devised a plan. They each contributed a bit of their poison to Tefen, whose poison now had the strength of seven scorpions. They would show the woman what it meant to mistreat a goddess. Meanwhile, a poor, humble woman opened her home, meager though it was, to Isis. As she and Horus settled in for the night, Tefen slipped underneath the door and went to the house of Usert, the rich noblewoman. There, Tefen stung her son with his mighty tail, and the poison flooded his veins until he was at the point of death. Usert, frantic, flew out of the house wailing for help, but none came to her aid. Her screams of fear and grief alerted Isis to her plight. Isis could not stand to see the suffering of an innocent child, so she commanded each of the scorpion's names in a binding spell. As she held the boy in her own arms, the enchantment took effect. By speaking the names of the scorpions, Isis could control the poison inside the boy's body, rendering it harmless. Usert, forever changed by this act of kindness and forgiveness, gave all her wealth to the humble woman who had so graciously opened her home to the benevolent goddess.

KHNUM / KHNEMU

Khnum was a very important Ram god who was associated with the Nile and creation. He is one of the earliest deities to emerge from archaeological evidence and was said to be the original source of the Nile.

GOD Ram or ram-headed.

ASSOCIATION/ROLE
Creator; potter; cataract; fertile soil.

MAIN CULT CENTER
Elephantine; Esna.

When the Nile flooded every year, it brought rich nutrients to Egypt in its silt and clay. Perhaps because the Nile deposited large quantities of clay every year, Khnum became known as a potter who made humans on his wheel. Some of his titles reflect this role: "Divine Potter," and "Lord of Created Things." The ram in ancient Egypt was associated with fertility and power, and the Nile was a source of both to the Egyptian way of life. In the ancient Egyptian language, the word for ram sounded like the word for spirit or "ba" of all living things. Because of this, it was said that Khnum was the ba of the sun god Ra, and eventually became merged with him as Khnum-Ra. In his association with the Nile, he was also known as the "Lord of the Crocodiles."

ICONOGRAPHY

Most often, Khnum is depicted as a ram-headed man with undulating horns, although in later dynasties, he was shown with short horns. He usually wears a short kilt and a long wig, and he is shown with the Atef Crown with feathers or two long plumes. Khnum is frequently shown sitting at a potter's wheel crafting humans to be placed in the mother's womb. Because Khnum was associated with fertility and creation of life, he was also associated with creativity and was the personification of creative force.

WORSHIP

Khnum's major cult center was the island of Elephantine at Aswan. In this region, he was known as part of a triad of gods, along with Satis and Anukis, who also enjoyed popularity there.

CREATION MYTH OF ELEPHANTINE

According to the Creation Myth of Elephantine, Khnum modeled the gods, humans, all animals, plants, and even foreigners who lived outside of Egypt on his potter's wheel. It was said that he paid particular attention to the human body, carefully making the blood flow over the bones and gently stretching the skin to make a perfect fit. It was said that he took especial care with the respiratory, reproductive, and digestive organs and the vertebrae. After he crafted all on his potter's wheel, it was said that he watched over human conception, labor, and birth. In addition to creating the body, he also created the ka of each person and could bless the child, if he wished.

The Creation Myth of Elephantine developed on the small island in the center of the Nile which stands opposite to the modern city of Aswan. It was here that Khnum was principally worshiped. His counterpart was a frog goddess, Heket, who was a goddess of childbirth. It was said that Khnum fashioned the first humans, who were then given to Heket to be placed inside the mother. This version of creation was written on the walls of a temple at Esna, surviving from the Greco-Roman period. His consort Satet was associated with the annual flooding of the Nile.

In another myth dating from the Second Intermediate Period, three pharaohs were born. Each birth was attended by several gods and goddesses, including Khnum. After they were born, he gave them health.

KHONSU (KHONS)

Khonsu was a moon god who was said to be the son of Amun and Mut, and as such, he was part of the important Theban Triad, along with those two aforementioned gods.

Scholars have traced his name from the verb "khenes," which means "to cross over," or "to traverse," and so he became "he who travels across the sky." Khonsu was the physical personification of the moon, and he, along with Thoth, marked the passage of time.

Khonsu was also said to protect those who travel at night, since his light shined in the darkness. He also had the titles "Pathfinder," and "Defender." The moon was linked with birth and conception, so it was thought among ancient Egyptians that when the moon was a crescent, women more easily conceived, and livestock were more fertile. In addition, because he was the son of Mut, he was associated with air, so when the moon was a crescent, it was said that people breathed fresher air. Finally, Khonsu's name was invoked in spells to protect against animals and to promote healing.

ICONOGRAPHY

Khonsu usually appears as a human, quite often as a youth. To represent his boyhood, his hair is usually a simple sidelock that was common among ancient Egyptian boys. He usually wears mummy linens, but his arms are not bound by the cloth. On his head, he wears a full lunar disk within a crescent. Sometimes he is shown with a beard to represent his godlike aspect. He is frequently shown with the flail and crook in one hand and a staff in the other.

WORSHIP

Khonsu's main cult center was Thebes, and during the 20th Dynasty, Rameses III began the construction of his temple at Karnak. He had many important festivals, such as the New Year's festival where his statue was carried in a long procession.

GOD Child with headdress of full and crescent moon.

ASSOCIATION/ROLE Moon.

MAIN CULT CENTER Thebes.

ABOVE: Khonsu pendant; **LEFT:** Representation of Khonsu; **OPPOSITE:** Image taken from Cnouphis-Nilus (Jupiter-Nilus, Dieu Nil).

Maat was the goddess of truth, balance, harmony, law, morality, and justice. She was also said to control the stars and seasons.

MA'AT (MAAT)

GOD Woman with a single feather headdress.

ASSOCIATION/ROLE Order, truth, justice; daughter of Ra, with of thoth.

ABOVE: This small figure represents Maat, goddess of truth and justice, and embodiment of an ideal world in equilibrium; **OPPOSITE, MAIN IMAGE:** Depiction of the Feast of the Beautiful Meeting; **OPPOSITE, INSET:** Depiction of Ancient artisans' village Deir el-Medina in Upper Egypt.

She was the goddess who brought balance and order out of the primordial chaos at the beginning of time. In ancient Egyptian beliefs, it was said that one of her feathers was used during the Weighing of the Heart ritual that took place in the Land of the Dead. The feather was placed on a scale, and the deceased person's heart was placed on the other end. If the person's heart was heavy with evil, it would tip the scale toward Ammit, who would eat the heart. If the heart was lighter than the feather, the deceased could pass on to paradise.

As the rulers of Egypt, the pharaohs were expected to uphold law and justice, and as such, they were often shown with the symbol of Maat to emphasize that role. Egyptians believed that the pharaohs ruled through Maat's blessing and authority. Often, the pharaoh's held the title, "beloved of Maat," to establish their legitimacy to rule.

Maat entered in Egyptian belief in the Old Kingdom, and by the New Kingdom, she was associated with Ra as his daughter. She was also associated with Osiris, the "Lord of Maat." Her husband was said to be Thoth, and her dual, opposite deity was Isfet, who was the personification of evil, injustice, and chaos.

Maat represented universal balance; if Ra created the world at the beginning of time, Maat set order to it. The ancient Egyptians believed that maat, or order and justice, must be always upheld and must be renewed with rituals. Maat also represented judgment, and she judged not only the deceased in the afterlife but also the king's right to the throne. It was thought that a righteous king could bring about bounty, peace, and wealth for the kingdom; likewise, if a king acted dishonorably or impiously toward the gods, he could bring about famine and destruction of the kingdom.

Maat also personified morality, and it wasn't just the king who was expected to uphold maat; all Egyptians, royal and commoner alike, were expected to keep maat in their daily lives and throughout their lifetimes. Maat wasn't a set of rules but rather the spirit of justice, and everyone was expected to act with honor and truth. Upholding this balance meant to ancient Egyptians that the unity of the universe would be preserved. They believed that the universe needed cosmic harmony to keep the peace among people.

ICONOGRAPHY

Although Maat was almost universally depicted as a human woman with a feather on her head, sometimes the feather itself stood for Maat. In funerary papyri and temple scenes, Maat is shown in the ritual of the Weighing of the Heart, where her feather is on the scale but sometimes the goddess herself crouches on the scale.

WORSHIP

Maat was an immensely important concept in ancient Egypt, and it permeated daily life and royal religious belief. However, Maat did not have many formal centers of worship and was usually incorporated into other gods' and goddess' temples. Still, a small temple was built in Karnak to her. Priests sometimes carried the title, "priest of Maat," which signified their authority to give judiciary rulings. In one ritual, the pharaoh presented a small statue of Maat to other statuses of Amun, Ra, and Ptah. This represented the king's pledge to maintain law, fairness, and order in his kingdom and vowed to dispense the gods' justice.

NEBET-HET, NEPTHYS

Nephthys was the daughter of Nut and Geb and was part of the Ennead.

GOD Woman with headdress of a basket and enclosure.

ASSOCIATION/ROLE Funerary; protective.

ABOVE: Nephthys Amulet; **OPPOSITE, MAIN IMAGE:** Stela in the Shape of a Pylon; **OPPOSITE, INSET:** Mourning Nephthys.

She was the sister-wife of Seth, and she was associated with funerals, death, mourning, night, darkness, protection, magic, embalming, and beer. She does not appear in many myths, although she does appear in the Myth of Osiris, when Osiris was murdered; she mourned him along with Isis, and she helped her sister Isis to recover his body. She always took her sister's side against Seth and was more loyal to her than the enemy of Osiris. In later Egyptian mythology, she had a son with Osiris, which produced Anubis. When she appears in the Pyramid Texts, she usually is alongside Isis, and they protect and support Osiris. Because of her link with Isis and Osiris, Nephthys was linked to the pharaohs as a protector. When she helped Isis in embalming and burying Osiris, Nephthys also became linked with funerary practices, and she was one of the four guardian deities of the canopic jars, and she guarded the lungs. In the Late Period, she became linked with Anukis, but she was most strongly associated with her sister.

Nephthys was also linked to beer and its abundant consumption. In some temple scenes, Nephthys is shown receiving offerings of beer from the pharaoh, and she in turn blesses him to drink without suffering the effects of a hangover.

As a goddess associated with the dark, it was thought that she gave the pharaoh the gift to see hidden things in the night. Her role as a goddess of darkness fits with her death associations as well as being the sister-wife of Seth. It was said that Nephthys assisted women in childbirth. A scroll called the "Westcar Papyrus," relates the myth of Nephthys, Isis, and Meshkenet, and Heket. They disguised themselves as dancers and traveled throughout Egypt, until they came to a temple of Amun-Ra. There, they met the wife of a priest who was pregnant, and they help her prepare to give birth to four sons, who became great heroes.

Finally, as she is linked with her sister Isis, the principal goddess of magic and healing, Nephthys was said to have healing powers as well. Many amulets and statues of her were made in order to summon her healing abilities and pass them to humans.

ICONOGRAPHY

Nephthys is most often depicted as a woman with hieroglyphs for her name above her head. There are also some illustrations of the goddess as a kite, which was associated with the wails of women during mourning. She, along with Isis, are sometimes represented as birds together, guarding the body of Osiris. In her female form, she was usually painted or carved at the ends of sarcophagi, to ensure protection of the deceased's body. Sometimes, Nephthys was placed at the head of the coffin while Isis was placed at the feet. In scenes where Osiris is shown as the god of the Underworld, the two sisters often accompany him on either side. If Osiris is on his throne, they sometimes appear behind him in their protective role.

WORSHIP

Nephthys was a very important goddess in funerary rites, but she did not have a formal cult of her own, nor did she have any temples dedicated specifically to her. However, she sometimes appears in statuary form in the temples of Isis. Over time, she became a popular amulet to be placed on mummies. After the 26th Dynasty, virtually every Egyptian burial included an amulet of Nephthys.

NEITH

Neith is one of the most important deities from ancient Egypt, and one of the earliest.

She held the title, "Neith, the great," and she enjoyed immense popularity through essentially all of Egypt's ancient history. Some archaeological evidence suggests that people worshiped her during the pre-dynastic and Early Dynastic periods. In some creation myths, she was the first creator of the universe and its governor. She was the goddess of the cosmos, fate, mothers, childbirth, hunting, weaving, war, wisdom, and water. She was the patron deity of Sais, and one of three patron deities of Latopolis (Esna). In some myths, Neith was the mother of Ra and Apep and later she was viewed as the mother of Sobek. Because she was associated with water, she was said to be the wife of Khnum. She was sometimes referred to as the "Virgin Mother Goddess," because she created herself in the beginning.

Neith held many important roles for ancient Egyptians, including being the goddess of Lower Egypt, a funerary goddess, a mother goddess, creator goddess, and warrior goddess. Her worship continued from the earliest of ancient Egyptian history until the rise of Christianity.

Goddess of Lower Egypt—Neith was without a doubt the most important goddess, and deity in general, of Lower Egypt. She came to personify the northern, Delta region, and she was said to protect Lower Egypt with her fierce, aggressive nature. Scholars posit that her name may have come from the word "nrt," meaning "she is the terrifying one." Her temple at Sais was sometimes called "The house of the bee," and the bee became an important royal symbol for Lower Egypt.

Funerary goddess—In the Pyramid Texts, Neith is said to watch over Osiris, along with Isis, Nephthys, and Serket. Each of these four goddesses were charged with watching over one side of a deceased's sarcophagus, just as they were responsible for watching over the four canopic jars. She was also a judge of the dead when they went to the afterlife. Neith was also seen as a goddess of weaving, and this was incorporated into funerary practice as the goddess who wove the bandages for mummies. It was said that she re-wove the world daily on her loom.

Creator goddess—Neith was closely linked to the waters of Nun, and she was regarded as the process of creation itself. It was said that she was the creative force at the beginning of time. By the Roman era, it was said that she emerged from the primordial waters as a self-generating deity and created the world before settling in

GOD Woman with red crown of lower Egypt holding shield and crossed arrows.

ASSOCIATION/ROLE Creator-goddess; warfare; weaving.

MAIN CULT CENTER Sais.

ABOVE: Neith suckling two crocodiles; **OPPOSITE, MAIN IMAGE:** Neith.

TOP: Tutu (son of Neith); **ABOVE:** Statuette of Neith.

Sais. In the myth of the Contendings of Horus and Seth, she is referenced as "the eldest, mother of the gods, who illuminated the first face."

Mother goddess—In some creation myths, Neith was the creator-goddess of all nature, so she was also seen as the mother of all. She was said to be the mother of Sobek, the crocodile god, as well as humans and all other gods. It was said that Neith supported and protected royal mothers, and in one depiction of her, she, and the goddess Serket hold up the bed that the queen and Amun slept in together when they conceived Queen Hatshepsut.

Warrior goddess—It was said that Neith had a fierce character, and she quickly became associated with weapons and warfare early in ancient Egyptian mythology. She was called the "Mistress of the Bow," and "Ruler of Arrows." In the Contendings of Horus and Seth, she was sought out for her wise council, but she threatened to become angry and make the sky fall to earth if the gods did not follow her advice. Over time, the Greeks syncretized her with Athena because of her associations with warriors. In this form, it was said that she made the weapons of soldiers and guarded their bodies when they died. She is also associated with Athena because of her association with weaving; part of the hieroglyph of her name bore similarities to a loom. In Greek mythology, Athena was the goddess who wove the existence of the world on her loom.

ICONOGRAPHY

There is archaeological evidence that ancient Egyptians worshiped her from very early on. A representation of her symbol was found on a boat from the Predynastic Period. In her human form, she is found depicted on a vase from the Second Dynasty. Neith is usually depicted as a woman wearing the Red Crown, sometimes holding a bow and arrow or harpoon. A symbol for Neith was two arrows crossed over a shield, and this symbol was found even in pre-dynastic times. She is often portrayed carrying the ankh (life) symbol and the was (power) scepter. The hieroglyphs of her name usually incorporate bows and arrows.

She could also be portrayed as a cow, usually kneeling, with the sun disk between her horns. This bovine representation was common at Sais

ABOVE: Illustration & Statuette of Neith.

and Esna. She came to be named as the "Cow of Heaven," who gave birth to the sun every day.

Neith was also represented as the uraeus and so with her aggressive, warlike nature, protected the pharaoh in her serpent form.

As a mother goddess, Neith is sometimes shown nursing small crocodiles at either breast or as a woman with a crocodile's head. Many amulets of her were made of this image. Her link with the Nile is seen in her representations as a fish because it was said that she turned into a fish to swim in the primordial waters before creation.

WORSHIP

Neith held prominence in ancient Egyptian culture from the earliest times. One of the earliest shrines discovered in Egypt is thought to be associated with Neith. In addition, she was one of the most important goddesses of the Early Dynastic Period. Her primary cult center was established in Sais during the Old Kingdom. Although early rulers emphasized Hathor, later rulers in the 5th Dynasty re-established her as one of the primary goddesses of Egypt. She also had a sanctuary in Memphis, and she was the counterpart to Ptah in southern part of Egypt. She was called the "Mistress of Mendes," so she commanded an important presence there as well.

Neith enjoyed high status throughout Egyptian history, especially in the beginning. Her influence waned during the Middle and early New Kingdom periods, but she regained importance in the 19th Dynasty. After the New Kingdom period, Neith enjoyed a surge in popularity, especially during the 26th Dynasty when the pharaohs emerged from Sais, her great cult center.

During the Greek and Roman times, Neith's temples continued to bring in revenue from trade from a nearby settlement. Neith was incorporated into other deities' temples, and she was worshiped alongside Khnum. A large festival was dedicated to her, and ancient Egyptians celebrated it on the thirteenth day of the third month of their summer.

NUT

Nut was the goddess of the sky and the dome of the heavens. It was said that she swallowed the sun in the evening and gave birth to it in the morning.

Interestingly, most ancient cultures depict the sky as a masculine deity, but in Egyptian mythology, the sky is feminine. Nut was the daughter of Shu and Tefnut, and her brother is Geb, the god of the Earth. She birthed four children: Osiris, Isis, Seth, and Nephthys. (In later Greek versions, Horus was added as her son as well.) In early Egyptian myths, she was the goddess of the nighttime sky, but later she became the general goddess of the sky.

Nut was seen as a wall separating the chaos of the universe from the ordered cosmos. It was said that her body was the night-time sky strewn with stars, and her four limbs touched the four cardinal directions.

It was said that her laughter was the thunder, and her tears were rain. Some scholars have said that she might have represented the Milky Way because the Book of the Dead refers to the large swath of stars across the sky, which is followed by a spell that invokes her name. In addition, some representations of Nut show her with stars on and around her body. Some Egyptian scholars have evidence that the Milky Way looked remarkably like a human with their arms and hands outstretched over their heads—just as Nut is sometimes depicted.

Nut was also associated with resurrection in Egyptian mythology. The dead were believed to become stars, and the stars passed through her body each night and were re-born the following night. According to the myth of creation from Heliopolis, Nut coupled with her brother Geb to produce the other gods and goddesses mentioned above. It was also said that Nut was the sacred ladder which Osiris used to ascend to the heavens. This symbol became known as the maqet and was placed in many tombs and coffins to protect the dead.

ICONOGRAPHY

Nut is usually shown as a nude woman bending over Geb, forming an arch. Sometimes she is supported by Shu, the god of air, and she touches the east and west horizons with her hands and feet, respectively. In this stance, she is shown to be a bridge in the sky, although she was usually imagined as the whole vault of the heavens. In many representations, Nut is shown with a water pot on her head, sometimes with the hieroglyph for her name.

Nut was also painted or carved on the underside of the lid of a sarcophagus, along with the solar disk of the sun being reborn. This placement was symbolic, as it not only depicted the goddess guarding the deceased but also depicted the sarcophagi as the medium for rebirth.

In addition, Nut was also shown as a sky cow. Her four hooves were the four cardinal points

GOD Woman, cow.

ASSOCIATION/ROLE
Sky; sarcophagus.

MAIN CULT CENTER
Sais

ABOVE: Nut (as frame) Painted wooden panel of Tabakenkhonsu; **OPPOSITE:** The sky goddess Nut swallows the sun, which travels through her body at night to be reborn at dawn.

of the compass, and in this bovine form, too, were the stars scattered across her body. Her legs were said to be the pillars of the sky, and Shu also supported her with upraised arms. As a female pig, she is sometimes shown suckling her young.

WORSHIP

Nut was the principal deity of the sky, but she had no formal temples or cult. She was very popular among the commoners of Egypt, and many amulets with her likeness were made to protect women's fertility.

Nut had many titles, including "Coverer of the Sky," "She Who Protects," "Mistress of All," and "She Who Holds a Thousand Souls."

OSIRIS

Osiris was one of the most important deities of ancient Egypt. He was a god of death, resurrection, and fertility.

He was the first son of Geb and Nut, and sibling to Seth, Horus (the Elder), Isis, and Nephthys. He was considered to be the king of the underworld, but he was sometimes meshed with Ra in this role. Osiris became the ruler of the land of the dead after his brother, Seth, murdered him (See "Myth of Osiris"). He presided over the judgement of souls where their hearts were weighed against the feather of Maat.

However, this role as a judge of the dead should not be equated with the concept of the Devil in Christianity; rather, Osiris protected the dead and helped them move on to paradise. Therefore, Osiris was a benign deity who helped people reach the land of peace in the afterlife. Moreover, he is usually depicted with a soft smile, seeming to signify that people should not fear him. His titles were "Lord of Silence," and "He who is permanently benign and youthful," and these suggest the great silence death brings and also suggests his victory over death. Interestingly, he was also referred to as "The Lord of the living," but this meant those "living" in the underworld.

Osiris is actually the Greek form of Asir. Some early forms of his name use the hieroglyphs for "throne" and "eye," which may suggest that his name meant "He sees the throne." The throne is also associated with his wife Isis, as it is a glyph used in her name. In later periods, Osiris was called "Un-nefer," which meant "Good Things Appear."

Some scholars believe that Osiris started out as a minor fertility god who later took on the characteristics of a god of the underworld. Because of his link with fertility, Osiris was also a god of agriculture. During the planting season, crops were sewn, and Osiris was seen to germinate symbolically; then, during the harvest, he was symbolically killed during reaping. Once the Nile inundated the land, bringing fresh soil and nutrients, the crops would germinate again, renewing the cycle of death and rebirth. It was said that the Egyptians were cannibals until Osiris and Isis taught them agriculture, and this myth emphasizes Osiris' role in bringing order out of chaos. Egyptians crafted small dolls out of dirt and corn seeds and placed them in coffins with the deceased. The seeds would sprout, representing the concept of life from death.

Over time, Osiris merged with other gods and took on their attributes. For example, his insignia is the same as an older god's, Andjety. He also shares the title, "Foremost of the westerners," with Khenty-imentiu. Osiris was associated with the west because the sun set every day, symbolically "dying." Often, necropolises were located on the western bank of the Nile. It was said that his birthplace was Rosetau in a necropolis, which symbolized his

GOD Mummified man with Atef-crown, holding crook and flail.

ASSOCIATION/ROLE Death; afterlife; rebirth; fertility; agriculture; see "Myth of Osiris."

MAIN CULT CENTER Heliopolis

ABOVE: Depiction of Osiris; **OPPOSITE:** Philae temple in Aswan on the Nile.

connection to the dead.

Moreover, it was thought that the ba of Osiris resided in the sacred ram Ba-neb-djedet, which was worshiped primarily in the Delta region.

The most important fusion of deities was that with Ra, and this is shown in his titles "Lord of the Universe," "Ruler of Eternity," and "King of the gods." Osiris was not only Ra's counterpart but came to be seen as part of his body. The ba of Ra descended to the underworld to unite with Osiris' body.

The idea of Osiris' resurrection was extremely important for Egyptian royal theology. Osiris represented the death of the old pharaoh, and the new pharaoh was said to be the embodiment of Horus, his son. This essentially helped lay the foundation for the lineage of kingship throughout Egyptian history. Osiris was also popular among common Egyptians because he represented salvation in physical form. There was not a need to fear death because there was the possibility of life after, and a good life at that.

ICONOGRAPHY

Osiris was usually depicted as a human mummy, most often a king with the curved beard, crown, and flail. His skin was usually green or black to represent necrosis but was also sometimes white like the linen wrappings of a mummy. However, his black skin may have also represented the rich, dark soil of the Nile, and likewise his green skin may have symbolized fertility and vegetation. He normally is shown wearing the White Crown of Upper Egypt or the Atef crown (a white crown with a plume of feathers and a disk on top). The Atef crown may have originated with the god Andjety. Because of his association with numerous gods, Osiris was often depicted with different, merged crowns. During the New Kingdom, Osiris was depicted with a broad collar and wrist bracelets.

The crook and flail were shown differently, depending on the region. Osiris is sometimes shown with his arms at his side, in others, crossed at the wrists. The earliest depiction of Osiris comes from the 5th Dynasty, where he is shown with a wig, but from the Middle Kingdom onward, he is shown with the White Crown. Osiris was linked to the djed, or column, so sometimes he appears as a pillar with human arms or a human mummy with a pillar head. In numerous wall scenes, he is shown lying on a funerary table with Isis and Nephthys mourning him.

WORSHIP

Although Osiris was not as ancient as some gods and goddesses, his cult was well-established by the 5th Dynasty. He was widely venerated throughout Egypt, and he had numerous cult centers. Because it was said that his body was scattered through Egypt, numerous cities claimed that they were the site of some of his parts. For instance, it was said that Athribis held his heart, and Biga, Edfu, Herakeleopolis, and Sebennytos were all important cult centers because they claimed parts of his limbs.

However, his most important cult centers were at Abydos and Busiris. Abydos is the oldest known sanctuary of Osiris and was the chief cult center in Upper Egypt. It was said that the tomb of Osiris was held there. Busiris was extremely important for Osiris in Lower Egypt, and even the name Busiris means "House of Osiris." It was said that Osiris' backbone was buried there.

There were numerous festivals dedicated to Osiris. One of them was during the fourth month of Akhet. Plays were enacted which symbolized important events in Osiris' life, death, and rebirth. The most important ritual took place in Abydos. His statue was carried from his temple to his traditional tomb.

Osiris was very popular among the common people of Egypt, and he was important as the representation of life, death, and rebirth. However, very few amulets of Osiris have been found. However, he was depicted frequently in funerary scenes, coffins, and tombs.

The cult of Osiris grew over time, and because of his association with Isis, it spread in popularity even beyond Egypt's borders.

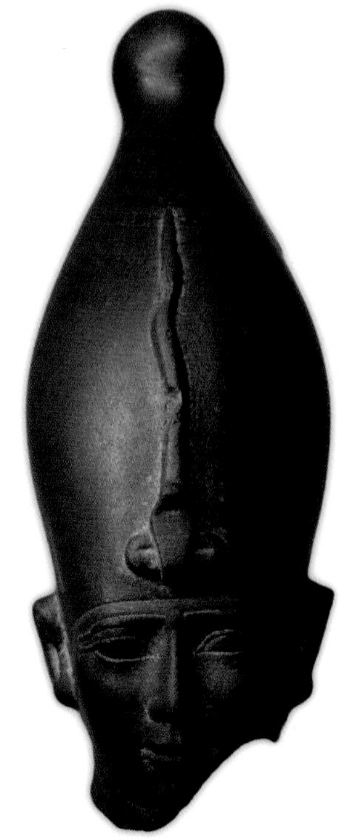

TOP: Head of the god Osiris; **ABOVE:** The gods Osiris, Anubis, and Horus. Wall painting in the tomb of Horemheb; **OPPOSITE:** The family of Osiris. Osiris on a lapis lazuli pillar in the middle, flanked by Horus on the left and Isis on the right.

5
4
3
2
1
6
7
8
9

PTAH

Ptah was a creator god and the patron god of craftsmen and architects

In mythology, he is the husband of Sekhmet, a warrior goddess and goddess of healing. In later eras, it was said that he was the father of Imhotep, the famous priest of Pharaoh Djoser (and architect of the Step Pyramid). He is part of a triad with Sekhmet and Nefertem, the god of the lotus flower. He is one of the oldest deities in Egyptian mythology, and he appears from the 1st Dynasty onward. Although he most likely started out as a local god, he grew to great importance in Memphis. He was Neith's counterpart as the god of Upper Egypt. Ptah held several important roles as a major god of Egypt.

Lord of Memphis—Ptah was the patron deity of Memphis, and because Memphis became the administrative capital of Egypt, Ptah's importance skyrocketed around the time of unification of Upper and Lower Egypt. Memphis was founded as the capital during the First Dynasty, around 3100 BC. Some scholars even think that the name "Egypt," is derived from the Egyptian phrase "Hut-ka-Ptah," ("the temple of the ka of Ptah,") rendered in Greek. Ptah was referred to as "Ptah, who is south of the wall," in contrast with Neith, who was associated with being "north." Ptah probably absorbed several local gods, and this is seen in a reference to him as "Ptah who is under his moringa tree," which suggested an incorporation of a lesser tree god of Memphis.

Creator god—Ptah was a god of creation who was known as a sculptor, which would lead to his association with craftsmanship as well. Like Khnum, it was believed that he formed everything in heaven and earth on his potter's wheel. In his form of a creator god, he embodied the masculine and feminine deities of Nun and Naunet, respectively. One creation myth emerged from Memphis in which Ptah created the world through his thought and powerful spoken word.

God of craftsmen—Perhaps concomitantly with his role as a creator, Ptah became associated with craftsmanship. With the rise of Memphis and the need for craftsmen to build the mighty empire of Egypt may have led to his rise in popularity. It was said that he was the smith of mankind and the progenitor of arts and crafts. During the Greek and Roman rule, he became syncretized with their god Hephaestus, who was the god of the forge and crafts.

God of supplication—Egyptians who needed prayers to be heard and answered often made them to Ptah. He was known as the "hearer of prayers," and there are many inscriptions of him with this title on temples.

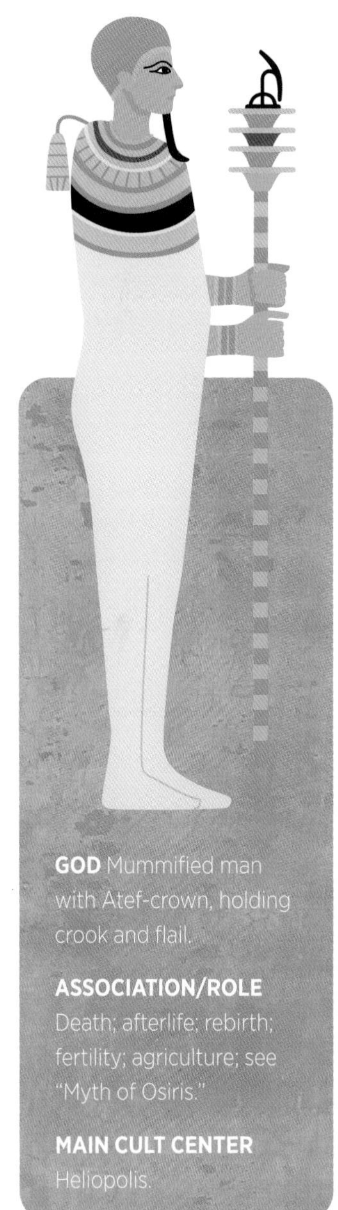

GOD Mummified man with Atef-crown, holding crook and flail.

ASSOCIATION/ROLE Death; afterlife; rebirth; fertility; agriculture; see "Myth of Osiris."

MAIN CULT CENTER Heliopolis.

ABOVE: Depiction of Ptah; **OPPOSITE:** Philae temple in Aswan on the Nile.

CREATION MYTH OF MEMPHIS

According to the Creation Myth of Memphis, Ptah was a self-engendered god who brought forth the universe by first conceiving all aspects of creation in his heart (which was thought to be the seat of thought for ancient Egyptians), he spoke his thoughts aloud, which then became physical reality. Ptah created the other deities (which then meshed well with the creation myth of Heliopolis in which his thoughts and speech formed Atum and the subsequent Ennead. He crafted stone statues out of wood, clay, and stone to act as the vehicles for ka of the deities. Everything after—animals, people, inanimate objects—were created by speaking their names.

This myth established the importance of the thinking heart. The ancient Egyptians did not know anything about the brain and instead thought that the heart was the vehicle of thought. (Which makes a certain degree of intuitive sense—when we are excited, our heart pounds; love feels as though it flows from our chest, etc.)

The power that names had is evident in this myth as well. One's name was considered the essence of a person, and it was thought that if someone knew an enemy's name, they could magically destroy them by writing it on an object, cursing it, and destroying the object. To ancient Egyptians, people survived by the utterance of their name, which is why burials with their name inscribed on coffins and tombs was so important. The Creation Myth of Memphis was inscribed on a slab of black granite, and it has been dated to around 700 BC. However, the myth itself is very old and probably dates at least to the Old Kingdom (around 2680 BC).

ICONOGRAPHY

Ptah was usually depicted as a male human, standing straight with his feet together, and holding a was scepter with the ankh and djed symbols. He is also usually seen with a sort skullcap, but sometimes has a small disk on his head with two tall plumes on either side, to represent his link with Osiris.

Ptah was associated with people who had dwarfism, as they traditionally worked as jewelers and artisans. Because of this, Ptah is sometimes depicted as a dwarf himself. However, this is based on writings of Herodotus, so it may be that the representations of dwarves simply symbolized workmanship and not the god himself.

WORSHIP

Ptah's chief cult center was at Memphis, although numerous temples were dedicated to him throughout Egypt. In addition, the sacred Apis bull also had a cult center at Memphis: it symbolized Ptah's physical manifestation.

TOP, LEFT: Amulet with Ptah on crocodiles; **TOP, RIGHT:** The Alabaster Sphinx outside the Temple of Ptah; **ABOVE:** Statue of the God Ptah.

ABOVE: Relief fragment depicting Imenet, Ptah and Amenhotep; **RIGHT:** Head of Ptah.

RA (RE)

Ra was a powerful, supreme creator-god in Egyptian mythology. He was considered king of the gods and creator of everything, according to the Heliopolis myth of creation.

Ra was the most important deity of all. He was an ancient deity worshiped from early times. He was so important that he frequently meshed with other deities to form composites, such as Atum-Ra or Ra-Horakhty (with Horus). He was seen as a divine father and protector of the pharaoh. He inhabits a primary position in importance, and his influence remained firm throughout Egyptian ancient history.

According to the Heliopolitan myth of creation, Ra emerged from the waters of Nun and either sneezed or ejaculated Shu, the god of air, and Tefnut, the goddess of moisture. They in turn begat Geb, the Earth, and Nut, the sky. It was said that after a dispute, Ra separated Geb and Nut. According to a prophesy, any child that Nut bore would one day supplant Ra as ruler, so he cursed her to not be able to bear children on any day of the year. However, Thoth crafted extra days from the moon, and Nut eventually gave birth to Isis, Osiris, Seth, Nephthys, and Horus (the Elder).

It was said that Nut swallowed Ra every night, as the sun set in the west. He then travelled through the Land of the Dead in his royal boat. He had to fight the serpent-demon Apep, but he was then reborn in the morning. His association with dawn linked him to the concept of rebirth, and this in turn linked him to the scarab beetle, which seemed to emerge spontaneously from a ball similar in shape to the sun. At sunset, he was linked to Horus.

ICONOGRAPHY

Ra had numerous images associated with him. He was depicted as a solar disk, usually protected by a cobra, and sometimes with outstretched rays. Ra was often depicted as male human with the body of a falcon, ram, or scarab. Ra was also shown as a falcon with the sun disk perched on its head. Because he was fused with so many other gods, he had numerous animal associations, including a phoenix, heron, serpent, bull, cat, and lion, among others.

One common image of Ra shows a scarab and ram-headed man both encircled by a solar disk; this represented the three essential roles of Ra, the rising, midday, and setting sun. Fused with Amun, he is shown as a man with a small solar disk attached to his crown. In his fusion with Osiris, Ra is shown as a mummy with the head of a ram, falcon, or scarab. In addition, there were many solar images attributed to him, such as sun disks, outstretched rays, flying vultures,

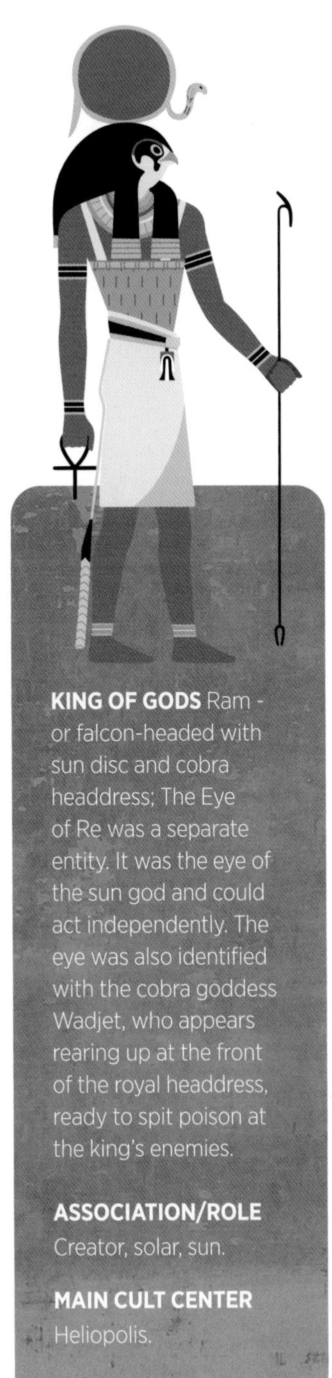

KING OF GODS Ram - or falcon-headed with sun disc and cobra headdress; The Eye of Re was a separate entity. It was the eye of the sun god and could act independently. The eye was also identified with the cobra goddess Wadjet, who appears rearing up at the front of the royal headdress, ready to spit poison at the king's enemies.

ASSOCIATION/ROLE
Creator, solar, sun.

MAIN CULT CENTER
Heliopolis.

ABOVE: Depiction of Ra; **OPPOSITE:** Stela of Shabaqo.

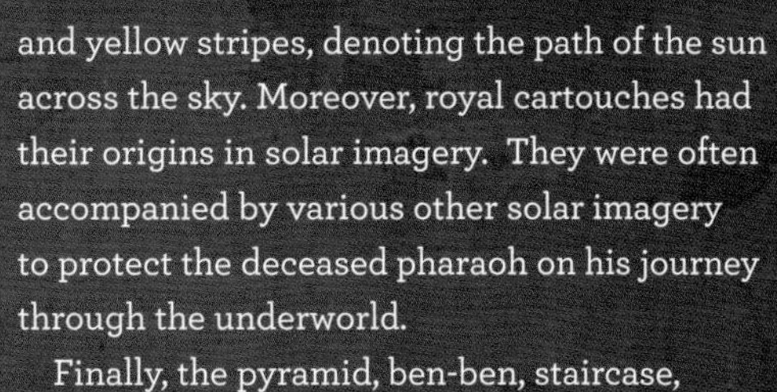

and yellow stripes, denoting the path of the sun across the sky. Moreover, royal cartouches had their origins in solar imagery. They were often accompanied by various other solar imagery to protect the deceased pharaoh on his journey through the underworld.

Finally, the pyramid, ben-ben, staircase, and obelisk were all architectural analogies of the sun or were created in its worship. Solar temples dedicated to Ra were built to let in sunlight, and Egyptians did not create statues to represent him; rather, the sunlight was thought to be a direct, physical manifestation of Ra in his temple.

Ra had numerous roles, in addition to being a creator-god. In Egyptian theology, the creation of the world had parallels to the creation of social order and especially kingship. Ra was considered to be the first king and thus set the archetype for pharaohs to come. Rulers were given authority under Ra's name, and he was closely associated with maat, or truth and justice. Those who were deemed unfit to rule Egypt (such as foreign invaders, like the Hyksos) were said to rule "without Ra." Additionally, Ra ruled both the heavens and the earth. His link as ruler of the earth shows the enormous importance the sun had for ancient Egyptians for their way of life. The sun made all life possible, from making crops grow to providing light and heat. The power of the sun was attributed to Ra, and so he became the central deity in the lives of Egyptians.

According to myth, Ra became too old and weary to rule. So the god Nun ordered Nut to turn herself into a cow and put Ra on her back and lift him up to the sky. Thus, Ra became the king of the heavens. Even the word "Ra" is the word for "sun," and it was said that the sun was his eye. Every day he crossed the great ocean of the sky in his boat, accompanied by Maat, his daughter.

Although Osiris was considered the lord of the underworld, Ra traveled through the land of the dead, and the two eventually fused to become Ra-Osiris. It was said that Ra ascended the heavens as a ba during the day to be joined with the body of Osiris at night.

WORSHIP

The first references to Ra come from the 2nd Dynasty, and by the 5th, his influence was powerful throughout Egypt, and he was closely associated with the pharaoh. By the 5th Dynasty, he was essentially the head of state religion, and he was without question head of the other deities. His cult was established at Heliopolis, but he was worshiped virtually throughout the entire region of Egypt. Numerous temples were dedicated specifically to him, but he was also incorporated into temples of various other deities.

Kings were called "the son of Ra," and many pharaohs built sun temples dedicated to the god. Over time, as Atum gained influence, the two merged to become one god, Atum-Ra. During the Middle Kingdom, Amun of Thebes gained prominence, but Ra still held sway, so he became Amun-Ra. The priests of Amun became so wealthy and powerful that there was a backlash against Amun among successive pharaohs, so during the New Kingdom, Ra regained some of his influence under his own name.

During this period, Ra reached his peak of influence, and many tombs included the image of Ra travelling by boat through the underworld. More sun temples were built during the 25th Dynasty: he even gained influence in the nearby kingdom of Nubia. During the Greek and Roman periods, he became linked with the god Zeus, and so remained enormously influential in the lives of common Egyptians. His name was incorporated into several common names of Egypt, and many amulets were crafted with his symbols. These were used in funeral rituals, given to the dead to protect them in the afterlife. Spells also invoked his name to right some injustice the enquirer had in their lives. However, his popularity began to decline after the Ptolemaic period, after numerous invasions and the rise of Christianity.

OPPOSITE, MAIN IMAGE: Fragment of a limestone stela of Djiho (Djedher); **OPPOSITE, LEFT:** Unfinished Stela of Amennakht of Deir el-Medina; **OPPOSITE, RIGHT:** Pyramidion of Khonsu.

RENENUTET

Renenutet was a goddess of fertility and the harvest, with her usual form being a snake.

GOD Cobra.

ASSOCIATION/ROLE
Harvest; nursing.

MAIN CULT CENTER
Faiyum.

ABOVE: Renenutet; **ABOVE, RIGHT:** Nepit, Renenutet and Hu as cobras.

She emerged from the Delta region, and is one of the most powerful serpent deities, whose gaze it was said destroyed her enemies. She was the wife of Geb in some traditions and the mother of Nehebkau, the snake god who guarded the entrance to the underworld. In the underworld, she was a fierce, fire-breathing cobra who could kill with a single look. In other traditions, she was the wife of Sobek or Shai, the god of destiny. It was said that Renenutet decided the length of a person's life and all the events in it. She was also the mother of Nepri, a god of grain. Her different titles suggest her association with harvests, such as "Lady of the threshing floor," and "Lady of the granaries." Perhaps because snakes guarded grain from rats and other rodents, she became identified as a protector goddess. As a grain goddess, she came to be identified with Osiris, and the Book of the Dead mentions that Renenutet is the mother of Horus. Therefore, in later traditions, she became associated with Isis.

Despite her fearsome aspects, she was associated with having a nurturing and protective nature, and she was identified with household and family life. It was said that she protected children from curses and bestowed

them with their "secret" name at birth. This aspect of her is reflected in her epithet, "She Who Rears," and it was thought that Renenutet protected and nourished the king at birth.

Renenutet is usually depicted as an erect snake with a sun disk and horns. Two plumes may be on top of the disk. She was also shown as a woman or a snake-headed woman. She had a harvest festival dedicated to her during the sewing of the crops and again in the summer when the crops ripened. She enjoyed great popularity in Fayum, where many crops were produced, Dja (modern Medinet Madi), and Terentius (Kom Abu Billo).

SERKET

Serket was the goddess of fertility, nature, animals, medicine, magic, and healing venomous stings and bites from snakes and scorpions.

In early Egyptian mythology, she was originally the personification of the scorpion. It is said that she was the daughter of Neith and Khnum, so she is therefore the sister of Sobek and Apep.

Her name refers to the deadly nature of scorpion stings, being "she who tightens the throat." It was believed that she had power over snakes and scorpions and could cure their bites. On the other hand, if a person was evil, it was said that she sent the scorpions to bite them in punishment. Because she was a protector against poisonous animals, it was believed that she protected the other gods and goddesses from Apep, the demon snake who attacked Ra on his nightly journey on his boat through the underworld. Because of her protective aspect from snakes and scorpions, many pharaohs took her as their patron.

Because venom often causes muscular paralysis (as well as death, which in turn causes stiffening), she was associated with embalmers and was said to be their protector. In addition, she was one of the four guardians of the canopic jars; she guarded the jar of the intestine. As a guardian, Serket thus gained an association with Isis, Neith, and Nephthys. Over time, Serket merged with Isis into one goddess. Serket was called "mistress of the beautiful house," which refers to the embalming pavilion.

Serket was also associated with motherhood through her link to scorpions. Scorpions were one symbol of motherhood in the ancient Near East, and in the Pyramid Texts, it is said that Serket nursed the king.

GOD Woman with scorpion on headdress.

ASSOCIATION/ROLE Funerary; protective.

TOP: Late period bronze figure of Isis-Serket; **ABOVE:** Depiction of Serket; **LEFT:** Serket with scorpion headdress.

SEKHMET

Sekhmet was a goddess of healing, of warriors, and a protector of the pharaohs. She was the most important of all Egyptian leonine deities.

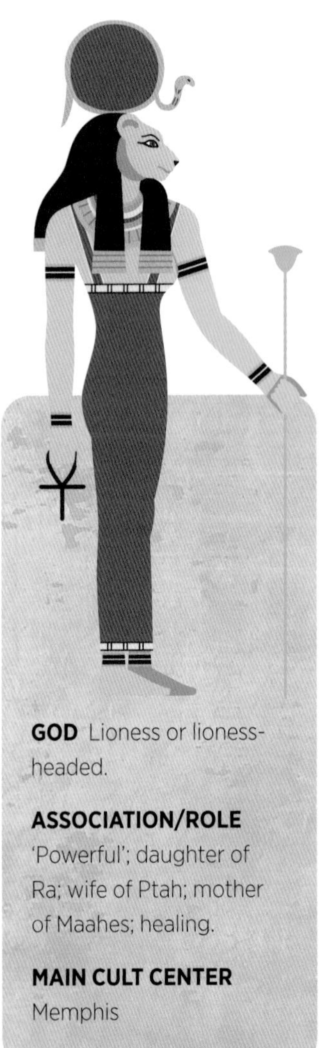

GOD Lioness or lioness-headed.

ASSOCIATION/ROLE 'Powerful'; daughter of Ra; wife of Ptah; mother of Maahes; healing.

MAIN CULT CENTER Memphis

She was as protective as she was destructive, embodying the fierce lioness. She was sometimes denoted as the daughter of Ra, wife of Ptah, mother of Maahes, (a lion god) and mother of Nefertum. Her names demonstrate her fierce character— "One Before Whom Evil Trembles," "Mistress of Dread," "Lady of Slaughter," and "She Who Mauls." Sekhmet was seen as the fierce counterpart to Bastet, who was the more domesticated version of feline qualities. In her protective role, it was said that she protected pharaohs in war, and when they died, she led them to the afterlife. She is often shown with the uraeus on her crown.

Because of her association with Ra, Sekhmet is a solar deity. She was the manifestation of Ra's power and was linked to the Eye of Ra. It was said that she breathed fire, and the winds of the desert were her scorching breath. Sekhmet was believed to cause disease and destruction. On the other hand, it was said that she could protect against the pestilence that afflicted ancient Egyptians.

ABOVE: Golden aegis devoted to Sekhmet; **MAIN IMAGE:** Sekhmet shown with her sun disk and cobra crown from a relief at the Temple of Kom Ombo; **TOP RIGHT:** Ra and Sekhmet; **OPPOSITE, LEFT:** Depiction of Sekhmet; **OPPOSITE, RIGHT:** Furniture plaque carved in relief with lion-headed figure.

DESTRUCTION OF MANKIND

In one myth, Ra learns that mankind plotted a rebellion against him. He wanted immediately to destroy the sorry humans, but he first sought the advice from his counsel. So, he summoned all the deities and brought them to his court. Shu, Tefnut, Geb, Nut, Nun, and Hathor, who came in her peaceful form. However, she could turn into the goddess Sekhmet when her ire was raised. He referred to her as his "Eye." The gods arrived in secret so the humans would not know that their plan was ultimately unmasked. When the gods arrived at Ra's court, Ra asked for their advice on what he should do with the humans. They responded that he should send Sekhmet out to slaughter the conspirators. Ra thus sent Sekhmet to destroy humans in punishment. However, after Sekhmet killed the men who conspired against Ra, her bloodlust was still unsatisfied, and she continued killing until she nearly wiped out the world's population. In response, Ra sent his messengers to find red ochre and mix it with beer to resemble blood. Ra's servants made 7,000 jars of beer, and they poured it on the ground and flooded the fields. Thinking it was human blood, Sekhmet drunk it all, and she became so intoxicated that she fell asleep. When she awoke, she stopped her vengeful slaughter. The whole experience had been too much for the aging Ra. He abdicated his throne and left the responsibilities of governing to Thoth. He left Thoth to teach the humans magic, writing, and literacy. Ra then ascended to the sky on the back of the Divine Cow. The earliest version of this myth was found on the famous sarcophagus of King Tutankhamun, from approximately 1330 BC. The writing style is from the earlier Middle Kingdom (around 2000 BC) so it most likely originated during that period. The myth deals with divine punishment, but the existence of a sort-of truce between the gods and mortals existed. Ra was ultimately merciful because the gods required people to tend to them, worship them, build their temples, and sacrifice offerings. Thus, the gods showed their beneficence if people worshiped them.

SETH

(SUTEKH, SETEKH, SET, SUT, SETY)

Seth was one of the oldest gods to emerge in Egyptian mythology, and he was worshiped from the Predynastic period.

GOD Unidentified quadruped or 'seth-animal' headed.

ASSOCIATION/ROLE Chaos; infertility; desert; storm (see "The Osiris Myth" p48–51, and "Horus and Seth" p52–55).

MAIN CULT CENTER Ombos Naqada.

He was the god of war, storms, and chaos, and many frightening natural phenomena, such as earthquakes, thunderstorms, and eclipses were attributed to him. Certain Egyptian words reflect the link between chaos, storms, and Seth. The words for "turmoil," "confusion," "storm," and "rage," all use his hieroglyph. Seth was the personification of anger and violence, and he served as the counterpart of Maat, the goddess of harmony. The day of his birth in the Egyptian calendar was considered an unlucky day. He also was linked with the desert and the lands beyond it. It was said that he was the brother of Osiris, Isis, Horus (the Elder), and brother-husband to Nephthys, but he had many other consorts and wives, such as the goddess Tawaret, the hippo deity of fertility and childbirth. He was also married to Neith, and her powerful character meshed well with his. He was part of the ancient Ennead of Heliopolis.

Although Seth had a reputation for being a god of evil, he was not always considered as such. Rather, Seth helped the dead ascend to heaven, and he protected the oases in the desert. It was said that he aided the pharaoh and protected Ra. Seth was considered to be strong, strange, and dangerous but not inherently evil. He was associated with numerous dangerous animals, such as the hippopotamus, crocodile, scorpion, pig, goat, antelope, and donkey. All these animals were thought to be unclean or particularly noxious to ancient Egyptians, so Seth could take on any or all of these guises. It was said that Seth was a black boar who swallowed the moon each month, which is why the light faded to darkness.

Seth played an important role in the myth of Osiris. He became jealous of his brother, either because Osiris was given the right to rule Egypt, or because Nephthys, his wife, slept with him and bore a son, Anubis with him. Either way, Seth plotted to kill Osiris by tricking him into a box, nailing it shut, and plunging it into the Nile. When Isis searched for the coffin of Osiris, Seth discovered it first, and dismembered the body of Osiris. He had the pieces strewn in the Nile, where fish ate parts of the body. Because of this, some fish, such as the carp, and oxyrynchus, became sacred to Seth. When Isis was able magically to conceive after putting the body of Osiris back together, she gave birth to Horus, who eventually grew up to battle with Seth for the throne in a decades-long war. Although Horus eventually won the right to the throne, Seth was given Anat and Astarte to wed as recompense for his losses. During their intense fighting, Seth dislodged the eye of Horus, which Thoth eventually healed, creating the "Eye of Horus."

Seth did not have any children. According to mythology, one of his testicles was torn off by Horus in retaliation for taking the eye of Horus. This rendered him infertile. It was said that he ate only lettuce, which was associated with fertility and male potency because it secreted a white, milky liquid reminiscent of semen. He was considered to be bisexual, and in some myths, he tried to rape both Isis and Horus. He was known as "the Red One," which symbolized both becoming red in anger as well as the "Red Land," or desert. It was said that he tore himself free from his mother at birth. His malevolent influence was said to be present during times of disease, civil unrest, and foreign invasion. Eventually, the Greeks identified him with their god Typhon, god of storms.

ICONOGRAPHY

Seth was originally depicted as the "Seth animal," which resembled a dog or jackal, with a curved head, tall, square ears, and an erect tail. It is unknown whether this animal was dog, jackal, or some other extinct canine, or a fantastical image of the imagination. He is sometimes shown crouching by the pharaoh in paintings and murals, in a show of protection. At times, the royal boat of Ra is pulled by the Seth animals, instead of the usual jackals. Over time, Seth came to be depicted anthropomorphically, with the body of a human male and the head of the Seth animal. Sometimes he wears the White Crown of Upper Egypt, especially during the New Kingdom era. Sometimes he is shown fused with Horus as a two-headed deity, perhaps

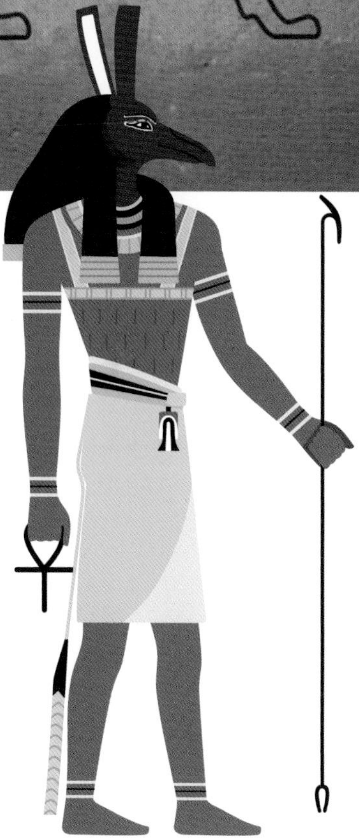

ABOVE: Depiction of Seth; **MAIN IMAGE, LEFT:** Seth on a late New Kingdom relief from Karnak: his figure was erased during his demonization; **MAIN IMAGE, RIGHT:** Depiction of he Seth-animal, Sha; **OPPOSITE:** Seth and Nephthys.

representing the fusion of Upper and Lower Egypt. As the protector of Ra, Seth is shown slaying the demon-serpent Apep in some depictions. During the first millennium BC, the Seth animal gradually disappeared from art, and Seth became more frequently shown as a donkey with a knife in its head, to represent symbolically his evil to be harmless.

WORSHIP

Seth most likely emerged as a local desert deity. Some of the first archaeological evidence for Seth comes from the Naqada I Period, (around 4000-3500 BC). During the 2nd Dynasty, he appears on the serekh (which was an embellishment used in writing to hold the king's name) along with Horus, so he was already very influential by this time. His earliest cult center, and most likely the town in which he originated, was Nubt, in southern Egypt. Nubt was one of the most important ancient settlements because of its rich gold deposits. The word "Nubt," comes from the word for gold, and Seth was sometimes titled, "He of Gold Town." There is also archaeological evidence that Seth was worshiped in the 19th Nome of Upper Egypt during the Pre-Dynastic era and over time came to be enormously popular in the 5th, 10th, and 11th Nomes as well. However, Seth was also influential in Lower Egypt; he had a cult center in the city of Pi-Rameses in the Delta region. Although he was associated with Upper Egypt, during the Second Intermediate Period, he became linked with the Hyksos, so he was seen as a force for evil. His character gradually shifted to become more neutral by the 19th Dynasty, but then with the rise of the Greek, Roman, and Christian theology, Seth once again became seen as a force of evil.

Various rituals existed to appease Seth or to show symbolically his destruction and thus break whatever evil influence held sway over a person or people in a city. Animals associated with him were sacrificed by the common people, and there were a few important rituals of sacrificial slaughter, such as the red ox or a desert bird. As early as the 1st Dynasty, a royal hippopotamus hunt would take place, in which the pharaoh hunted a wild hippo and killed it, to symbolize the victory of Horus over Seth. In popular religion, his name was frequently invoked in magical spells in which he was called on to aid someone against their enemies or other hostile deities and supernatural beings.

ABOVE: King Ramses III, and the gods Horus and Seth; **OPPOSITE:** Bas relief of Seth and Anubis in the tomb of Ramesses IX.

SHU

Shu was one of the primordial deities of air and sunlight.

GOD Man with feather on head; lion-headed.

ASSOCIATION/ROLE "Eye of Ra".

MAIN CULT CENTER Heliopolis; Leontopolis.

ABOVE: A depiction of Shu; **RIGHT:** Shu statuette.

He was the personification of wind, clouds, and earth's atmosphere, and the light that illuminated the world at the beginning of creation. He marked the separation of night and day, as well as the land of the living and the dead. It was said that he breathed life into all living beings. The clouds were thought to be his bones, and he held the ladder that the deceased traversed to reach the heavens.

According to one creation myth, Atum created himself, then created Shu and Tefnut, the goddess of moisture, and they in turn produced Geb, the god of Earth and Nut, the goddess of the sky. In one myth, Shu separated Nut and Geb after Nut swallowed the stars and Geb became angry at her for consuming their offspring. In another telling, his children were overly attached to each other and so Shu interceded and separated Nut and Geb. It was thought that four pillars held up the separation of the earth and sky, and they were known as the "Pillars of Shu."

Shu was also associated with light, and he is most closely linked to the moon and Khonsu, perhaps because his wife Tefnut was also closely associated with lunar qualities. He was also linked to Ra by way of protecting him from the demon snake Apep, as Ra travelled through the underworld. In one myth, Shu defeated Apep but was so weakened from the fight that Geb turned against him. Shu abdicated his throne, leaving Geb to rule the earth, and he returned to the heavens to protect Ra. He is usually depicted anthropomorphically with a headdress of ostrich feathers, clutching a was scepter and an ankh. At other times, he is shown as a single ostrich feather, which represented his airy nature and the breath of life.

SOBEK

Sobek was the god of crocodiles, and he was an ancient deity, worshiped from at least the Old Kingdom until the Roman period.

He was the most important of the crocodile deities, and he was eventually syncretized with the Greek god Helios. In some traditions, it was said that Sobek created the world, who rose from the dark, primordial waters to establish order. He was a god of the Nile, sometimes called "Lord of the Waters," and it was thought that his tears or sweat formed the river. He was tied to fertility, since it was his eggs that created the universe. In some myths, he is the son of Neith, and his fierce nature is seen in his title of "He Who Rages," and "the one who takes women from their husbands, whenever he wishes, according to his desire." Some traditions state that his father was Seth, and he sometimes aligned himself with the forces of chaos rather than creation. He was known as the father of Khonsu, Horus, or Khnum in some regions of Egypt.

Because of the association of a crocodile's ferocity, he became a symbol of pharaonic might and a patron deity of the army. Moreover, the word for "sovereign" used the hieroglyph of a crocodile. It was thought that Sobek protected the pharaoh from dark magic, and many pharaohs incorporated his name into their royal one. In some areas of Egypt, a tame crocodile was worshiped as his physical manifestation on earth, but in other regions, crocodiles were hunted without remorse. Sobek usually appears as a crocodile or crocodile-headed man. In either form, he often wears a headdress with a sun disk and horns, to connote his association with Ra.

GOD Crocodile or croc-headed.

ASSOCIATION/ROLE Pharaonic might.

MAIN CULT CENTER Kom Ombo; Faiyum.

TOP: This statue of Sobek was found at Amenemhat III's mortuary temple; **ABOVE:** Plaque with head and shoulders of a priestly figure and Sobek; **LEFT:** Sobek bearing the falcon head of Re-Harakhti.

TEFNUT

Tefnut was the Egyptian goddess of moisture and was also associated with lunar and solar imagery.

As a lunar goddess, she embodied moisture, and as a solar goddess, moisture was absent. Her name means "Moisture," and it derives from the Egyptian word for "moist" and "spit." It is from this play on words that it is believed that Tefnut emerged from the spit of Ra when he created the universe. As a moon, she was considered to be the "Eye of Ra," and she embodied the gentler aspects of precipitation, such as rain, mist, and dew. However, as a solar deity, she was known as "the Lady of the Flame," and she was considered to be the protector of Ra and so took on the form of the uraeus. She was not the only goddess to have this role, as Mut, Bastet, Isis, Sekhmet, Hathor, Wadjet, and Nekhbet were also considered to be the uraeus.

Tefnut was the daughter of Ra and sister-wife of Shu. She was usually represented as a lioness or a woman with a lion's head. A solar disk with a rearing cobra head usually encircled her and she carried a scepter and ankh.

One myth tells the story of Tefnut drying out the land of Egypt. She got into a fierce argument with her father, Ra, so she left Egypt, taking all the water and moisture with her. The land dried up, crops and animals died, and people suffered greatly. Ra then sent Thoth and Shu to retrieve her. When she returned, the inundation of the Nile came again, bringing fertility once more to Egypt's fields.

Her main cult centers were at Heliopolis, and at Leontopolis in the Delta.

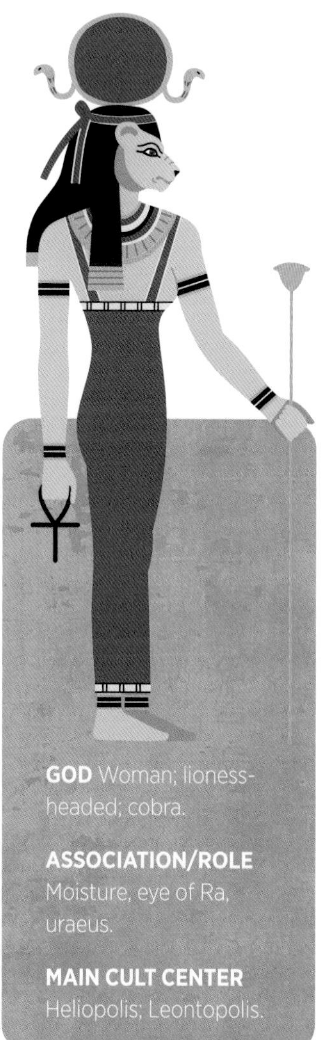

GOD Woman; lioness-headed; cobra.

ASSOCIATION/ROLE Moisture, eye of Ra, uraeus.

MAIN CULT CENTER Heliopolis; Leontopolis.

ABOVE: Depiction of Tefnut; **LEFT:** Carvings depicting Tefnut at the temple of Khnum; **OPPOSITE:** Hieroglyphic sculpture of the lioness-headed goddess Tefnut.

THOTH

(DJEHUTY, TEHUTY, TAHUTI, TEHUTI, ZEHUTI, TECHU, TETU)

Thoth was a god of the moon, writing, learning, creator of languages, patron of scribes, and advisor of the gods.

GOD Baboon; ibis or ibis-headed.

ASSOCIATION/ROLE Moon; knowledge; scribes.

MAIN CULT CENTER Hermopolis Magna.

It was said that he was the wisest of the gods, and many magicians ascribed their power to him. It was said that he was the inventor of magic, medicine, and law.

One of the creation myths holds that Thoth created himself with a word of power, and through his song, he created the other deities of the Ogdoad, which included the gods Nun, Heh, Kuk, and Amun and the goddesses Nunet, Hauhet, Kuaket, and Amaunet. In another version of the creation myth, he was an ibis who laid eggs from which Ra emerged. In the myth of Osiris, he was responsible for restoring the eye of during his dealings with Seth.

Thoth most likely started out as a local moon deity but over time gained influence in Egyptian religious belief. It was believed that Thoth created five extra days out of moonlight that he won in a game from Khnum. From those five days, Nut was able to bear children. Because Khnum lost so much light, it was believed that the moon waxed and waned each month.

As the patron of scribes and the written word, it was said that he maintained the library of the gods with his wife, Seshat (goddess of writing). His titles reflect his role as a scribe of the gods with "Lord of the Divine Body," "Scribe of the

MAIN IMAGE ABOVE: Thoth; **LEFT:** Inlay frieze (cutout detail) depicting Thoth as the ibis with a maat feather; **OPPOSITE, LEFT:** Depiction of Thoth; **OPPOSITE, RIGHT:** Stone statue of Thoth represented as a baboon.

Company of Gods," and "Counsellor of Ra." He stood on Ra's royal boat every night as it made its way through the underworld.

ICONOGRAPHY

Thoth was usually depicted in two main forms, an ibis, and a baboon. Baboons were thought to be intelligent by ancient Egyptians, as they were often in groups "chatting" amongst themselves. The ibis represented the search for knowledge because it plunged its beak into the river mud searching for food. As a baboon, Thoth was usually sitting, with a large man, with its legs drawn up close to its body. The baboon was usually associated with lunar deities, and Thoth as a baboon was usually depicted with a lunar disk above his head sitting within a crescent, to symbolize the different phases of the moon. As an ibis, Thoth could appear as the bird or as an ibis-headed man. Many depictions of Thoth show him at the Weighing of the Heart ritual where he carefully records the fates of the souls.

WORSHIP

Thoth was widely worshiped in Egypt from early periods onward. His chief center of worship was Hermopolis, and there is some archaeological evidence that Thoth had a cult center in the Delta region in early Egyptian history, but certainly by the New Kingdom, Thoth had gained widespread popularity and importance for both royalty and Egyptian commoners. Thoth was so important that there were burial grounds dedicated specifically to ibises and baboons, such as the one located at Saqqara. During the New Kingdom, pharaohs often took on names incorporating his into theirs. For instance, Tuthosis meant "Born of Thoth." Scribes in particular held Thoth in great reverence, and it is said that they made a small libation sacrifice of their ink every day by pouring out a drop of water that they dipped their brushes into. Amulets of Thoth appeared with his image of an ibis or baboon, and many were worn by scribes. Because Thoth was the god of magic, his name was invariably invoked during magical spells and incantations.

WADJET

Wadjet was one of the earliest Egyptian goddesses, worshiped from the pre-dynastic period onward. As a cobra goddess, she was a symbol of sovereignty.

Her name means "The Green One," or "She of the Papyrus." The name "the Green One," might refer to green snakes or the green Delta region which she inhabited. Together with goddess Nekhbet (who represented Upper Egypt), she was believed to protect the king. She was the personification of Lower Egypt. One of the ruler's five names was His Nebty, or "two ladies," names, referring to the goddess. She appeared as the uraeus ("she who rears up") on the king's forehead, ready to spit venom at an unsuspecting enemy. One of her titles was "The Mistress of Awe" or the "Mistress of Fear."

Military inscriptions describe her as slaying the monarch's enemies with her fiery breath. She was sometimes depicted as the nurse of Horus, linking her with Isis. She is usually represented as the rearing cobra that protected both gods and kings, often attached to the solar disk. In murals and paintings, she is frequently shown seated along with the vulture Nekhbet on two baskets, which was an image originating in the 1st Dynasty. Over time, she fused with Nekhbet and was sometimes shown as a vulture or a serpent with wings (and vice versa--a cobra wearing the White Crown usually represents Nekhbet). She was also said to be an "Eye of

Ra," and as such, she appeared as a lion or as a cobra with a lion's head. Amulets of Wadjet were very common among Egyptians. Her shrine was called the "per-nu" or "House of Flame," it was often depicted in funerary decoration and existed from pre-dynastic times. The innermost of the four funerary shrines of Tutankhamun took the per-nu form.

GODDESS: Cobra; Lioness.

ASSOCIATION/ROLE
Tutelary goddess of Lower Egypt; Uraeus; Mother of Nefertem.

MAIN CULT CENTER
Buto.

ABOVE: Statuette of Wadjet in the name of Akanosh, son of Pediamenopet; **LEFT:** Wadjet illustration; **OPPOSITE:** Relief of Wadjet at Hatshepsut temple.

3

OTHER DEITIES

Of the countless gods of Ancient Egyptian mythology, only a fraction have survived to be analyzed in modern times. Of those recorded, many are known only in name, with little or no significant sources of background information to be found—but all were significant at one point or another throughout Egyptian history. What information can be found relating to these less-popular deities is collected here.

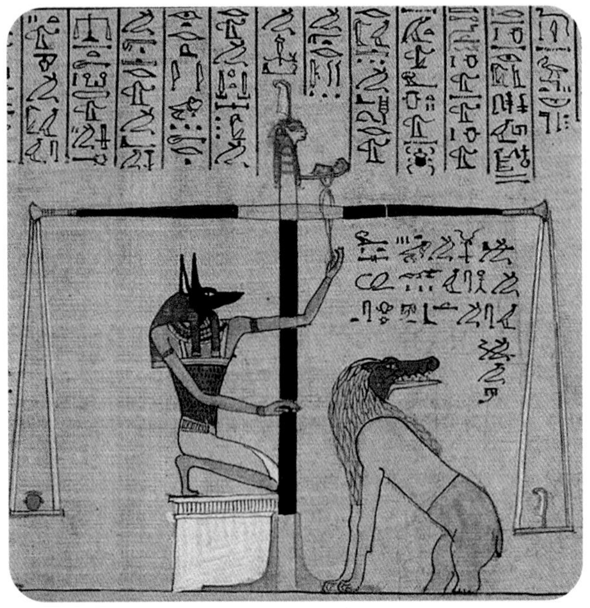

TOP: Ammit waiting to be fed hearts; **ABOVE:** Ra slaying Apep.

AMMIT

DEMON DEITY: was responsible for devouring the hearts of those who had done wrong during their lifetime, thereby denying life after death. It was represented as part crocodile (head), part lion (front legs) or panther, and part hippo (back legs).

APEP

(APOPHIS; APEPI)

Apep was the demon snake that was a great adversary of Ra when he journeyed through the underworld each night. He was the personification of the powers of dissolution, darkness, and non-being. This huge serpent was believed to exist from the beginning of time in the primordial waters which preceded creation. It was through this that he would continue to exist in an endless cycle of attack, defeat, and re-attack.

As the Ra traveled through the underworld, the serpent would try to defeat it by drinking the river water to stop the boat or by hypnotizing Ra. On murals and depictions, he is often shown ritualistically cut up into pieces. Epithets include "evil lizard, opponent, and enemy, world-encircler, and serpent of re-birth." He is associated with frightening natural events such as unexplained darkness, storms, and earthquakes. Although in the original myth, Seth protects the boat of Ra and uses magic and force to subdue the serpent, he eventually became identified with him, as a symbol of forces hostile to the other gods.

ANAT

As a goddess of war, she was to protect the king in battle. She is depicted with a lance, axe, and shield and most often wearing a tall crown with feathers. She is also called, "Mother of All the Gods," and "mistress of the Sky." Sometimes regarded as the consort of Seth or the fertility god Min. She originated in Syria-Palestine as a deity of the Canaanites and Phoenicians.

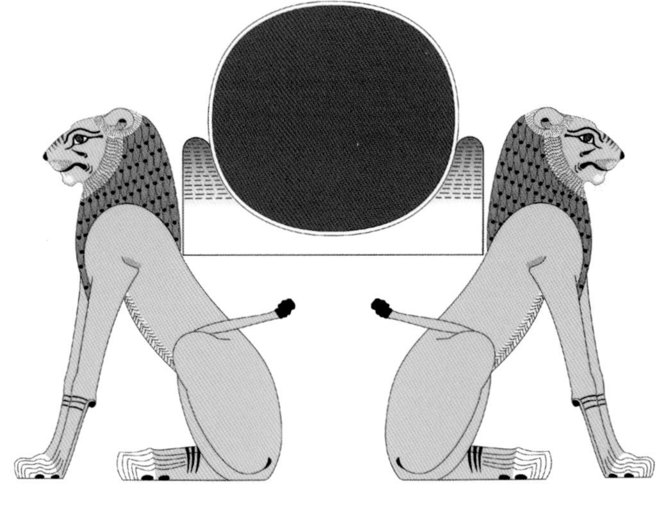

AKER

Aker was an earth god who controlled the junction of the western and eastern horizons. He was the divine personification of eastern and western horizons (which signified the entrance and exit into and out of the Netherworld. He is important in funerary texts and imagery. He is usually represented as two lions sitting back-to-back, or as a piece of land with a lion or a human head at each end (one facing east and one facing west).

ASTARTE

Interchangeable with Anat; Also associated with war (specifically horses and chariots) and protected the king in battle. Syrian in origin. Usually represented as a naked woman riding a horse and wearing the atef-crown or bull's horns on her head. Regarded as either Ra's daughter or Ptah and thought to be one of Seth's consorts.

BABA

At his most dangerous, baba was believed to murder humans and feed on their entrails. Depicted as a baboon. Associated with aggression and virility. Sometimes his genitals was said to be the bolt on the doors of heaven, and at other times it was the mast on the ferry in the Netherworld. Believed to be able to ward off snakes and to control darkness and turbulent waters.

TOP: Aker iconography; **LEFT:** Statuette figurine of a goddess with a horned headdress, possibly Astarte; **ABOVE RIGHT:** Babi (or Baba) as a baboon crouched with an erection.

ABOVE: Small figurine of the god Hapi; **LEFT:** Inlay of the hieroglyphic sign "heh" meaning "millions of years"; **OPPOSITE:** Heket relief in Temple Rameses II, Abydos.

HEKET

(OR HEQUAT)

Heket was a goddess in the form of a frog, associated with birth and re-birth. She helped the dead king on his journey to the sky. She was considered a consort of Khnum (who made the first humans on his potter's wheel), she gave life to the figures, and as a goddess of childbirth, she shaped the child in the womb and gave it life.

HAPI

(OR HAPY)

God of the inundation of the Nile, and one of the Four Sons of Horus. Fertility god.

Hapi is portrayed as a man with pendulous breasts to emphasize his fecundity and with papyrus or lotus flowers on his head. His body is often shown as green or blue. He lived among the caverns in the rocks at the First Cataract and one of his main cult centers was near Aswan.

HEDEDET

Hededet was a scorpion goddess. She is equal to Serket in several ways, in form and function, but she was later associated with Isis. Hededet symbolizes motherly qualities, nursing, and caring. Amulets often bore her image of a seated goddess with a scorpion on her head and nursing a child.

HUH

(OR HEH)

This frog-headed god was personification of formlessness and infinity. His consort was the snake-headed goddess Hauhet. He was often depicted as a human holding a palm-rib in each hand. One of the Ogdoad (group of eight primeval deities) of Hermopolis. He appears on royal regalia as a charm to ensure longevity.

The name "Khepri" comes from the Egyptian word for the scarab or dung beetle.

KHEPRI

MYTHOLOGY

So how did a god associated with a beetle also come to be known for the rising sun? Ancient Egyptians observed that scarab beetles roll their dung into balls, and this may have reminded them of the huge ball of the sun "rolling" across the sky. In addition, scarab beetles lay their eggs in the dung balls, and so the young eventually emerge (as though spontaneously). The Egyptians thus equated the ball with life, as new life emerged, just as the sun is responsible for bringing new life into creation. In addition, the Egyptian verb "kheper," means "to develop" or "to come into being," and thus Khepri was linked to development and life.

Khepri was the personification of the rising sun, and formed a tripartite with Ra, the personification of the midday sun, and Atum, the setting sun in the evening. Because of this, he is sometimes referred to as "Atum-Khepri."

ICONOGRAPHY

The most common depiction of Khepri is in the form of a scarab beetle, or of a scarab-headed man. Other times, he is shown with the body of the insect fused with the bodies of other creatures, such as falcons or vultures, with their outstretched, feathery wings, tails, or avian legs. Still other times he is shown with a scarab body and the head of a ram, to symbolize the unity of Atum-Khepri as both the rising and setting sun.

WORSHIP

Although the scarab beetle was the most popular amulet of ancient Egypt, and thought Khepri is carved into many temples, painted on walls, and made into huge statues, he did not have an official cult center. Nevertheless, the enormous popularity of the scarab amulet shows that he was one of the most ubiquitous deities in ancient Egypt. An enormous sculpture of a scarab beetle at Karnak Temple shows the importance of the scarab to pharaohs of ancient Egypt.

ABOVE: Dung beetle on his dung ball; **OPPOSITE:** Relief panel showing two baboons offering the wedjat eye to the sun god Khepri, who holds the Underworld sign.

GODDESS: Woman, panther.
ASSOCIATION/ROLE
Associations: protector against snakes and scorpions, mongoose, ocelot.

MAFDET

Mafdet is one of the oldest ancient deities, and her mention goes back to the 1st Dynasty. She was a protective deity, and she was associated with either a feline, such as a small ocelot, or mongoose. She was known for her ferocity, attacking snakes and scorpions. In the Pyramid Texts, she protects Ra, leaping toward a snake and attacking it with her razor-sharp teeth and claws. According to myth, she helped piece Osiris back together along with Isis.

At times, she was paired with the goddess Hededet, in her role as protector. Sometimes she is associated with divine punishment, as she appears in scenes of afterlife judgment as an executioner. Because of this role, she was also linked with a (symbolic) instrument of punishment, which was a curved pole with a knife at the end. In her mongoose form, she is sometimes shown running up this pole. She was the personification of legal justice. It was said that she ripped out the hearts of evildoers and laid them at Ra's feet, as cats sometimes do with rodents or mice with humans.

She was an apotropaic deity, so ancient Egyptians invoked her to ward off evil spirits or seek protection. An ancient spell used to cast out demons or ghosts from the household involves her. Egyptians would recite a spell over a phallus-shaped piece of bread, with the name of the evil spirit inscribed on it. Then, the loaf was wrapped in strips of meat and fed to a cat. When the cat devoured the now-potent loaf, it was believed that Mafdet destroyed the influence of the malevolent supernatural being.

Mafdet is often depicted wearing the skin of a cheetah.

MANDULIS

Mandulis was a local god of the Nubian region but was also worshiped in Egypt. His name in Egyptian was actually Merwel, but he is usually known by the Greek rendering of his name. A text called the "Vision of Mandulis," equates him with Apollo. He is also known as the companion of Isis. His main cult center was his own temple, the Temple of Kalabsha at Talmis and also at Ajuala but he was also worshiped at the Temples of Petesi and Pihor at Philae. He grew in popularity during the Roman rule of Egypt, and in some texts, he is referred to as the "Sun, the all-seeing master, king of all, all-powerful Aion." The Aion was a Greek deity that was associated with time, the orb circling the universe, and the zodiac.

Mandulis was usually shown in anthropomorphic form, with a crown of ram-horns, sun disks, and cobras. He could also be depicted as a human-headed bird.

TOP: Two fragments that form a depiction of Mafdet as Mistress of the Hut Ankh (Mansion of Life). She holds a staff with her front right paw; **OPPOSITE:** Mandulis from the Temple of Kalabsha in Nubia.

MEHEN

Just as there were dangerous and evil serpent deities that threatened Ra, so too there were protective ones as well. Mehen was a coiled serpent god, who protected Ra on his nightly descent into and journey through the underworld. The serpent was said to exist as nine, concentric circles, which were "roads of fire," that protected Ra. He was also known as one who had authority over criminals, which usually meant enemies of Ra. Mehen did not have his own cult center but rather was used in myth and ritual spells. Some scholars have traced the "coiled serpent board game" ancient Egyptians played as far back as the Predynastic Period to the image of Mehen.

MENTU

Mentu was a falcon-headed god of war. He is usually shown wearing a headdress of a sun-disc and two plumes. His cult center was at Thebes from the 11th Dynasty onward, but gradually gave way to Amun. He fought the enemies of the gods and he saw the victory of Egyptian kings over their enemies. He came to symbolize aggressive aspects of the pharaohs. Later, he became associated with a black-faced white bull called Buchis.

MERETSEGER

She was a local cobra-goddess of the mountain overlooking the Valley of the Kings at Thebes. Her name means, "She who loves silence." She watched over a necropolis, and she was venerated by workers in the valley, who left inscriptions on stones to strike down those who committed crimes with blindness or snake poisoning, and also offered care to the repentant.

MESHKENT

She was a goddess of childbirth, often identified with the birth brick Egyptian women used to give birth. She is sometimes shown as a woman with a brick on her head. As a funerary goddess, she helped the deceased be re-born into the afterlife. It was said that she was present at the judgement of the dead. Finally, she is also associated with determining the destiny of a child at birth.

INSET, ABOVE: Meretseger; **OPPOSITE:** Mehen Pharaoh Ptolemy IV Philopator (222–204 BC) adoring Montu, in the "Place Of Truth" of Deir el-Medina.

TOP Amulet of the god Mahes; **LEFT:** Amulet of the god Min.

MAHES
(OR MIHOS)

Mahes was a god of war, and he was associated with war, protection, weather, knives, lotuses, and devouring captives. He was a son of Bastet and Ptah (or Sekhmet). As the son of Bastet, he inherited her leonine nature, and his name means, "He who is True Beside Her." He also bore titles such as "Lord of Slaughter," the "Wielder of the Knife," and "The Scarlet Lord," perhaps referencing the blood drawn in battle or slaughtering his enemies.

Mahes was a fairly recent addition to Egyptian mythology, as he only becomes frequently mentioned in the New Kingdom, although references to him also exist from the Middle Kingdom as well.

His main cult center was in Taramuand Per-Bast, where Bastet and Sekhmet also had their centers of worship. The Greeks knew this city as "Leontopolis," or "lion city," further connecting him with lion imagery. At this temple, tame lions were kept, and the Greek historian Aelian wrote in a text that they roamed freely, were fed oxen, and that when they ate, Egyptians would play music during their feeding. He frequently was depicted on small amulets and bronze statues.

In Egyptian written language, male lion hieroglyphics were used in words to denote power, such as prince, masthead, or strength, and it was the symbol for the word power itself.

MIN

As a god of fertility and male potency, Min was represented in semi-mummified human form, his left hand holding his erect phallus and his right arm raised, sometimes with a flair that rests on his fingertips, suggesting sexual penetration. His headdress had two tall plumes. Emblems of his cult were the lettuce (which was a symbol of potency, possibly because of their shape and possibly because of their milky sap) and possibly a lightning bolt, or barbed arrow. He was an ancient deity, regarded as the protector of the mining regions in the Eastern desert. His main cult centers were at Koptos and Akhmim. The Greeks eventually identified this god with Pan, and over time, he merged with Amum. He was an early agricultural god, who ensured a bountiful harvest by his great fecundity. Pharaohs in the New Kingdom celebrated festivals in honor of Min as part of the ritual to celebrate the renewal of the kingship.

ABOVE: Votive stele for a Mnevis bull, 12th century BCE, from Heliopolis; **LEFT:** Block Statue of a prophet of Montu and scribe Djedkhonsuefankh, son of Khonsumes and Taat.

MNEVIS

Mnevis was another sacred bull, like the more famous Apis bull of Memphis, and second only to him in importance to the ancient Egyptians. He was known as the divine bull of Heliopolis, and his Egyptian name was Mer-Wer, but he is more frequently referenced by the Greek version of his name, Mnevis. Over time, he came to be associated with the power of Ra and gained more importance than his humble beginnings as a minor, independent deity. This bull was granted great respect and privileges in Egyptian culture and was said to provide wisdom and oracles in the same manner of Apis. He was known as the herald of Ra, who brought messages to humans and made Ra's will known to mortals. Through time, the priests at Heliopolis claimed that Mnevis was the progenitor of the Apis bull, in an attempt to bolster his importance.

Like other sacred bulls, there could be only one designated Mnevis bull alive at a time, and like the Apis bull, the selected bull could only have a completely black coat without any markings. In his artistic representations, he is usually shown with a solar disk and uraeus between his horns.

MONTU

A falcon-headed god of war, Montu was most famous and most popular in Thebes and its environs. He appears as early as the Old Kingdom in archaeology, but it was during the 11th dynasty in Thebes that he gained widespread popularity. Although he was worshiped as his own deity, he became linked with Horus and gained the name, "Horus of the strong arm." As a god of war, several pharaohs took on the name, "Montuhotep," or "Montu is content." Rulers who wanted to be known for their military might described themselves using Montu's name, with phrases like such as, "fought like Montu in his might."

Montu was usually depicted as a falcon, human with a falcon head, but also sometimes as a winged griffin. He usually carries a khepesh (Egyptian sickle-shaped sword), intimating at his aggressive, warring nature. Like Ra and other falcon deities, he wears the sun disk and uraeus on his head, but is usually distinguished by the two, tall plumes on the headdress as well. In later dynasties, he is shown in the form of his sacred bull, Buchis, or as a bull-headed man.

His main cult centers were all in Thebes or in areas surrounding Thebes, such as Medamud, Karnak (where he had his own temple), Armant, and Tod. Amulets were made with his image, and sometimes took the form of four falcons side by side, representing the four sites of worship.

ABOVE: Nineteenth dynasty statue of Mut; **LEFT:** Small figurine of Nefertem .

MUT

Mut was a Theban goddess normally depicted as a woman wearing a brightly colored dress. She wears a headdress shaped like a vulture along with the combined crown of upper and lower Egypt. She was so important at Thebes that she eventually became the wife of Amun, so became the symbolic divine mother of the earthly king. It was said that she gave birth to Khons with Amun. She became The Eye of Ra and was presented as a lion-headed goddess and because of that, she became fused with Bastet.

NEFERTEM

(OR NEFERTUM)

Nefertum was a god associated with the lotus blossom and represented as human male with blossom on his head. Sometimes equated with Horus as the "child of the sun." He is sometimes represented as a man wearing a lotus-shaped headdress with two plumes and other times with a lion's head. The Creation Myth of Hermopolis Magna states that the sun rose from the primeval lotus flower and Nefertem was closely linked with the sun god. Referred to as, "The lotus blossom which is before the nose of Ra." Also "protector of the Two Lands," (Upper and Lower Egypt). He was worshiped at Memphis as the son of Ptah and Sekhmet. Finally, he is also sometimes referred to as son of Bastet, Wadjet, or Sekhmet.

NEKHBET

Nekhbet was a vulture goddess and the patron deity of Nekheb, which was the capital of the 3rd nome, or principality, of ancient Egypt. Because this city was located close to Nekhen, which was the capital of Upper Egypt, she became the patron deity of Upper Egypt, and eventually, along with Wadjet, the deity of all united Egypt. With Wadjet, they were known as the "Two Ladies."

She is most often represented as a vulture, either with her wings outstretched or standing in profile. Nekhbet is often shown holding the circular shen hieroglyph in her claws, representing eternity. Because she was linked with Wadjet, she was sometimes depicted as a serpent (and on the flip side, Wadjet was sometimes shown as a vulture). As a serpent, Nekhbet usually wears the White Crown. Finally, she was sometimes shown as a woman wearing a vulture cap.

TOP: Depiction of Neper; **ABOVE:** Nun and Naunet; **LEFT:** Statuette of Mut.

NEPER

Neper was a minor grain deity who appears early in ancient Egyptian mythology, possibly as a link between the early development of agriculture and the rise of civilization. He was especially associated with barley and emmer wheat. His name means, "lord of the mouth," which refers to grain as the main sustenance of Egyptians.

Osiris eventually overcame him in popularity, as he was known as a god of agriculture and of the dead. Thus, Neper eventually took on the title, "The One who lives after dying," since Osiris was linked to the afterlife. He eventually became assimilated with Osiris, but he was still important in his own right. The hieroglyphs for his name include the word for "grain," and in some paintings, his body is shown dotted, representing grains of corn. Egyptians connected this god of grain to the god of flooding, reflecting the dependence of the harvest on the annual flooding of the Nile. Hapy, the god of inundation, was at times known as "The Lord of Neper."

Neper was an important deity of harvest, prosperity, and grain. His main cult center was in Fayum. He is linked with the cobra goddess Renenutet, who was also a patron goddess of the harvest. At times, he is depicted as a child suckling on Renenutet, although the oldest surviving depiction of him is as an older man with three grains above his head.

NUN

Nun was the divine personification of the primordial waters of chaos, which preceded creations. Described as "eldest father," and "maker of humankind." After creation had taken place, chaos was believed to continue to exist beyond the edges of the universe, and in the Netherworld, and was the place of social outcasts and demons. Sometimes represented as a baboon, or with a frog's head, or in human form with a beard. Sometimes depicted as holding the solar barque aloft.

SOKAR

God associated with earth and fertility but particularly with death and the cemetery of the capital city of Memphis. Became syncretized with Osiris and Ptah. In the Pyramid Texts, Sokar is described as the maker of royal bones. Represented as a mummified man, sometimes with the head of a hawk. Also portrayed as a mound of earth with a boat on top, containing the head of an eagle. Cult center was at Memphis; during his festival, his devotees wore strings of onions around their necks. Onions were used in the embalming process of a mummy.

Many real-life aspects of Ancient Egypt were mythologized over time. Animals such as cats, ibises, and scarab beetles were held sacred and even directly influenced the physical depictions of the gods, and several historical figures ascended into myth after—and sometimes during—their lifetimes. This chapter details some of the most culturally-significant creatures of Ancient Egypt (both real and fantastical), historical figures who were revered as gods in their own right, and a selection of Ancient Egyptian myths, fables, and folk tales.

4

MONSTERS, CREATURES AND MORTALS

CATS

Cats were enormously important in ancient Egypt. They were considered sacred animals, and they not only were significant in daily life but also in religious life as well. Over time, they became symbols of divinity, protection, fertility, good luck, the sun, motherhood, and domesticity.

While it is commonly thought that the Egyptians worshiped cats, this is not strictly the case. As we'll see, the religious significance of cats was a bit more complex, as with many things in ancient Egyptian culture.

Interestingly, the Egyptians gave us the word for "cat." It originally stems from a North African word for "animal," quattah. Once conquerors invaded Egypt and spread their empire outward, other European languages began to adopt the word. In French, the word for cat is chat; German, katze; Italian, gatto; Spanish gato; and Swedish is katt. Moreover, the slang term for cat—"puss," or "pussycat," also comes from Egypt in that it is derived from the word Pasht (another name for Bastet, the cat goddess of fertility, domesticity, and protection).

HISTORY

The ancient Egyptians had a variety of cats in their lives, both large and small—lions, panthers, jungle cats, and smaller desert cats, and the entrance into their personal lives came from the advent of crop domestication, growth of agriculture, and civilization. The world's first domesticated cats have been traced to what is now Turkey, around 10,000 years ago. As people domesticated crops, such as wheat and other grains, they began to store the excess in granaries. Naturally, this attracted rodents, who fed on the grain. In turn, wild cats came to hunt and eat the rodents. Humans eventually kept cats on hand, perhaps attracting them with free scraps and affection in gratitude.

Mitochondrial DNA analysis has shown that all the world's domesticated cats can be traced to this subtype (the Felis silvestris lybica) in the Near East, and by 6500 years ago, they had spread out to Europe, Africa, and Asian. Their original color was sandy (perhaps as camouflage in the desert around them), which looks a lot like a Mackerel tabby. Although they most likely originated in Turkey (or concurrently in Egypt, as some have speculated), Egyptians have been credited with "turbocharging" domestication. As cats grew in importance, keeping both rodents out of their grain and staving off the infectious bacteria they carry, Egyptians began to breed cats, and

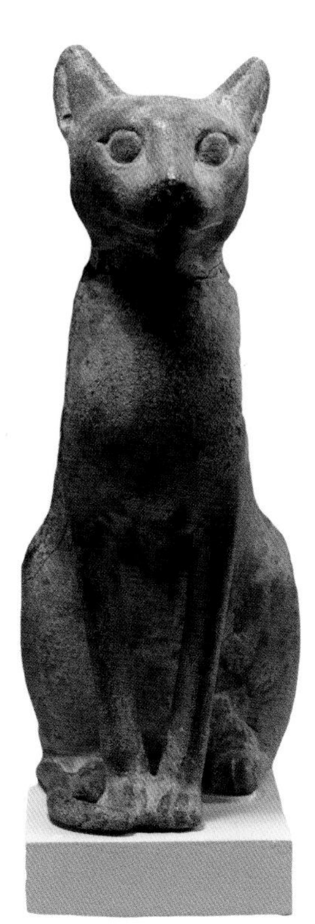

ABOVE: Cat statuette; **OPPOSITE:** Cat killing a serpent.

they most likely selected ones that were more social, less territorial, and more amenable to living with humans. Cats were bred for their tameness and eventually became part of the Egyptian's daily lives.

The archaeological record hints at this process as well. There are records of cats as early as the predynastic period, approximately 5,000 years ago. In addition, archaeologists have found cat and kitten burials as early as 3800 BC, so they had already reached a level of importance sufficient to be considered for ritual burial. Early representations of cats show them in their hunter role, such as hunting rats or birds. However, as time passed, they began to appear in tamer, more domesticated scenes, such as sitting under chairs at dinner, wearing collars, and sitting next to women.

ROLE AND PURPOSE

Cats provided pest control, a hunting aid, and companionship both during life and, for the ancient Egyptians, in the afterlife as well. Although we now live in relatively rodent-free zones, the ancient Egyptians had to contend with a number of disease-carrying rats, poisonous snakes, and venomous scorpions. These tiny creatures could be anywhere—in nooks and crannies, in dark corners, in clay jars, and in the grain (which would be spoiled by their presence). Cats were able to prevent loss of food and to also provide protection from the deadly animals that threatened their lives.

Eventually, cats also became hunters alongside their humans for birds and fish in the marshes and along the Nile banks. Finally, cats were beloved pets. The Egyptians not only appreciated them for their practical purpose, but also as a valued member of the household. Humans came to protect and cherish the felines that kept their homes safe and who provided friendship and companionship. Cats were depicted in paintings throughout Egypt's history, which means that they became enormously important in daily life.

Egyptians also used cats during the burial process. In ancient Egyptian belief, a body was mummified and buried so that the soul could inhabit it in the afterlife, and this applied to cats as well. Mummified cats were buried with their owners so that the owners could return and inhabit the body of their cat, if they chose, or the cat could continue with them in the afterlife. Mummifying cats became so important that Egyptians began to breed cats specifically for the purpose of being ritually killed and mummified. Eventually, a huge industry developed, and millions of cats were bred between 700 BCE and 300 CE, when the cat breeding industry reached its zenith.

IMPORTANCE

It is hard to state the full importance of cats to ancient Egyptians. They admired and revered cats of all sizes for their complexity and duality, especially as duality was an important concept in Egyptian cosmology. All felines possess grace, fertility, and gentleness, along with their more ferocious aspects of protection, aggression, swiftness, hunting, and lethal claws.

In the "Instruction of Onchsheshony," text from the Ptolemaic period states, among its hundreds of lines, that one should not "laugh at a cat." This probably does not refer to literal laughing at a household feline but rather not scoffing at the divinities associated with cats and respecting them, as they may appear in feline form.

Egyptians had a variety of interesting practices related to how special cats were for them. For example, Herodotus, the ancient historian, reported that if a house caught fire, the focus was not on trying to stop the blaze but to rescue their cat. In addition, they were so beloved that ancient Egyptians named or nicknamed their children "Mitt," (which means

ABOVE: Sarcophagus of Prince

ABOVE, BACK: Statuette of Bastet; **ABOVE MIDDLE:** Cosmetic Vessel in the Shape of a Cat; **ABOVE FRONT:** Cat Statuette intended to contain a mummified cat.

cat) for girls. In addition, since cats were thought to bring good luck, if an Egyptian dreamed of a cat or cats, it was thought that that person would receive good fortune.

The government also had a hand in the daily treatment of cats. Since cats were bred, some people began to export cats to other countries. However, the government came to prohibit this practice, as it wanted to keep the sacred feline relegated to Egyptian borders. This law was so strict that an entire branch of government was developed to deal with the issue of smuggling, and they even went so far as to send out agents to other countries to bring back the cats that had been smuggled out. As far as written records go, the penalty for killing a cat (even by accident) was death, with the exception of the ritual mummification process. However, many agree that this law more than likely existed much earlier.

As far as pets go, ancient Egyptians mourned cats as they would a family member. If a cat died, Egyptians observed many mourning practices that show just how important the cat was in their lives. As a sign of mourning, owners would shave off their eyebrows and consider themselves in mourning until their eyebrows grew back. Egyptians of all social classes buried their cats, and they sometimes traveled long distances to bury their beloved pet in a cemetery dedicated to animals. Egyptians are credited with developing the world's first pet cemetery, and by 1000 BC, gigantic cat cemeteries with tens of thousands of cats were fairly common throughout the nation. Relics of mummified cats were so common that when the British took control of Egypt, they began exporting the cat mummies as fertilizer.

Not only did cats have practical importance in the daily lives of Egyptians, but they were also an emotional component.

POPULARITY AND ICONOGRAPHY

Cats may have gained popularity for their practical roles in Egyptian's lives in any case, but it was the royalty and upper echelons of society that made them popular with the masses. This makes a certain amount of sense; in order to have enough grain to attract rodents, you need to be rich enough to have lots of grain. Royals not only kept smaller house cats but large cats as well and spoiled and pampered them to no end. They dressed them in jewels, crafted exquisite collars for them, and fed them delicious treats. Eventually, cat ownership trickled down to the poorer classes of Egyptians.

As with many significant aspects of Egyptian life, cat motifs became part of art, fashion, and home ornamentation for both rich and common households. People wore necklaces and earrings with cat motifs, and cat amulets were very popular gifts around New Year's as a sign of good luck.

People decorated their homes with cat paintings and sculptures, from small to massive, images of cats were carved into sarcophagi, and even home décor reflected the popularity of cats. Chair legs, bedposts, headboards, and game pieces have all been found with cat images. Even tiny amulets have a remarkable degree of detail, and it is clear that the artisans put their devoted attention to crafting such work.

Finally, the festival of Bastet was enormously popular with ancient Egyptians, as it was a time of revelry, dancing, feasting, and drinking. People celebrated with the hopes of becoming pregnant or to celebrate the cat goddess and her benevolence and protection. Thousands of people would arrive at Bubastis to celebrate, and the festival would last for days.

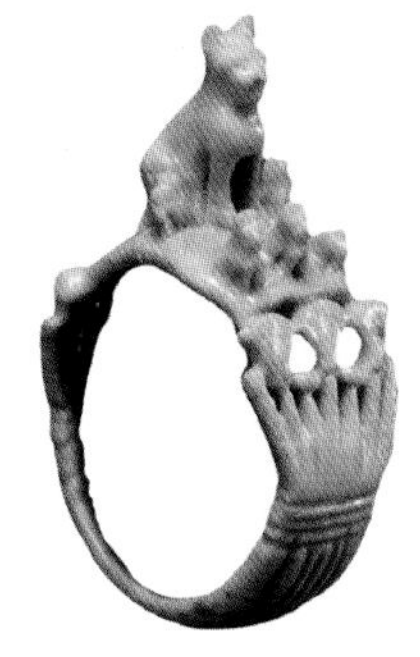

TOP: Cat figure used as a handle; **CENTER:** Cat amulet; **ABOVE:** Ring, featuring cat and kittens.

CATS IN ANCIENT EGYPTIAN RELIGION

Felines were a part of ancient Egyptian religion in both depictions of their gods and goddesses, their symbolism, and certain rituals and celebrations (such as the festival of Bastet). Some of the gods and goddesses that have cat imagery include Bastet, Sakhmet, Mut, Tefnut, Shesemtet, Pakhet, Mafdet, Bes and Wadjet.

As mentioned, it is uncertain whether ancient Egyptians actually worshiped cats; rather, they represented divine aspects of the gods, and believed that cats held a bit of divine energy within them. In addition, Egyptians believed that gods could take on the form of animals, cats included. Cats were not necessarily worshiped as gods themselves but rather honored as the potential vessels the gods could inhabit and the gods could choose to take on their likeness. In this way, cats served as a daily reminder of the power of the gods.

In short, they were as sacred to the Egyptians as the cow is to modern Indian Hindus today. By keeping a cat in their home, they believed that the gods would bless them with good luck and good fortune and protect their home. Cat gods and goddesses were the personification of the tenderness of mother cats as well as their fierce protectiveness. Cats also symbolized fertility, most likely because they have multiple kittens in a litter. Therefore, cats were often depicted lying underneath a woman at a dinner table or surrounded by kittens in paintings and statues. It was believed that a woman stood a better chance of getting pregnant if she honored the cat goddess Bastet.

Cats became linked to the sun for many reasons. They had similar coloration to the sun, with yellow and orange fur. They love the warmth and basking in the sunlight. Cats were also linked to the sun for their dual nature. The sun could be a source of life and energy but also a threat to survival in the scorching desert. Egyptians equated the cat's dual nature with that of the sun, both as a source of life and danger. Thus, many goddesses with feline traits were associated with the sun and were often depicted as daughters of the sun god, Ra, as lionesses or lion- or cat-headed women with sun disks on their heads.

TOP: Many goddesses with feline traits were associated with the sun and were often depicted as daughters of the sun god, Ra, as lionesses or lion- or cat-headed women with sun disks on their heads; **ABOVE:** Cat with the image of Bastet on its breast.

THIS PAGE: Examples of mummified cats.

Finally, ancient Egyptians mummified their cats both in their owner's ritual burials and as offerings to the gods. By placing their cats in the same tomb as their owner, the belief was that they could be reunited in the afterlife. Mummified cats were presented as offerings in the hope of a favor from the gods. As sacrifices, supplicants would ask the gods for specific wishes or prayers, such as long life, health, children, or for general protection. These votive sacrifices became a means to appease potentially angry gods if infertility was an issue or to seek additional help with personal matters.

Priests developed large "catteries" that supplied cat mummies. For example, some point to the thriving trade at the Temple of Bastet in Tell-Basta as an indication of how large the cat mummy industry was. It was forbidden to kill a cat, except for the express purpose of it becoming mummified as a sacrifice to the gods.

Bastet, along with Sekhmet, was arguably the most important cat goddess. She not only watched over the personal lives of Egyptians, but also watched the world and guarded Egypt from invasion.

Cats remained an important part of Egyptian religious life until the rise of Christianity under Roman rule.

The Bennu Bird was a self-created being who, according to myth, helped create the universe. It was said that it was the ba of Ra. According to myth, he flew over the primordial waters of Nun, landed on a rock, and gave a mighty call that helped shape creation.

BENNU BIRD

It was said that the Bennu bird appeared each morning in the form of the rising sun and shined from the top of the famous tree in Heliopolis, where he renewed himself.

The Bennu bird is linked with the sun and rebirth, and it may have been inspiration for phoenix. The Greek historian Herodotus wrote that the people in Heliopolis worshiped a bird that lived for 500 years before it died and resuscitated. He describes the bird as a large eagle with red and gold feathers, which may have been symbolic of the sun. He wrote that the people built a funeral pyre for the egg. However, Egyptian sources do not describe its death. The word for "phoenix" may derive from the word "Bennu."

It became the sacred bird of Heliopolis, closely associated with Ra and Atum, and depicted on obelisks, and benben stone. In Pyramid texts, it appears as a yellow wagtail. In the Book of the Dead, it is represented as a grey heron with long, straight beak, and a two-feathered crest. Therefore, it may be that the Bennu bird was originally a large species of heron that is now extinct. The Book of the Dead included spells for being transformed into The Bennu bird. Some depictions of the Bennu bird show it perched on a benben stone, linking it with the myth of creation.

ABOVE: Closely associated with Ra and Atum, in the Book of the Dead, the Bennu bird was a large gray heron with a two-feathered crest, and possibly linked with the Egyptian myth of creation.

THE SACRED BULL (APIS)

There were many bull cults of ancient Egypt, such as the cult of Buchis, Mnevis, but the most famous is the cult of the Apis bull.

It was regarded as a manifestation of Ptah, but unlike totems (which were thought to merely be a magical link) it was thought that the bull was a host to the god himself. When Ptah and Osiris merged, the Apis bull became associated with Osiris as well.

The Apis bull had to have very specific markings. It had to be black with special markings of a white diamond on its forehead, double the number of hairs on its tail, the sign of a scarab under its tongue, and the image of a vulture on its back. It was thought that a flash of lightning made the cow conceive the Apis bull.

When a new Apis bull was discovered, there was always a celebration. The mother cow was held in high esteem and given the title, "Isis cow." The festival of the Apis bull lasted for seven days, and the sacred bull was led through streets as people gathered to watch and cheer. It was thought that any child who smelled the breath of the bull would be able to read the future.

When a new Apis bull was born, the new bull would be brought to the cult center at Memphis, transported by a ceremonial boat built specifically for its transport and decorated with special markings. The old bull would be ceremonially drowned in the Nile. The old bull was then mummified and buried in a granite sarcophagus in an underground catacomb called Serapeum, at Saqqara. The sarcophagus could be enormous, weighing approximately 60 tons. The dead bull became identified with Osiris and was known as Osiris-Apis or Osorapis.

BELOW: Stele dedicated to the sacred bull Apis

The serpopard is a mythical animal about which very little is known. It is not mentioned by name in any historical records, and all that scholars know is from various depictions of a creature with the body of a leopard and the head and neck of a snake.

SERPOPARD

LEFT: Serpopards pictured on one side of the Narmer Palette.

Even the word "serpopard," is a modern mashup of the words "leopard" and "serpent." One theory is that they represented masculinity and vitality; other theories say that they represented chaos and the barbarians who lived outside of Egypt. This is because of the Narmer Palette, in which Narmer, the first king of a unified Egypt, is shown defeating his enemies on one side of the palette, with the serpopard on the other side. Interestingly, the creature is also featured in Mesopotamian art from around the same time periods. Just as in Egyptian art, they are seen in pairs with their necks twined around each other.

One famous image of the creature is on the Narmer Palette, and the serpopard was a popular image to put on cosmetic palettes from the predynastic period of Egypt. In Mesopotamia, they were motifs on cylinder seals.

There is even doubt as to whether the image is actually of a feline and a serpent, as it could be a long-necked lioness. It usually has a tuft of fur at the end of its tail. It does not have any spots, and it also has round ears like a lioness, unlike a serpent, which does not have any ears at all. Moreover, it is not depicted with any serpentine features, such as scales, flickering tongue, or a reptilian head shape.

They could represent a connection with royalty, as lionesses were associated with the protection of Egyptian royalty. It has been suggested that the long necks are an exaggeration to frame the mixing area of cosmetics.

Imhotep was a real historical figure who was the Great vizier, or chief minister, of the Third-Dynasty king Djoser (c. 2667–2648 BC).

IMHOTEP

LEFT: Statuette of Imhotep.

Imhotep was the architect of Egypt's earliest monumental stone structure, the Step Pyramid Complex of Djoser at Saqqara, the chief burial site at the time for the capital at Memphis. He was also the high priest of the sun god Ra at Heliopolis. An inscription on a statue of the king honors him as a master carpenter and sculptor. He may have been one of the first to use stone columns to support a building.

He was one of the very few non-royals of Egypt to become deified. He was deified during the Late Period, some 2,000 years after his death. He was identified with the Greek god Asklepios as a god of wisdom and medicine. However, there are no texts that mention his name as a physician from his lifetime. His cult lasted into the Roman period, and there is evidence that Egyptians poured out drink offerings in his honor.

Imhotep gradually became associated with intellectual pursuits, such as medicine, healing, and architecture, but then later was equated with Thoth. According to myth, his mother was a mortal and his father was Ptah. Other myths state that since his father was Ptah, his mother was Sekhmet (since she was the consort of Ptah).

One myth of Imhotep states that there was a famine which lasted for seven years, and Imhotep was the wise priest who told Pharaoh of the connection between the god Khnum and the rise of the Nile. Another myth states that Imhotep disguised himself to save the sister of a pharaoh, and another in which Imhotep fought an Assyrian sorceress in a duel of magic.

One day, all the great gods were assembled in a mighty council, and Amon-Re ruled over all as the King of the Gods.

THE BIRTH OF QUEEN HATSHEPSUT

Then Amon-Re declared, "There have been many pharaohs in the Kingdom of Two Lands, and some of them have pleased me greatly. Khufu and Khafra, who built the great pyramids; Amenhotep and Thutmose, who conquered many lands and made the people worship me and bring great offerings and sacrifices."

He gazed around at the gathering of gods. "Now a great, golden age is upon us. And it will take someone with the strength of a man but the wisdom of the fairer sex. I will create a great queen to rule over the land of Khem."

At this, a gasp arose among the gods. Never before had a woman ruled over Egypt. Amon-Re held up a hand for silence. "Yes, she will rule over Egypt, but I will bless her to rule over the lands of Syria, Nubia, and even far-distant Punt as well." Isis was the first to speak after Amon-Re's declaration. "Father of All, if you create a queen, I will bestow my blessing and wisdom upon her."

Then Thoth spoke up. "Oh Lord, I know the perfect maiden for this great work. Her name is Ahmes, and she is the most beautiful woman in the world, strong of limb, and sound of mind. She is the new bride of the god Pharaoh Thutmose, who has earned your blessing through his mighty works and conquests. It is Ahmes who will be the mother of the great queen you will create. Currently, she is in the palace of the Pharaoh. Let us go to her."

Thoth transformed himself into his favorite form, an ibis, so that he could fly swiftly through the air. In this disguise, he flew to the palace of Pharaoh Thutmose at Thebes, then to the great chamber with splendid, painted walls, where Queen Ahmes slept.

Thoth cast a spell over the whole palace, down to the last servant, so that everyone fell into a deep sleep. Even the Pharaoh slumbered but only his body would awaken by Thoth's spell. Through the spell, his three spiritual parts, the ba, ka, and khou left his body but hovered near it. The now-empty body of Thutmose was ready for Amon-Re to inhabit.

RIGHT: Life-sized statue of Hatshepsut; **OPPOSITE PAGE:** The Mortuary Temple of Hatshepsut.

Amon-Re came to in-dwell in Thutmose for a little while. The king's ka took the place of his body on the bed, lying still in the shape and form of Thutmose, while the ba took the form of a bird with a human head, and the khou as a hovering flame.

When Amon-Re entered the body of Thutmose, light seemed to shine from him, and when he walked down the dark halls of the palace, all was illuminated. As he passed through the corridors, a lingering aroma of sweet perfume was left behind. He wore a glittering necklace of precious stones, bracelets of pure gold, and two tall plumes rose from his headdress.

Amon-Re opened the double-doors made of solid ebony, decorated with silver, and entered Queen Ahmes' chamber. He found her lying on a beautiful, golden bed in the shape of a lion. He walked to her and held the divine symbol of life, the Ankh to her nose, and the holy breath of life flowed into her. The couch rose and floated in the air. In her sleep, it seemed to the Queen that she was bathed in a soft light, and she saw nothing below or above her except for the delicate, golden mist.

She heard the voice of her husband say softly, "Rejoice, fortunate queen, for you shall conceive and give birth to a daughter who shall be the child of Amon-Re. She shall reign over Egypt and be the ruler of the world." As he spoke the words, they seemed to echo into the distance. After that, Queen Ahmes sank into a deep, dreamless sleep. Amon-Re returned to the Pharaoh's bed chamber, where the ba, ka, and khou hovered over the bed of Thutmose. Amon-Re left his body and the ba, ka, and khou returned from whence they came. However, Amon-Re's work was not completed. He summoned Khnemu and said, "Take your clay and set it upon your wheel, Oh Potter, who forms the bodies of humans, and craft my daughter, who shall be called Hatshepsut. She shall be born to Queen Ahmes and King Thutmose in the royal palace of Thebes."

ABOVE: Head of an Osiride statue of Hatshepsut; **MAIN IMAGE, LEFT:** Statue of Hatshepsut; **OPPOSITE PAGE:** Sphinx of Hatshepsut.

ABOVE: The Female Pharaoh Hatshepsut; **MAIN IMAGE:** THe Great Hypostyle Hall at the Temples of Karnak; **TOP RIGHT:** Fragment of the head of Queen Hatshepsut; **OPPOSITE PAGE:** Statue of Queen Hatshepsut.

Nine months later, Hatshepsut was born, strong and healthy, and there was great rejoicing in Egypt. When she lay in her cradle, Amon-Re came in his own form, accompanied by Hathor and her seven daughters, who weave the web of life for all. He gave her a kiss in the center of her forehead, so that she would be blessed and become a great queen. Then he spoke to Hathor and her daughters: "Weave your golden web and let me see her life."

So Hathor and her daughters began their work, and the life of Queen Hatshepsut was revealed to them. In their web, they saw Hatshepsut as a beautiful little girl, kneeling in the temple at Karnak, as Horus anointed her head with the waters of purification, while the other gods and goddess looked on. Then their web revealed Hatshepsut beside her human father, Thutmose, as they journeyed throughout Egypt, to be hailed by the common people as the great and future queen.

Amon-Re saw Hatshepsut being crowned as Pharaoh, the only woman to rule Egypt, except for Cleopatra the Greek. Then Amon-Re saw in the web Hatshepsut seated on the great throne of Pharaoh, as the kings of the earth bowed before her and brought her rich and costly gifts. Amon-Re saw Hatsheptsut's great expeditions to the distant land of Punt, to the lands of the south, and their return, bringing treasures from those lands to Egypt, gold, and incense.

Finally, Amon-Re saw within the web the great mortuary temple of Hatshepsut, with all the images that Hathor had revealed in her web of fate painted on the temple walls.

Many tales exist of the achievements of Se-Osiris, whose name means, "The Gift of Osiris," who was the greatest magician that Egypt had ever known, even at the age of twelve.

SE-OSIRIS AND THE SEALED LETTER

One day, all were seated in the great throne room of the Pharaoh's palace in Thebes. The princes and nobles were gathered to pay homage to the king. Suddenly, the Grand Vizier burst through the doors and prostrated himself before the Rameses, the Pharaoh.

He cried out, "Life, health, and strength to you, Oh Pharaoh! A wicked Ethiopian has come to your court. He stands seven feet tall and demands an audience with you, saying that the magic of Egypt is nothing compared to the magic of Ethiopia."

"Let him enter," commanded the Pharaoh. Soon, a huge, Ethiopian man strode into the throne room. He bowed low to the ground in honor of the king.

He said, "Mighty Pharaoh of Egypt, I have a challenge for you to test the magic of Egypt. In my hand is a sealed letter. If any of your priests, scribes, or magicians can read what is written within without breaking the seal, then the worth of your magic shall be known. If not, I will return to Ethiopia and tell my kind and any who will listen that your magic is weak, and all will mock you. Your name will be derided among my people."

The Pharaoh was angry and troubled by this challenge, so he sent for his son Setna, who was known as the greatest magician at that time. Setna, too, was dismayed by the Ethiopian's challenge, but he said, "Oh my father, let this mischievous barbarian rest in your house. Let him eat, drink, and sleep in your best chamber, save yours, until your court is assembled next. Then I will present you with such power that will prove that our magical arts in Egypt are far superior to any foreigner's.

"Let it be so," replied Pharaoh Rameses, and the Ethiopian was escorted to the Royal Guest House.

Now, although Setna had spoken confidently, he was secretly quite distressed. He was the most skilled magician, had read the Book of Thoth, and was the wisest man in the land. However, he could not read the contents of the scroll without breaking the seal and unrolling the letter.

He returned to his own palace and lay down on his couch to think, but he looked so pale and forlorn that his wife came to tend him, thinking that he was sick. Their son, Se-Osiris, came as well. Setna told his family of his troubles, and his wife burst into tears at their plight. However, his song laughed with glee.

ABOVE: King cobra; **OPPOSITE:** Statue of Ramses II at the Great Temple of Abu Simbel, Egypt.

"My son, why do you laugh so? Why do you do this when I tell you of my troubles that will affect all of Egypt."

"Because your trouble is not really trouble at all. It is actually an opportunity to bring glory to Egypt and the gods. We will humble this overbearing Ethiopian and his king, and everyone shall know the power of Egypt. Wipe your tears, mother, and stop your sighing, father, for I will read the sealed letter."

Setna immediately jumped up from his couch and gazed at his son, who was no more than twelve. "You will do this?" he asked. "Truly? But how will we know you are up to the task?"

"Take any papyrus scroll you like from your room, and I will read it without breaking the seal," replied Se-Osiris.

And so Setna did as Se-Osiris said, and he read a scroll fetched from the study, and he read the entire contents while it was still rolled and sealed with wax.

The next day, the Pharaoh summoned his court once more, and when all had gathered in the great throne room, he sent his Grand Vizier to bring the proud Ethiopian before him.

The huge wizard walked into the great hall with hardly a bow to Rameses and held up the scroll. He said, "King of Egypt, let your magicians read what is written, if they are able, or else admit that our magic of Ethiopia is greater than yours."

Pharaoh motioned to his son, Setna. "My son, please answer this insolent barbarian."

"Oh Pharaoh, such a cur as this does not deserve to be matched against a magician in his strength, which is why I present my son, Se-Osiris, who is but twelve, to stand against him."

A murmur of shock and laughter rippled through the court as the small boy stepped forward to meet the gigantic Ethiopian who clutched the sealed letter in his hand.

Then Se-Osiris spoke up. "Oh Pharaoh, life, health, and strength to you! I will meet the Ethiopian's challenge. The scroll tells the tale of a Pharaoh of Egypt from five hundred years ago as well as a king of Ethiopia. In this tale, the king of Ethiopia sat in his marble palace far away to the south. In the shade of sweet-smelling plants, the greatest magicians of Ethiopia sat talking together. One said, "We are greater in magic than all the Pharaohs of Egypt. I could bring a great darkness over Egypt that would last for three days."

Another responded, "And I could bring a deadly blight that would ruin its crops for a season."

And so they each went on, telling of the horrors that could be wrought upon the Kingdom of Two Lands, until at last, the chief of magicians said, "And upon the Pharaoh himself, I could summon him here with magic and have him beaten five hundred times with a rod, then carry him back to his palace in Egypt, all within five hours."

When the King of Ethiopia heard this, he said to the magicians before him, "Tnahsit, my Chief Magician, if you do as you have said, I will reward you with riches greater than any magician has ever received."

So Tnahsit bowed and set to work at once. He crafted a litter and four bearers in wax, chanted powerful spells over them, then breathed life into them. He bade them to bring the Pharaoh to Ethiopia that very night.

Se-Osiris asked the Ethiopian if it was all true what he had spoken. When he had nodded his assent, Se-Osiris continued.

All happened just as the Chief Magician had promised. The Pharaoh was lifted from his bed, carried to Ethiopia, then beaten with five hundred strokes of the rod, then taken back to Egypt all within five hours.

The next morning, his back burned in great pain, and he summoned his court and all his magicians to tell him of the shame. He said, "I must avenge myself upon the King of Ethiopia," said the Pharaoh. "And I must take vengeance upon his magicians and protect Egypt from these barbarians."

So the Pharaoh summoned his Chief Magician, Kherheb, and commanded him to seek the counsel of Thoth in his great temple.

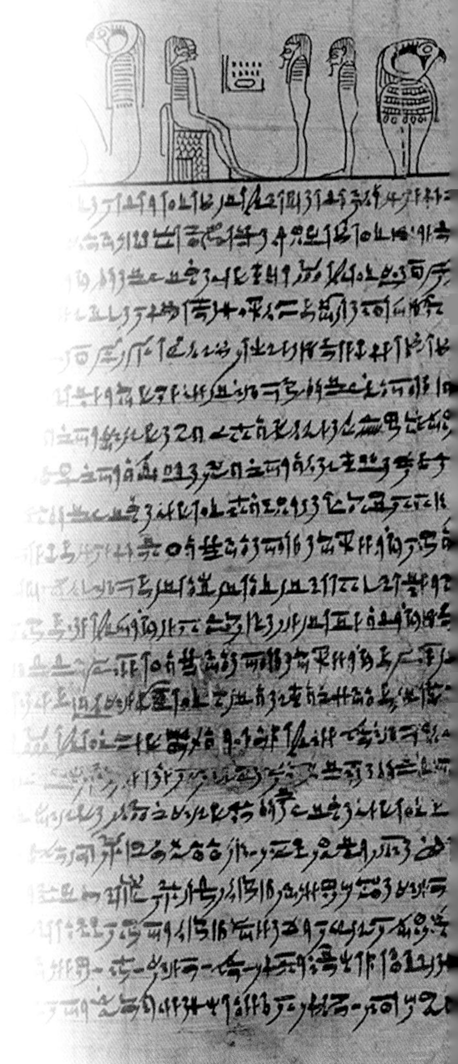

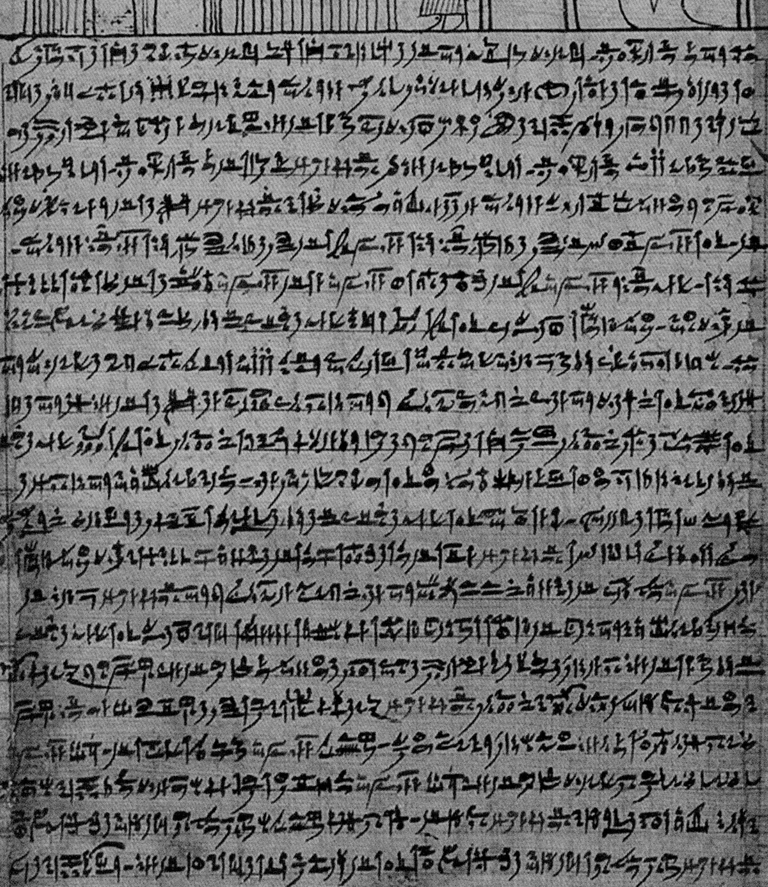

Kherheb slept in the temple of Thoth, and Thoth came to him in a dream and told him all that must be done to protect Egypt and restore the honor of the Pharaoh.

The next night, the Ethiopian litter-bearers once again stole into the royal palace to carry away the Pharaoh to Ethiopia to be beaten. However, the magic which Thoth had taught to Kherheb was so strong that they could not enter the royal chamber or even lift their arms to raise the Pharaoh onto the litter. They faded away and were never seen again in Egypt.

In the morning, Kherheb prepared a magic litter of his own with four bearers who went into Ethiopia, stole the king, and brought him into Egypt, where he received five hundred lashes with a rod before the entire court. And once that was complete, the litter-bearers took him back to Ethiopia. The king awoke the next morning sore, and he immediately sent for his chief magician to protect him. However, the chief magician of Ethiopia could do nothing to protect the Pharaoh. Three times, the magic litter-bearers of Egypt returned to Ethiopia

ABOVE: Papyrus scroll.

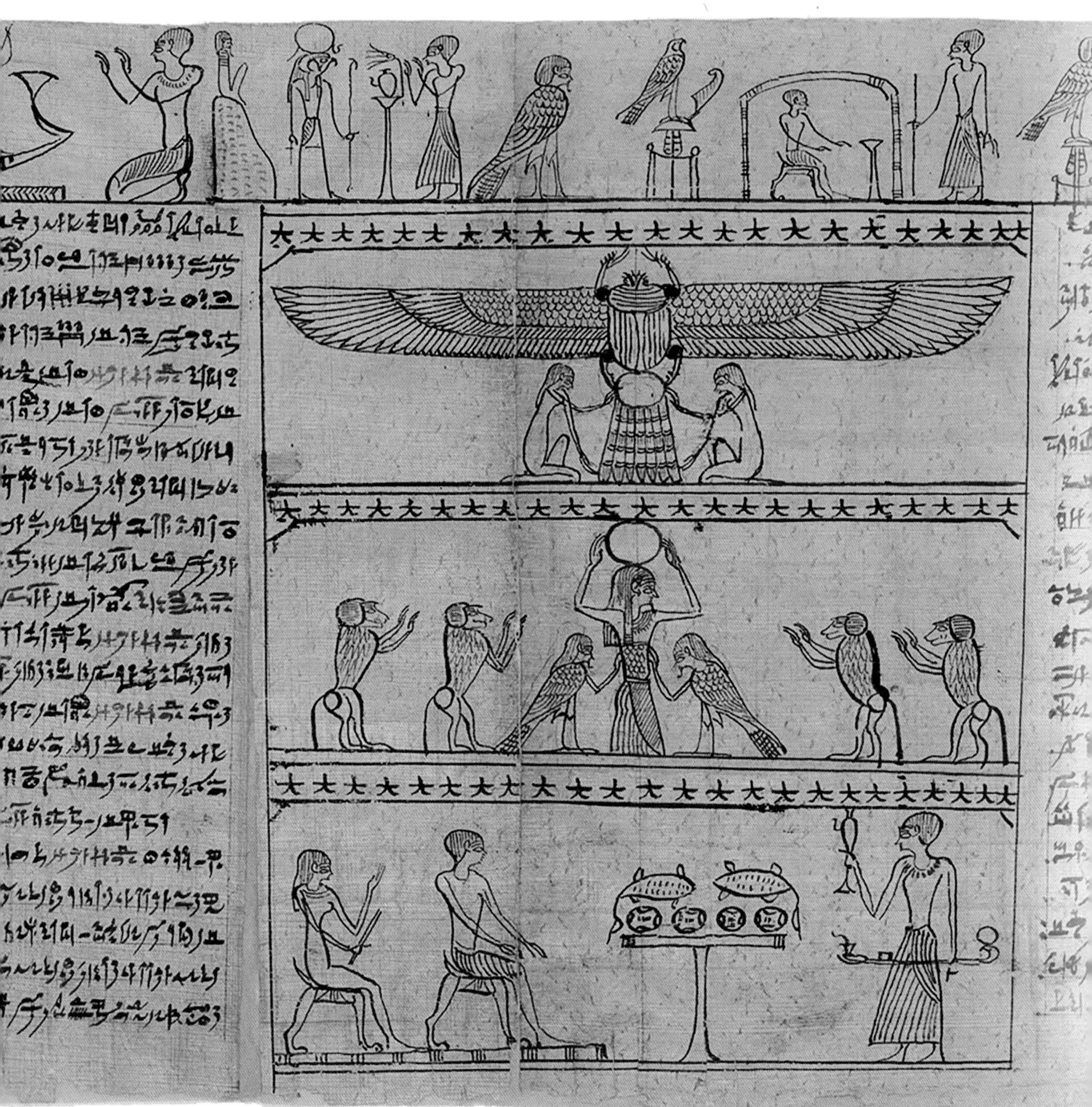

to take the king, beat him, and return him. So, the king of Ethiopia cursed his chief magician, Tnahsit, and cast him out of the kingdom because his magic was weak and could not protect him. The king said, "May you wander the earth in life and death, until you bring vengeance upon Egypt and her Pharaoh, and until you prove that there is no greater magic than that of Ethiopia.'"

Se-Osiris finished reading the sealed letter and said, "And so, Ethiopian, tell us. Are these not the words of the sealed letter you have in your hands? Answer truthfully or may Amon-Re smite you where you stand."

The Ethiopia fell to his knees and cried out, "Indeed, those are the very words written on the scroll, mighty magician!"

The Grand Vizier broke the seal of the letter and read aloud the contents before Pharaoh and all his nobles. All of the contents were exactly how Se-Osiris had spoken.

Then the Ethiopian said humbly, "Mighty Pharaoh, the challenge is complete. May I leave in peace?"

The Pharaoh had just lifted his hand to give leave to the foreigner, but Se-Orisis spoke up quickly, saying, "Oh Pharaoh, do not let him depart! This wizard has the Ba of Tnahsit within him. He is the same wizard of five hundred years ago who brought shame to Egypt. Should not there be a final battle between the magic of Egypt and that of Ethiopia?"

Rameses the Great nodded and touched his grandson with his royal scepter, saying, "You are Kherheb today; finish what Kherheb began five long centuries past." Then he turned to the giant man and said, "Black dog of the south, if you have the magic to stand against Egypt, then show it now."

The Ethiopian only laughed and replied, "White dog of the north, I defy you! Soon Seth will take you and Apep will soon feast upon your Ba. Behold!" Then he waved the sealed scroll as if it were a wand and pointed it at the floor in front of Pharaoh, muttering a powerful spell.

Immediately, a huge snake reared up, hissing; its forked tongue flicked menacingly, and its fangs were bared, ready to strike. Although the Pharaoh was frightened, Se-Osiris only laughed, and he raised his hand. In response, the giant cobra shrank into a tiny, white worm, which Se-Orisis plucked up and threw out of the window. Howling with rage, the Ethiopian waved his arms, shouting curses and incantations. A huge black cloud rolled through the throne room, casting everything into darkness as black as midnight in a tomb, and as dense as smoke from burning bodies.

But Se-Osiris only laughed again. He gathered his hands and took the darkness, crushing it together until it was no larger than a child's ball and tossed it out of the window.

The Ethiopian became crazed with the desire to win. He waved his arms and yelled a powerful word, and at once, wall of flames shot up from the floor and moved rapidly toward the Pharaoh to consume him and any who were unlucky enough to be in its path. But Se-Osiris merely blew upon the wall of flame, and it doubled back in on itself, then wrapped around the Ethiopian. He gave a great cry, as the flame consumed him, then dwindled, and eventually went out like a candle flame. Only a small pile of ash remained of the wizard from Ethiopia. Se-Osiris said, "Farewell, Tnahsit! May your Ba dwell elsewhere and never come to Egypt again."

That was just the beginning for the grandson of Rameses the Great. Se-Osiris went on to become the greatest magician Egypt had ever known.

ABOVE: Nefertiti; **OPPOSITE:** Papyrus scroll.

EVROPA

Once upon a time, in the days of Ancient Egypt, there ruled a Pharaoh called Amasis. He was threatened by the Persians, who were conquering the world.

RHODOPIS

THE GIRL WITH THE RED ROSE SLIPPERS

So to buffer his kingdom against the invaders, the Pharaoh invited Greeks to live in the north of Egypt, where the Nile meets the Great Green Sea. He gave the Greeks an entire city called Naucratis.

In this city by the sea, there lived merchants who plied their wares in the many markets. Spices, cloth, jewelry, and colorful birds were bought and sold, along with incense, perfume, and slaves. One such merchant was a wealthy Greek called Charaxos, and though he originally came from the island of Lesbos, he loved Naucratis, and settled there after he had become wealthy.

One day, as he was strolling through the marketplace, he came to the square where slaves were sold. Although he had plenty of slaves, he walked to the stone rostrum to satisfy his curiosity. When he arrived, he saw the most beautiful girl he had ever seen. She had white skin with pink cheeks and lips as red as roses. Her eyes and nose suggested that she was Greek, and Greek she was. Filled with determination, Charaxos decided to pay as much as it took to buy the beautiful slave woman. When the bidding began, Charaxos easily bought her, as he was one of the wealthiest merchants in the city.

Now, unlike most merchants of his day, Charaxos was a kind master. He took her to his home, where he gave her fresh clothes, warm food, and a comfortable bed to sleep in. When she awoke, they dined on fresh bread, figs, and honey, and having earned her trust, the woman began to tell Charaxos her story.

Her name, she said, was Rhodopis, and when she was a little girl, she had been kidnapped by the Hyksos, the feared sea peoples who terrorized islands and coastal towns. They had taken her from her home in Greece and sold her to a rich man with many slaves on the island of Samos. Although her life was not difficult, she missed her home deeply. One of the slaves had always been kind to her, a man named Aesop, who, though ugly, told fabulous stories of talking beasts, wise animals, and foolish humans. However, when she came of age, her master decided to sell her to make money, so he had her shipped off to Naucratis.

OPPOSITE: The ancient Greek geographer, historian and philosopher Strabo. It's speculated by some academics that the merchant Charaxos mentioned in the story of Rhodopis, is, in fact, Strabo, though this is disputed.

As she told her story, she told it simply, without embellishment or self-pity. The more Charaxos listened to her, the more he was filled with sympathy for the poor woman's plight, for he knew what it meant to grow up poor with very little. So, he came to love her as his own daughter and spoiled her with presents of jewelry, beautiful clothes, and a pair of gorgeous rose red slippers. He even gave her her very own house with a little garden in the center. All these things she cherished, for Rhodopis had never known such kindness as Charaxos had shown. Now she had her own slave girls to attend her, and she was just as generous with them as Charaxos was with her. She might have spent her life with him, had not a strange event changed the course of her life.

One day, she was bathing in the marble pool of her private garden, while her attendants watched over her bejeweled dress and her precious red slippers. She idled in the pool, for it was a very hot summer's day, and the sun was particularly strong. All was peaceful and quiet. Until an eagle came swooping out of the sky. It shrieked and dove straight down, as if it would attack the group of slave girls by the pool. They cried out and dropped everything in their hands—including Rhodopis' clothes and shoes. They hid among the richly scented flowers and trees of the garden. Rhodopis rose from the water and hid among the shadows, staring at the eagle in fear and fascination.

The eagle swooped down and picked up one of the rose red slippers with one of its talons. Then, just as quickly as it came, it flew away to the south, still carrying the slipper.

Rhodopis wept at the loss of her slipper, not because of its worth but because she was sorry to have lost anything that Charaxos had given her. She was sure that she would never see it again. The bird flew nonstop to Memphis, then towards the palace of the Pharaoh. At the time, Pharaoh Amasis was sat in his great, opulent courtyard, surrounded by his nobles and commoners alike, as he heard their cases to dispense justice. The eagle swooped over the courtyard, frightening some of them and dropped the red slipper right into the Pharaoh's lap. Several nobles reacted in surprise, and indeed Amasis was shocked to have a slipper

MAIN IMAGE: Memphis. **OPPOSITE:** Sandals from the Tomb of Yuya and Tjuyu.

seemingly fall from the sky into his lap. But as he inspected the delicate shoe, he admired the craftsmanship and quality of the article. He knew that it was a shoe worthy of the feet of someone beautiful, and who must be lovely enough for a Pharaoh. Immediately, Pharaoh Amasis issued a decree:

"Let my messengers go forth throughout my kingdom, into every city and every town, even to the very borders. Take this rose-red slipper, which the divine eagle of Horus has brought to me, and find its mate, for whosoever this shoe belongs to will be my mate in life and in the afterlife."

No sooner had the Pharaoh spoken these words that his messengers and guards bowed and swore that they would find the woman who owned the rose red slippers.

Many months they searched, through Heliopolis, Tanis, and Canopus, until, finally, they came to the city of Naucratis. They were weary from searching so they entered a tavern where Charaxos was just finishing his meal. Charaxos saluted them and, seeing their poor, tired faces, offered to buy them all a meal and a tall glass of beer. When Charaxos asked what brought them to the city, they answered that they were looking for a beautiful woman

who was missing a rose red slipper. Whoever it belonged to would become the Pharaoh's wife. Immediately, Charaxos knew that it was Rhodopis that they searched for. Although he was deeply torn between sorrow at his loss and joy for the good fortune of Rhodopis, he ultimately knew what he had to do. He escorted the messengers to her house and bade them enter. When the messengers showed Rhodopis the mate to her slipper, she cried out in joy, for it had been returned to her. She held out her foot, and the messengers placed both slippers on her feet. Then, they bowed before her and said, "The Pharaoh bids you come to his palace at Memphis, where you shall be treated with honor and given a high place in his Royal House."

When she heard these words, Rhodopis was excited at her turn of fortune, but in her loyalty to Charaxos, she refused to go unless he came with her. And so, going with her, Charaxos departed with the entire party as they made their way to Memphis. Yet he knew that he would have to give her up.

When they arrived at the Pharaoh's palace, Amasis was astounded at her beauty. He was sure that the eagle had been sent by Horus and that the gods meant her for his wife. Not only did he place her in the Royal House of Women, but he made her the Head Wife, the Queen and Royal Lady of Egypt. As for Charaxos, the Pharaoh blessed him with titles and riches for taking such good care of Rhodopis during her years with him. And so Rhodopis and Amasis married, and they lived many happy years together until the end of their lives and met each other in the afterlife as well.

MAIN IMAGE, ABOVE: Horus statue in Edfu Temple; **TOP LEFT:** Eagle; **ABOVE LEFT:** Ivory sandaled foot; **OPPOSITE:** The Sphinx at Memphis.

Once upon a time, there lived Rameses the Third, who defeated invasions from outsiders, encouraged trade, and patronized great architectural works such as Egypt had never known. Egypt grew prosperous under Rameses, and because of this, he became the richest Pharaoh of all.

THE TREASURE THIEF

His treasure grew, as he exacted tribute from lesser kings around the land, and he grew wealthy with gold, silver, precious stones, incense, beautiful and costly wood from the land of Lebanon, and many silks and spices. But the trouble with owning such bounty was that it soon outgrew the spaces in which to store it, and the more it grew, the more Rameses feared that someone would steal it.

So he summoned his Master Builder, Horemheb, who was the greatest of all builders in Egypt. The Pharaoh commanded him, "Build a great treasure house, hewn of the thickest stone, so that no man may chisel his way in, neither through the walls nor the ceiling, nor dig a hole and come through the floor. Build a great pyramid that can hold all my treasure so that no thief may ever enter."

Horemheb bowed low before the Pharaoh and paid homage to him, prostrating himself. He replied, "I will build such a treasure house for you that will put all other pyramids to shame, and no man will be able to force his way into it."

Immediately, Horemheb sent his stonemasons to quarry the hard rock in the desert to make blocks. Day and night they worked, and once they hewed the stone from the desert cliffs, they carried it on sledges to be transported down the Nile on boats. There the stones went to Thebes, where the temple of Rameses was already being built.

Under the direction of the Master Builder, a great pyramid was erected, so that a treasure chamber was in the middle. The entrance was made of a series of doors, some were sliding doors of stone, while others were made of iron and bronze. Finally, when the treasure was transported to the pyramid, the final detail was set in place: the doors were locked and sealed with Pharaoh's seal.

But as the Master Builder, Horemheb had a few tricks up his sleeve. He had said that no thief could force his way in, but that was because he built a secret passage with a stone on a pivot, so that it appeared as solid as any part of the wall but when pushed in exactly the right spot, a hidden spring revealed the entrance to the treasure chamber. No force

ABOVE: Relief from the sanctuary of the Temple of Khonsu at Karnak depicting Ramesses III; **OPPOSITE:** Wall relief of Rameses III.

would be necessary for those who knew the secret. He kept this secret for all his life, until he was on his death bed. He told his two sons about the hidden entrance just before he drew his last breath. His sons buried him with all honors in the Tombs of the Nobles in Thebes. After they had honored their father, they began to apply their knowledge of the great treasure chamber. They easily entered and helped themselves to the treasure.

The Pharaoh's treasure was now steadily disappearing, but he did not understand how the thieves could possibly enter, for the royal seals were never broken. The Pharaoh soon began to obsess over his treasure and its loss, so he commanded that traps be built, set within the chamber itself. This was done in secret, and the brothers knew nothing about it. So, the next time that they entered, the first brother stepped across the floor toward the many chests, and the trap sprung and caught him. He knew immediately that he would not be able to escape.

He cried out, "Brother! I am caught in this deadly snare, and not even all your wisdom and cunning can free me. I will most likely be dead by the time the Pharaoh sends his guards to check the treasure. If by some miracle, I am not dead, I will probably be tortured until I tell everything, including your complicity—and then I will be put to death. Either that, or the guards will recognize me, and so catch you and you too will die a miserable death. They may even come for our beloved mother as well. So, I beg of you, draw your sword, and cut off my head and take it with you to be buried. I will die quickly and easily and hopefully pass the judgement of Osiris. No one will recognize me, and you and Mother will be safe from Pharaoh's wrath."

Although the second brother tried to free the first from the trap, it was useless. He agreed that it was better for one of them to die rather than their whole family, so he drew his sword from its sheath. He swung straight and true and lopped off the head of his brother. He carefully wrapped it in cloths, closed the stones carefully behind him, and left the pyramid. He then buried his brother's head with all honors and reverence, so that he might pass into the afterlife.

When the morning light broke over the horizon, Pharaoh Rameses went to the treasure chamber and was shocked to find the headless body of a man in one of his traps. But he was still confounded because his royal seal had not been broken on any of the doors and the second brother had erased all their footprints leading in and out of the chamber.

Still, more treasure was missing from the chamber, so Pharaoh was more determined than ever to catch the thief. He commanded that the body of the first thief should be hung on the outer wall of the palace, with guards standing nearby to catch anyone who may try to take it for burial or who mourned near it.

When their mother heard that the body of her son was hanging on the palace wall, and therefore could not be given the sacred burial rites, she cried and could not be consoled. She turned to her son who remained living and said, "If your brother's body remains unburied, he will never know peace in the afterlife or come before Osiris to sit in judgement. He

MAIN IMAGE: Valley of the Nobles, with the largest collection of private tombs.

MAIN IMAGE: Temple of Rameses III; **INSET, BELOW RIGHT:** An ancient model of donkeys and drivers.

will wander forever, a ghost, lost for all time. Therefore, you must bring me his body, or I will go to Pharaoh myself and beg for it, in the hope that he will show mercy for the love he bore for Horemheb, his Master Builder. If he learns that you are the Treasure Thief, at least I will bury you with your father with all the sacred rites, and both you and your brother shall be laid to rest so that you may pass on to the afterlife."

Initially, her son tried to convince her that the burial of his brother's head was enough to satisfy the gods.

"Surely it is better for one of your sons to lie unburied than for both of them to die?" he asked her.

But she refused to listen, and so the second brother promised to do all he could to recover his brother's body.

Disguising himself as an old merchant, he loaded two donkeys with skins of wine and set out along the road that led to the palace wall. As he passed the place where his brother's body hung, and where soldiers guarded it, he made the donkeys bump against each other. In addition, he had secretly poked holes in the wineskins, to make it appear as though the donkey's sharp harnesses had damaged them. The wine began to flow out of the skins and onto the ground, and the Treasure Thief howled loudly about the loss of his wine, pretending to be upset to attract the notice of the guards.

As soon as they saw what was happening, the guards ran to help the merchant save the wine.

"You might as well drink it," said the false merchant. "Otherwise, it will simply be wasted, for the wineskins are broken and cannot hold it."

The soldiers were more than happy to help themselves to the wine, and soon they had drunk all the wine from the damaged skins, and it went straight to their heads.

"Thank you, my gallant rescuers! Here, take another skin in my gratitude for saving my wares." So, he sat down to share more wine with them, and they did not refuse yet another skin when it was offered. Soon, they were so inebriated that they laid down on the ground and slept soundly, snoring loudly with their mouths open. By that time, it was night, and so under the cover of darkness, the Treasure Thief took down his brother's body from the wall, wrapped it in the empty wine skins, and carried it away on one of his donkeys. He went back to his home where he and his mother buried the body with all the sacred rites, and the funeral was completed by morning.

When the morning came, Pharaoh discovered that the body had been taken, and his rage was swift as the Nile and just as mighty. He took the guards and beat them with rods as punishment for their drunkenness and foolishness. Now Pharaoh simmered with determination to catch the Treasure Thief, so he summoned his own daughter in a plan to catch him. He disguised the royal princess as an elegant lady from a far-distant land and told her to go to one of the taverns near the city gates and offer herself in marriage to the man who could tell her the cleverest and wickedest deed he had ever done. So the princess stationed herself in one of the taverns, and she attracted much notice by her odd questions. But the Treasure Thief saw through her guise straightaway, and he was as equally determined as the Pharaoh to outdo him in cunning. So he took the arm and hand of a man who had recently been executed for treason and hid the limb under his cloak. He walked to the tavern to visit the princess in disguise.

"Great lady," he said. "I want you as my wife." He was not lying, for the princess was very beautiful and very clever, even though she was under the command of the Pharaoh.

"Then tell me the cleverest yet wickedest thing you have ever done, and I will accept your offer of marriage, if it outshines all the rest that I've received."

So the Treasure Thief told her everything that had happened thus far with his brother, how he had stolen the treasure with him, how he cut off his head, and how he had stolen the body right from under the noses of the soldiers who were supposed to guard it. The princess, despite orders from the Pharaoh to capture the man, found herself enthralled by his cleverness and ways of storytelling, and found herself falling in love with him. Still, she was commanded by the Pharaoh to capture the Treasure Thief, so she called out to her attendants, who were stationed nearby.

"Help! Come quickly, for I have captured the Treasure Thief!" And she grasped hold of the arm of the thief.

Or so she thought. When the attendants came, he had slipped away into the darkness, leaving the Princess clutching the dead man's arm. Although she was furious for being tricked, she also admired how clever the thief was. When the Pharaoh heard what had passed, he gave up attempting to punish the thief. "This man is far too daring and clever to punish. This man has wisdom given by the gods, and I cannot go against that, for he is the cleverest man in my kingdom." He then summoned his messengers and said, "Proclaim through the city that I will pardon this man for his crimes and moreover, I will reward him handsomely if he will serve me faithfully."

Thus, the Treasure Thief earned a place in the Pharaoh's royal court and became a loyal servant to him. The Pharaoh showered him with riches and gave him his daughter, the royal princess to marry. He never needed or wanted to enter the Royal Treasure Chamber again.

ABOVE: Tomb Treasure; **LEFT:** The Mortuary Temple of Ramesses III.

Once there was a prince of Egypt called Thutmose, who was the great-grandson of the great Queen Hatshepsut.

THE PRINCE AND THE SPHINX

Although he had dozens of brothers and sisters, he was the Pharaoh's favorite son, and he was chosen to succeed him when the time came. But, because of the favors bestowed on Thutmose, his brothers were jealous and bitter, and constantly plotted against him to make him seem foolish, and weak. Sometimes they tried to paint him in a bad light to the people and priests of Egypt, to make them believe that Thutmose was cruel or extravagant or did not honor the gods, and so would make a bad king. At times, there were even plots to kill him.

Thutmose became troubled and greatly unhappy. Although he loved his father, he spent less and less time at court in Memphis or at Thebes. Rather, he rode with the soldiers on expeditions into Upper Egypt or across the great desert to the seven oases. Soon, the Pharaoh began to notice his son's absence and commanded him to spend time in festivals or at court. Thutmose attended these meetings, but would slip away whenever he could with a few close friends. Sometimes in disguise to hunt in the desert or to spend time in the great cliffs at the edge of the city. Thutmose was an excellent hunter, superb with bow and arrow, and consistently shot his target with ease. He could drive his horses across difficult terrain and track antelope for miles across the desert. If he wanted a challenge, he would hunt the savage lions and hippos along the Nile.

It was during one such festival that Thutmose desired to leave. After he had made his official appearance, he left the festival of Ra at Heliopolis and took his bow to hunt at the edge of the desert. He took his two closest friends with him and drove his chariot up the steep, rocky road, all the way to the great Step Pyramid of Djoser. They rode past the scrub and stunted trees, past the cultivated fields, and even past the stone wasteland, into the Libyan desert where they rested for the night.

At the first light of morning, they hunted as many antelope as they could, and when it became too hot in the midday sun for any movement, much less hunting, they stopped for rest under an oasis of palm trees. As they rested, Thutmose realized that they were not far away from the great Pyramids of Giza. Because he wanted to be alone, and to pray to the god

ABOVE: Ritual statuette of Thutmose III; **OPPOSITE:** Dakhla oasis is one of the seven oases of Egypt's Western Desert.

Horus in his form of Harmachis, he climbed into his chariot and drove it to the three great pyramids, leaving his two close friends behind. The journey was easy, for the sand was smooth and firm, and as he approached the pyramids, he was filled with awe. They towered into the sky, appearing to reach the heavens, and the midday sun illuminated their sparkling, white marble peaks, and the polished sides appeared as liquid gold.

While these would have been wondrous enough, a gigantic head and neck of stone caught Thutmose's attention. He almost didn't notice it because it was nearly buried in the sand. Its body had the form of a lion with the head of a Pharaoh—the colossal statue was that of Harmachis, the god of the rising sun. Originally, the Pharaoh Khafra had carved the sphinx out of a natural outcrop of solid rock, and he had given the sphinx his own likeness as his face.

During the many long and lonely centuries, the sands of the desert had blown against the Sphinx, burying it little by little until almost nothing could be seen except its head and shoulders.

For a long, long time, Thutmose simply stared up at the majestic head, which was crowned with the royal headdress of Egypt, with the uraeus on the brow and folds of linen surrounding the face to protect the head and neck. Although the noonday sun was intense, and Thutmose was soaked in sweat from the heat, he prayed to Harmachis for help concerning all his troubles.

"Tell me," he prayed. "Whether it is my destiny to become the Pharaoh of Egypt, when my enemies hound me so and wish to see me dead."

Suddenly, the great stone statue began to stir. It appeared as though the Sphinx was trying to throw the sand off it, struggling beneath the weight. Sand trembled and fell in small clumps but there was too much on top of it for its struggling to do any good. Its gaze fell on Thutmose, and his eyes were no longer carved stone of lapis lazuli but real eyes that shone with life and light. Although he was a god, his gaze was kind and merciful. The Sphinx then spoke to Thutmose in a great, booming voice, as loud as thunder but as soft as feathers.

"O Thutmose, Prince of Egypt, heir of Hatshepsut, and beloved of mine. I am Harmachis, your father—the father of all Pharaohs of Egypt. You indeed will wear the Double crown upon your head, if you so choose,

MAIN IMAGE, LEFT: Horus in the form of Harmachis; **RIGHT:** Statue of Pharaoh Khafra; **OPPOSITE:** The sphinx of Thutmose.

if you so desire it. You will indeed sit upon the throne if you so choose. Lesser kings will bow before you, will bring you tribute, and your people will give you what is rightfully yours—if you so choose, if you so desire it. Besides all this, you shall have many long and happy years, health, and strength."

"Thutmose, my favor is with you, and my heart yearns to give you every good thing, and your spirit shall always be entwined with mine. But look at how the sand has hemmed me in on all sides so that I cannot move. It binds me, smothers me, and hides me from your eyes. Promise me that you will honor me, as a good child honors his father. Prove that you are my son and promise that you will help me. Draw near to me, and I will be with you always, guiding your steps and making you a great and glorious king."

Thutmose was astounded at all he heard and saw. The light shone from the eyes of the Sphinx so brightly that it dazzled the prince and the world around him spun and went black, and he fell to the ground unconscious.

When he awoke, the sun was setting, and the shadows of the desert had stolen over him. The sands were pink and purple in the fading, evening light. Slowly, Thutmose rose to his feet, and as he did so, he remembered the powerful vision that the Sphinx had given him. Thutmose turned his face toward the Sphinx and cried, "Harmachis, my father! I call upon you and all the gods of Egypt to bear witness to my oath. If I become Pharaoh, the first act of my reign shall be to free your image from the sand and build a shrine to you carved in stone, telling with the sacred writing of Thoth all you commanded and how I fulfilled it."

Then Thutmose climbed into his chariot and sped away back to the oasis, where he found his two loyal friends, who had begun anxiously searching for him.

Thutmose returned to Memphis, and from that day on, the gods bestowed their favor with him. Not long after, the Pharaoh proclaimed Thutmose as his heir to the throne, and soon after Pharaoh Amenhotep passed into the afterlife with Osiris, and Thutmose became the King of Egypt. He did as he promised to the Sphinx and dug the sand around it, so that it was restored to its glory. Thutmose lived a long, fruitful life and had a glorious reign, becoming one of the greatest Pharaohs of Egypt.

Once upon a time, an unkempt and disheveled stranger came to the court of the Pharaoh. He patiently waited at the gate until it was his turn to ask for an audience with the king of Upper and Lower Egypt.

THE SHIPWRECKED SAILOR

When his turn arrived, he bowed low and humbly asked the gatekeeper for admittance, as he had strange and marvelous tales to tell the Pharaoh. The gatekeeper took one look at his ragged clothes, dirty face, and poor appearance and refused his request. No king would want to be in the presence of such an unsightly peasant. However, the stranger protested that his tales were worth hearing, and that the gatekeeper wouldn't regret letting him through.

"Very well," said the guardian of the Pharaoh's inner chamber. "You may tell your tale to me, and I will judge whether it is worthy of the king's ear. But be warned: you had better not waste my time."

The stranger settled himself in and began his story:

"Although I appear as nothing more than a poor beggar, I am a nobleman from a long and illustrious lineage, and it was my destiny to be an overseer of the Pharaoh's mines in the far-distant land of Kush. The day came when it was time for me to assume my position, and I had to board a ship to cross the Sea of Reeds. This was no simple task for me, as I had always had a fear of the great, dark sea, stretching infinitely into the horizon. However, the ship appeared sturdy, built of quality wood, and the finest of mariners crewed her. Their hearts were as fierce as Mahes, and there was nothing, not tempest, nor wave, nor perils of the deep that frightened them.

"However, Shu did not smile on us, for the as soon as we alighted upon the open waters, a great and mighty tempest befell us. The waves rose above our heads; the winds howled, and the sails snapped to and fro. The storm had neither mercy nor remorse in crushing us in its fist. Men were swept from their posts, and though our captain was experienced, he could not take back control of the ship. The winds ripped the rigging down, oars were lost, and men drowned as a giant wave crushed the ship and broke it to pieces.

"Only I survived the great and terrible storm. All others sank to the bottom of the sea. I had the good fortune to find a timber, which kept me afloat. For three days, I drifted alone on the surface, in the aftermath of the storm. My throat

ABOVE: Statuette of the deity Shu, the personification of the wind, clouds, and the earth's atmosphere, and the light that illuminated the world at the beginning of creation; **OPPOSITE:** "The Sea of Reeds" has historically been interpreted as meaning the Red Sea.

became parched with burning thirst, and my stomach shrank from hunger. By the grace of the gods, the waves tossed me onto an island, and I kissed the sand in happiness.

"When I had recovered my strength enough, I looked around me and saw that it was a beautiful, fertile island. The waves were turquoise, and brightly colored fish filled the shallows. Bushes laden with figs and grapes dotted the island, along with berries, melons, and golden grain. The streams were cold and sweet, the sweetest water that I had ever tasted. I drank until I thirsted no more. After that, I ate figs until I was satisfied and gave thanks to all the gods for my deliverance.

"I began to explore the island when suddenly an enormous crash shook the earth beneath my feet. It was so loud that I thought an earthquake or another tempest was upon me. The trees shook and bent, and through the forest, a huge serpent emerged, rearing up before me. It was truly awful and terrible to behold, yet glorious and magnificent. This snake was more than forty feet in length, and its mouth was as large as an ox. Its scales were golden, each the size of a man's hand, and its belly was as blue as lapis lazuli. A beard more than two feet long sprouted from its chin, like our king's beard. But most terrifying of all were its eyes, which gleamed with intelligence and cunning. This was no mere serpent but a crafty one. I fell to my knees in fear."

The serpent opened its mouth to speak, and its voice boomed across the island.

"Small creature," it said. "Why are you here in my kingdom? Speak. But I warn you, if you say anything that I have not heard or knew before, then I will eat you whole, and you will fill my belly."

"At once, the great serpent took hold of me in its powerful jaws, and carried me to its lair, where it released me. It fixed me with its stare, and I felt as helpless as a mouse, enchanted by the eyes of a cobra. My muscles were paralyzed in fear, but eventually, I got up the courage to speak. I related the entire story of my voyage to Kush, the mighty storm, and being shipwrecked upon the island and my fallen mariners. Upon listening to my tale, the snake softened its gaze and was compassionate to my plight.

"He said, 'Do not be afraid, small human. Cheer up, for only the benevolence of the gods could have spared you further misery. Welcome to my peaceful realm. This is a blessed and bountiful island, and you will want for nothing. Here, there is food, water, the air is pure without plague; no insects live here to annoy the inhabitants. I am the king here, and like others of my kind, I have the power of prophesy, and so I will impart you with this gift: I tell you that when the moon has waxed and waned four times, a ship will come and you will board, and you will reach your home.'

"I began to weep with gratitude. I declared that when I reached home that I would take a return ship laden with offerings of the sweetest perfume, sacred oils, donkeys, birds, and the finest robes. I promised that I would bring him my personal fortune as a gift to my savior.

"But the serpent only laughed in response. He was of such a size that the ground rumbled beneath me in his laughter."

"He responded, 'Egypt does not possess such perfumes as I require or want. Those are all ordinary incenses. As the king of this island and the Prince of Punt, I possess so many sweet perfumes of a finer quality than you could ever bring that I have no need of more. I have no use for robes, donkeys, or birds. Moreover, my

BELOW: An aged and old fig tree; **OPPOSITE, TOP:** Ripening figs, for many thousands of years one of the region's favored fruits; **OPPOSITE, BOTTOM:** A fine relief sculpture of an egyptian cobra, or serpent.

island is hidden from mortals, and once you leave here, you will never see me or the island again. So, relax, and be content to stay here with me a little while, and simply savor the pleasure of being alive.'

"After that, I walked with the serpent over the various paths of the island, and we talked about everything under the sun, the ways of man, the course of stars, and the mysteries of life. The great snake told me that others of his kind lived on the island, all philosophers, and all who did not eat human flesh.

"Just as the serpent foretold, the moon waxed and waned four times, and one day a ship appeared in the distance. I climbed a tree so I could see if it was a friendly or enemy ship, but as soon as I saw the banner of Horus, I knew that I was saved. I was overjoyed at the sight but stricken with sadness, as I would have to say goodbye to the serpent who had given me my life, knowledge, and my freedom. But he would give me even more before I left. He kept carefully out of sight of the other sailors as the ship approached and bestowed upon me many gifts of precious perfumes, ivory, cassia, kohl, sturdy wood, apes and monkeys, gold, silver, and other precious jewels. 'Goodbye, my friend. In two months, you will be reunited with your family, but you will never forget me.'

"He then slithered away into the dense foliage

ABOVE: A contemporary model of an Egyptian boat.

of the forest, and I have never seen him since.

"We set sail that day, the crew welcoming me as though a long-lost brother, for they thought I had been alone all that time. They stored my cargo below deck, and our path was swift. As we sailed away, I stood in the stern of the ship, watching the mysterious island fade from sight, as a dream fades upon awakening.

"And so, here I am, at the gates of the palace, for though I wear nothing but beggar's clothes, I hold in my possession the entire wealth that the serpent gave to me, and I offer these things to the Pharaoh, in gratitude and humility."

The guardian of the gate could hardly speak for wonder at the tale. He sent two guards to verify the treasure that the man spoke of. Meanwhile, he ushered the traveler into the presence of the Lord of the Two Lands. Once the guardian of the gate had verified that the traveler spoke the truth of his wealth, he related this to the Pharaoh. The noble traveler then told his entire story to the Pharaoh. So pleased with the tale was the Pharaoh that he allowed the shipwrecked sailor to keep all the gifts that the serpent king had given him; moreover, he bestowed upon the traveler numerous ranks and titles, and the sailor returned home, with his new wealth and position. Thus ends the tale of the shipwrecked traveler.

Once upon a time in the north of Egypt, in the delta region near the Great Green Sea, lived a peasant man with his family.

THE ELOQUENT PEASANT

Although they were poor and did not have much in the way of money or goods, they were happy and lived joyfully with each other. The peasant loved his family dearly, and he often told stories and jokes to lighten the load of the daily struggles of his class. He earned money by trading salt and rushes that would eventually be made into parchment. Every day, he took his wares into the nearby town to sell in the market, and he would return with that day's food and other necessities. Whenever he came home, his wife and children shouted with joy to see him, for he always came back with a story from the city.

Now, to get to the town and the market, the peasant had to pass through lands which belonged to a rich and powerful family from the house of Fefa. Sometimes, he would happen upon a tenant-farmer named Tehuti-nekht, who was mean, bitter, and selfish. Over time, Tehuti-nekht gradually expanded his meager plot of land closer and closer to the banks of the Nile, which encroached on the peasant's path, so that it became difficult to pass without setting foot on Fefa land.

One day, Tehuti-nekht saw the peasant driving a donkey laden with salt and rushes of the finest quality, which would be sold to make excellent parchment. Greedy, Tehuti-nekht schemed a way to take the peasant's goods from him. So, he took a fine shawl and spread it on the ground, so that one edge marked the boundary of his land, while the other edge touched the waters of the Nile. The happy peasant was singing as he approached, and Tehuti-nekht shouted at him to stop.

"Do you not see that your dirty, foul-smelling donkey will trample my good shawl?" Tehuti-nekht bawled at the peasant. Not wishing to be involved in a conflict, the peasant merely replied, "Very well, I will try to avoid it." He then led his donkey into the field of barley, smiling and singing all the while. But Tehuti-nekht shouted at him again: "Your silly donkey has ruined my crop! And now he is eating it!"

"This is unfortunate, but there was no other way to pass," answered the peasant.

"I claim your donkey as compensation for my lost crop of barley." Tehuti-nekht thus grabbed

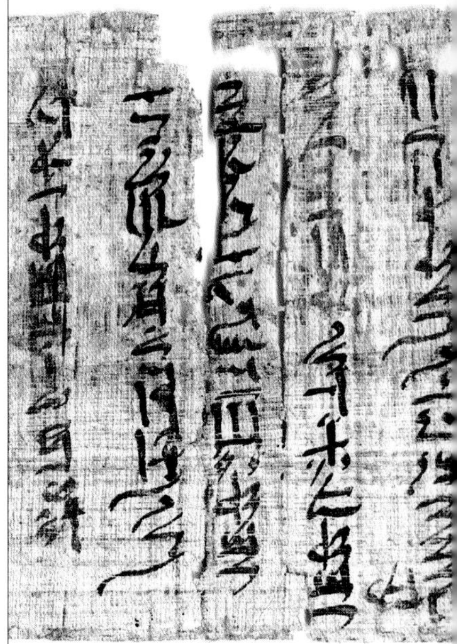

ABOVE: A papyrus fragment of part of the *Eloquent Peasant* story; **OPPOSITE:** Peasants harvesting papyrus.

hold of the rope attached to the donkey and guided it toward his home. Unfortunately, all of the other donkeys the peasant had followed after the first.

The poor peasant despaired and vowed that he would seek justice. "I will bring my complaint before the high steward Meruitensa, and you will see justice."

But Tehuti-nekht only laughed in response. "Do you think to threaten me with your idle words? I am the right hand of the great steward Meruitensa." He then took a stick and beat the poor peasant.

Thus did the peasant go to the high Steward Meruitensa but with a heavy heart, for he had little hope that the high steward would listen to him. He presented himself to Meruitensa, and he found that the lord was preparing to go on a voyage. Nervous, the peasant bowed low into the dust and begged for the steward to hear his story. The steward left the matter in the hands of his scribe, so the peasant told of the injustice done to him at the hands of one of the steward's tenant-farmers. With a tongue like silver, the peasant related all that Tehuti-nekht had done to him, his trickery and theft of his donkeys. So impressed was the scribe with the peasant's power of speech that he gave the matter to his master, the steward, to decide, as he determined that it was a matter of law. The peasant came before the high steward, but he threw up a hand before the peasant could speak.

"Let him bring forth a witness who may testify to the event in question," commanded the steward, not addressing the peasant directly. "If his case is proven true, it may be that Tehuti-nekht will face punishment, to be beaten or to have a fine raised against him."

But the peasant said this in response: "Great lord, you are the mightiest of all stewards, the most just in all the land, and who protects those who cannot protect themselves. I am but a poor man who has been deprived of the few possessions he owns. Alas, there was no one else around when Tehuti-nekht beat me and robbed me of my salt, reeds, and donkeys. However, there are many who can vouch for my honor, who can testify that I have always lived by the law and have worked hard all my life. Surely you cannot take the word of a greedy

ABOVE: Workers and their donkey harvesting the fields; **OPPOSITE:** The banks of the Nile river.

man such as Tehuti-nekht over my own, even though he is a villain and a rascal, and I am but a humble peasant."

The great steward, admittedly, was flattered by the peasant's description of him, as he considered himself worthy of all the description of the peasant. And despite all his misgivings of the peasant, he was astonished and impressed by the eloquence of the peasant, and marveled that an uneducated man could make such a passionate speech.

Although the peasant spoke truthfully, the steward was in a quandary. He did not wish to condemn Tehuti-nekht, for in doing so, he would alienate all the other tenant farmers who worked for him. So, to delay the verdict, the steward said that he would confer with the wisest advisors in the land, and that the peasant should come again and present his case once more. That evening, when the moon was full and the air was sweet, the steward sent for his scribe to write a letter to the Pharaoh.

The steward wrote, "O Lord of the Two Lands, there is a peasant whose goods have been stolen. He possesses such eloquence that I suspect that he has been given a gift from the gods and he carries their blessing. Tell me, what should I do with such a man?"

The Pharaoh wrote back that the high steward should have the peasant's speeches written down, and that in the course of bestowing justice, his family should be given grain and meat to eat while the case was decided. However, added the Pharaoh, the steward should not tell anyone that it was of the Pharaoh's doing. And so, as the peasant spoke his case, he added more details to it, and every word was carefully written down by the scribes, and a copy was sent to the Pharaoh each night. And every night, a messenger came to the peasant's house with bread, meat, and beer in such large quantities that the peasant and his family dined well and had leftovers for the next day.

One day the high steward became bored with the peasant's speeches. So, when the peasant once again came to plead his case, the high steward sent him away. However, not deterred, the peasant stood beneath his window and pleaded ever more passionately. The speeches

LEFT: Model of a Chief Steward's boat; **BELOW:** The beautiful temple of Philae, and its Greco-Roman buildings, seen from the Nile river; **OPPOSITE:** Ancient egyptian papyrus with a painting of the Nile river traffic.

continued, until the high steward threatened to beat the peasant. Finally, the high steward sent guards to the peasant's house. At first, the peasant and his family were afraid that the peasant had gone too far, and that everyone would be fed to the crocodiles in the Nile. But the news was that the peasant and his family were summoned to appear before the Lord of the Two Lands in the capital far away. So, the peasant and his family boarded the high steward's barge and set sail down the sacred Nile. As they traveled, the family saw such wonders as they had never seen: huge cliffs, the waving stalks of grain, glorious cities that were grander than anything that they had ever seen, fleets of mighty ships on the river, and finally, the wondrous pyramids. When they arrived at the Pharaoh's palace, they had to crane their necks and shield their eyes. It was so tall it seemed to touch the very sky itself.

When the peasant and his family were brought before the mighty king, they threw themselves on the ground in prostration. In a gesture that shocked his entire court, the Pharaoh descended from his throne and raised the peasant and his family with his own hand.

"I consider you a friend," said the Pharaoh. "Your speeches have entertained me and my court for weeks. Your honesty shines from your words like the light of my father Ra. It is clear that you are a good man."

For once, the eloquence of the peasant failed him, as he stood gaping at the Pharaoh. The Pharaoh continued. "I did so enjoy how you depicted the high steward as a rather pompous fellow; most would never besmirch the name of their betters, but you are right in this case. In the matter of your stolen property, I decree thus: you will be raised to the rank of a high lord, and that the property of Tehuti-nekht shall be given to you. In addition, you will be my overseer and administer my estates in the region of the Great Green Sea, and all the riches thereof shall be yours in proportion to your status."

No sooner had the words left the Pharaoh's lips that his servants rushed to obey his decree. The property of Tehuti-nekht was stripped from him and given to the humble and eloquent peasant, who became the Pharaoh's trusted minister.

First, a warning to all who read: This is a tale with no end. It was originally on a papyrus scroll but it became damaged, and the end of the tale is lost forever.

THE DOOMED PRINCE

Once upon a time, there was a king who was greatly troubled at heart because he desired a son, yet none had been born to him. He prayed to all the gods to grant his request, and they blessed him therewith, for he had been a good and righteous king. So, in time, he wife became pregnant and bore a son. When he was born, the Hathors came into his room and stood over him to decide his destiny. They said, "His death shall be by the crocodile, or by the serpent, or by the dog." All those who heard the fate grieved, and the servants ran to tell the king what the Hathors had foretold. When the Pharaoh heard the news, he feared for his son, so he commanded that a house be built in the mountains, filled with everything the boy could ever want, so that he would have no need to leave the house.

One day, when the boy had grown some years into a strapping youth, he went up to the roof of the house one day, and he saw a dog following a man. He turned to his servant and asked what the strange creature was, for he had never seen it. The servant replied that it was a dog, and the boy immediately wished to have one for his very own. When he asked the king for a dog, his father did not deny him, because he loved him so and did not wish for him to be sad. Time passed and the boy and dog grew together. However, as a man, the prince was restless and wished to see more of the outside world. When he was told the decree of the Hathors, he sent a message to his father, saying, "Why, then, am I kept a prisoner when I am fated to die in any case? Let me follow my own path, and let the gods fulfil their will, however they may."

The Pharaoh knew that his son was right, and said, "You are free to go wherever you wish."

And so the prince was free to do as he willed, just like other men. He trained with weapons to hunt, and the dog followed him wherever he went. He left the house, set out for the east country, and let his whim dictate his path. He hunted and lived on the game of the wild desert. Soon, he came to the land of Nahairana, and met the chief there. Now, this chief had only one daughter, and he had built a house for her that stood seventy stories tall, with seventy

ABOVE: Depiction of an offering to the crocodile-god Sobek. Detailed on a box that may have been used for temple rituals; **OPPOSITE:** The Seven Hathors and a depiction of an ancient egyptian dog.

windows. He proclaimed that whoever could climb the palace and reach his daughter's window would be her husband.

When the chief of Nahairana met the prince, he welcomed the youth to his land and showered upon him gifts and treated him with honor. As they sat down to dine, the chief asked the youth where he came from. He answered, "I come from the great land of Egypt, and I am a son of an officer there. My mother died when I was young, and my father has since taken another wife. When she gave birth, she only loved her own children and grew to hate me. So, I fled their house as a fugitive, and I have not returned." The chief and his family felt very sorry for him.

One day, the prince saw many men climbing the walls of the palace, and he asked why they did so. They told him of the chief's decree that whosoever could scale the walls and reach the tallest window of the princess's chamber would marry her. The prince, having seen first hand how beautiful the princess was, decided to try for himself. He climbed the dizzying heights and managed to reach her window. The princess was very happy that the prince had accomplished the feat, for she wanted to marry him. She kissed and embraced him, and in her happiness, sent a messenger to her father, telling him of the success.

When the chief asked which of the youths had reached his daughter's window, the messenger replied that it was the fugitive from Egypt. The chief grew very angry and vowed that a fugitive from Egypt was not fit to marry his daughter. He ordered him to be found and driven from the land, back to Egypt. An attendant who was sympathetic to the prince ran to tell him and the daughter, but the princess clung to the prince and refused to let go. She swore by the gods that they would marry and be together, even in the afterlife. "If he is taken from me, I will neither eat nor drink, and I shall die!" The chief was told of his daughter's vow, but he did not listen. He sent soldiers to slay the poor prince, but the daughter once again clung fast to him and swore, "By the god Ra, if he is slain, then I will die before the setting of the sun. If we are parted, then I will draw nary a single breath more."

Her message was once again delivered to the chief. The chief commanded that his daughter and the prince be brought before him in his throne room. Although both trembled, the chief

ABOVE: Two bas reliefs depicting serpents at the temple of the goddess Hathor, in Dendera; **OPPOSITE, ABOVE:** Egyptian dogs; **OPPOSITE, BELOW:** the goddess Hathor.

embraced the youth with love, saying, "I see that my daughter loves you greatly. Therefore, I will love you as a son." Then the chief gave his daughter to the Egyptian youth to marry and gave him a rich dowry of lands and cattle besides.

Many happy years passed, and one day the prince told his wife what the Hathors had decreed saying, "I am fated to die one of three ways—by a crocodile, by a serpent, or by a dog."

At once, her heart was filled with a great and terrible fear. She immediately drew a knife to slay the dog that was at his side, saying, "Let me kill the dog that follows you then." But he stayed her hand, for he could not kill the animal that had been so faithful to him, which he had raised since it was a pup.

Finally, the prince desired to return to the land of his birth, but his wife would not let him go alone, so she went with him. During their journey, they came to a town near the edge of the Nile. In the river lived a terrifying crocodile that plagued the town, and which sometimes carried off children in the night. In this town lived a strong and mighty man who did not want the crocodile to terrorize his village, so he would bind the crocodile. When it was bound, the strong man felt at peace and could travel. When the sun rose, he returned to his house and the crocodile would escape its bonds. Then, the man would re-bind the crocodile every night. This continued for some months.

When the prince and his wife passed into the village, they did not fear the crocodile, for it had been bound up by the strong man, and they rested easy in their house. One night, the prince fell asleep on the couch, but his wife had the habit of remaining awake for a few hours, to make sure that nothing happened to her husband. That night, she filled a bowl of milk and placed it by his side in case he should thirst in the middle of the night. While he was sleeping, a serpent slithered from a hole in the house, and it tried to bite the prince. But his wife, seeing the serpent, gave it the milk to drink, so that it became drunk and lay helpless on its back. When it couldn't move, the wife drew her dagger and cut off its head. When her husband woke up, his wife explained all that had happened. "See," she said. "The gods have given you one of your dooms, and you have escaped. Surely, they may give you all three to pass over you."

Then the prince made sacrifices to the gods and praised them. One day not long after, the prince went into his fields, his faithful dog following him as always. His dog began to chase some wild game, and he jumped into the river. The prince followed his dog to the river. Upon hearing the commotion, the crocodile crawled out of its hiding place. He said to the prince, "Behold, I am your doom..."

THE AFTERWARD

Unfortunately, that is all there is to know about the story. Was he devoured by the crocodile? Did his dog betray him or lead him to greater danger? Or did he manage to escape all three dooms? Let the reader dream up the ending as they so desire...

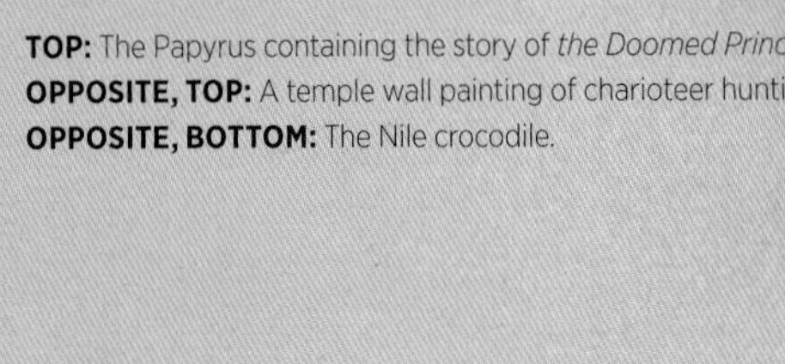

TOP: The Papyrus containing the story of *the Doomed Prince;* **OPPOSITE, TOP:** A temple wall painting of charioteer hunting; **OPPOSITE, BOTTOM:** The Nile crocodile.

THE GOLDEN LOTUS

Once there reigned Sneferu, the father of the Pharaoh Khufu, who commissioned the Great Pyramid of Giza.

ABOVE: Pharaoh Kufra; **OPPOSITE:** Sneferu, and the Egyptian lotus flower.

Sneferu was such a good Pharaoh that he had no wars, nor troubles within his kingdom, and so he often found he had lots of time to spare. Although he was Pharaoh, and could have whatever he wished, he found that nothing could satisfy him. One day, as he wandered through the halls of his great palace in Memphis, he sought out various pleasures, but none could fill the hole in his heart. So he summoned his Chief Magician, Zazamankh, for he thought, "If any man can entertain me and show me new wonders to lighten my heart, it is the wise magician. Bring me Zazamankh."

The servants went immediately to the Temple of Wisdom and sought out the Chief Magician for the Pharaoh. Once he was brought before Pharaoh on his throne, he said, "I have searched throughout my palace for something that will delight me and make my heart glad but have found nothing. Conjure something in your wisdom that will give me pleasure."

Then the Chief Magician replied to him, "O Pharaoh, I advise you to go sailing down the Nile, to the lake below Memphis."

But the Pharaoh waved away his suggestion. "That is nothing new. I have already sailed upon the Nile and to the lake."

"This will be no common expedition," said Zazamankh.

"Especially if you follow my advice to the letter. Send for the fairest maidens from the Royal House as your rowers. They will row for you, and on this voyage, you will see the beautiful birds of the lake, the greenest fields, and the lush grass and papyrus reeds that grow along the Nile, and your heart will be glad."

The Pharaoh's eyes lit up at the thought. "Hmm, perhaps this will be interesting. Very well, I place you in charge of this voyage. You may speak with my power and command my servants to do all that is necessary to prepare."

Then the Chief Magician bowed low to the ground and honored the Pharaoh. Next, he summoned the servants and attendants of Sneferu and said, "Bring me twenty oars of the finest ebony wood inlaid with gold. Make the blades of light wood inlaid with electrum."

Some of the servants bowed and immediately went to fulfill his command. Next, he turned

BELOW: Botanical painting of the Egyptian lotus; **BOTTOM:** Model of a typical paddling boat. Boats of this particular type appear in representations of the "pilgrimage to Abydos".

to other attendants and said, "For the rowers, choose twenty of the fairest maidens in the Royal House of women. They should be virgins without blemish, slim and lovely, as fair in face as they are in limb, with long, flowing hair."

Then those servants bowed and rushed to fill the command.

Finally, he turned to a third group and said, "Bring forth twenty nets of golden thread and craft twenty fine garments for them. They shall all be fitted with jewelry of gold and malachite. Each of them shall wear a golden lotus upon her head, made of electrum and malachite."

They, too, bowed, and did as he commanded. Very soon, the Pharaoh embarked on his journey in his Royal Boat, while the maidens rowed, dressed in their fine garments of gold with golden lotuses on their heads to hold back their long, flowing hair. As they rowed down the Nile, the Pharaoh gazed at the shining waters and the beautiful women, and his heart grew light at the sight, and the whole voyage seemed to become the golden days when Osiris would return to rule the earth. One of the maidens was stationed at the head of the boat, and she sang a song to keep the rowers in time. She was the fairest of all the maidens and had the loveliest voice.

But an odd mishap fell upon the happy party. One of the maidens raised her oar and accidentally brushed the head of the girl who sang to keep the tempo of the rowers. The oar swept the golden lotus off her head, and it sank into the water. The maiden cried out and leaned over the boat to try to find it. She stopped singing, and when she stopped, all the rowers stopped their task, for they relied on her for the tempo.

The Pharaoh rose from his throne on the boat. "Why have you ceased rowing?" he asked.

The maidens replied, "Our steerer stopped singing and no longer leads us."

"Why, then, have you stopped leading the rowers with your beautiful song?" asked the Pharaoh.

"Forgive me, O Pharaoh," said the fairest maiden with a sob. "But one of the oars struck my head and swept away the beautiful golden lotus from my hair, the one that your majesty gave to me, and it fell into the water. It is now lost forever."

The Pharaoh simply waved his hand and said, "Keep rowing. I will give you another."

But the poor girl could only cry and said, "I can have no other golden lotus but the one you gave me."

Then the Pharaoh replied, "There is but one man who can find the golden lotus, and he is Zazamankh, the great magician. Bring him here."

ABOVE: The Great Pyramid.

So the Chief Magician came before Sneferu in his silk pavilion on the royal boat and knelt before the king of Egypt. The Pharaoh said to him, "Zazamankh, greatest of magicians, I have done as you advised, to the letter. My heart is light and glad, and my eyes have delighted in the sight of the beautiful waters, the verdant pastures, and the beautiful women. This journey has seemed to be in the golden days when Ra ruled the earth or when Osiris shall return from the Duat. But one of the maidens is distraught for the golden lotus that sat atop her hair has fallen into the lake, and now she ceased to sing. The rowers cannot keep time with their oars. This fair maiden cannot be consoled but weeps for her lost lotus. I wish that the golden lotus be restored to her, so that the joy will return to her soul, and she will sing once more.

"Pharaoh, I will do what you ask. For one of my wisdom and magic, it is a simple matter. But it will be an enchantment the likes of which you have never seen, and it will fill you with wonder, as I promised, and make your heart glad with joy of new things."

Then Zazamankh stood at the front of the Royal Boat and chanted potent spells and words of power. He held out his wand over the water, and the lake parted as if it had been cut with a sword. The lake was many feet deep, and there came to be a wall of water where there had been none before. Zazamankh guided the boat gently along the cleft in the lake, until it rested on the bottom of the lake, where there was a bit of ground as firm and dry as the land above. Right next to the boat lay the golden lotus. The fairest maiden cried with joy when she saw it and jumped over the side of the boat, picked it up, and placed it in her hair. Then she climbed back into the Royal Boat and took her place at the head of the company. The Chief magician waved his wand, and the waters began to rise once more. The Royal Boat slid up the wall of water, until it rested on the surface of the lake once more. The great cleft sewed itself together, and the waters became unified once more. A light breeze rippled over the surface of the lake, as if nothing had ever happened. The heart of Pharaoh was filled with wonder, and he cried out, "Zazamankh, you truly are the wisest of magicians! You have kept your promise and have shown me such wonders on this day. I shall reward you greatly with all that you may desire, and I will give you a seat in my Royal Household."

Then the Royal Boat continued its voyage, sailing gently over the lake toward the glow of the setting sun. The maidens dipped their oars of ebony and gold into the sparkling waters and sang a song to keep the tempo. And the Pharaoh was glad indeed.

THE SEVEN YEAR FAMINE

In the eighteenth year of the Pharaoh Tcheser, the whole southern region, the Island of Elephantine, and the district of Nubia, were ruled by the high official, Mater.

ABOVE: Pharaoh Djoser.

The king sent a message to Mater informing him that his region was in great peril because for seven years, the Nile had not flooded and so for seven years, the earth had been dry and barren, producing no grain. Moreover, there were no vegetables or fruit, and the people had very little to eat. Such scarcity there was that men robbed one another, if they had the strength, which they frequently did not for hunger. Children cried because their bellies were empty, young men collapsed from weakness, and the elders fainted and laid themselves down to die. This troubled the king greatly, and so he sought the help of the god, Imhotep, the son of Ptah, who had once saved Egypt from famine. However, Imhotep did not respond, and Tcheser grew despondent and sent a messenger to Mater and asked him to tell him where the Nile rose, and which god or goddess was responsible for the flooding each year.

In response to the summoning, Mater left immediately for the royal palace and gave him the requested information. He reported that the Nile flooded from the Island of Elephantine, which was the site of the first city that ever existed. From the blessed island rose the sun, which spread its heavenly rays on mankind. There was a spot on the island from which the river flowed, it was a double cavern, which was the shape of a woman's bosom. From this spot, the Nile-god watched the river and when it was time, it rushed forth and filled the whole country. The guardian of the flood was known to all as Khnemu, and it was his charge to keep the doors closed that held in the river and he opened them when it was the proper time.

Mater also described the temple of Khnemu at Elephantine and told the Pharaoh that the other gods had blessed the Nile. He told the Pharaoh of the various sacrifices that he could make to this god and to make obeisance to him, so that the Nile could once again flood and bring its life-giving power to the people of Egypt. So the Pharaoh went to the Island of

MAIN IMAGE: The famine Stela located on Sehel Island in the Nile near Aswan; **TOP:** Statuette of Imhotep; **ABOVE:** Statuette of Khnemu / Khnum.

Elephantine to appease the god Khnemu, to offer sacrifices to him, and to ask if there were anything amiss that he could rectify. It was a long and arduous journey to the holy island, but the Pharaoh eventually reached it. He entered the temple and prayed for many days, asking Khnemu to appear.

Finally, Khnemu revealed himself to the Pharaoh and said, "I am Khemu, the Creator. I am he who created himself. I am the Nile that rises and who gives health to those who toil. I am the guide of all mankind, the Almighty, the father of the gods, and the mighty bringer of life. I am the primeval waters without which no life could exist."

When Tcheser asked why the Nile had not flooded for seven years, Khnemu replied, "My shrine is broken and in disrepair. No one has bothered to restore it in seven years, even though there is plenty of stone in the hills not far from here."

Khnemu said these words with compassion and not a trace of bitterness, for it was not his way. But as soon as Pharaoh heard these words, he said, "O mighty Khnemu, I will send for stone-masons this very day to repair your shrine. And I will issue a decree to last forever that the land on either side of the Nile will be set aside as an endowment, to protect your shrine and maintain its upkeep. A special tax shall be levied on the people surrounding this island for the protection of the priests and the maintenance of your temple. I will write this in stone so that it may last forever, and I will set it in a prominent place so that all may know."

The Pharaoh went and did all that he had promised. When the shrine was restored, the god of the Nile appeared to Tcheser once more and said, "Because you have been faithful and kept your word, the Nile shall rise every year, as in the old days, and the waters of life will give life to Egypt."

Thus ended the famine.

In the ancient days, there lived two brothers, who were as alike as sea and sand, fire and water, day and night.

THE BLINDING OF TRUTH BY FALSEHOOD

The first was very handsome, good, and kind. He listened to maat, and so he was called Truth. However, his brother was his opposite in every way: he was ugly, his heart was heavy with sin, and he was deceitful, so everyone called him Falsehood.

One day, Truth needed a knife, so he asked to borrow one from his brother. Falsehood grudgingly loaned it to him. After he had finished with the knife, Truth placed it in his home but promptly forgot its location in his absent-mindedness. When he went to give the knife back, he could not find it and so was very upset. Truth begged his brother's forgiveness, and he promised to replace the knife with another one.

"Yes," sighed Falsehood deeply. "But that knife was special. The blade was made with rarest metals, its handle fashioned from hard cedar from Lebanon, and the sheath was the finest leather, carved with the likeness of a god."

"I do not remember such a blade," said Truth.

"Even so, that is my claim, and if you do not replace it with one as equal to the original, I will demand legal recourse," said Falsehood.

Truth could not hope to find a knife as the one Falsehood had described, so Falsehood took them before the court of the Nine gods at Heliopolis. Falsehood pointed at his brother and accused him of losing his precious, rare weapon. Truth did not say anything in response because he could not fathom why his brother would lie so outrageously.

However, since Truth offered no defense, the gods ruled in favor of Falsehood, and asked what Truth's punishment should be. "Let his eyes be struck from his head, all his property will become mine, and let him be a servant in my house," responded Falsehood. The gods carried out the sentence immediately, and even then, Truth did not protest. Truth was led, now blind, to his brother's house where he was made a door-keeper, and to listen for intruders.

In a rare display of guilt, Falsehood felt bad over what happened to his brother. But he could not bear the guilt and so commanded two servants to take Truth to a den of lions where he would be torn apart and eaten. The two servants sadly led Truth to the den of lions, and

ABOVE: Egyptian knife; **OPPOSITE, ABOVE:** A bas relief of an ox; **OPPOSITE, BELOW:** The surviving papyrus of *The Tale of Two Brothers*.

they lamented the loss of their former master. They decided that they could not carry out Falsehood's command, but they could not bring Truth back to their new master's house. So, they took Truth far away in the rugged mountains and left him with some food and water. There, they thought, some merciful traveler might find him, or the gods would be kind to his plight. Truth wandered the mountains helplessly, and the little food and water the two servants had given him was quickly consumed. Truth laid down on a rock to die, abandoning all hope.

However, a beautiful lady and her entourage came passing through the mountains. She saw Truth's handsome face, even without sight, and immediately took pity on him. She took him to her mansion, where he was bathed, given fresh clothes, food, and wine. The woman soon fell in love with Truth because he was the most handsome man that she had ever met. Now, because he was her servant, they could not be seen sharing a bed together. Nevertheless, Truth came to share her bed every evening and returned to his lodging before the morning light. She soon became pregnant and gave birth to a son, as handsome and good in nature as his father. He grew up strong and healthy, and he quickly became the best in his schooling, as he was far more intelligent than any of his classmates. However, although he was smart, strong, and handsome, his classmates taunted him for not knowing his father. He begged his mother to tell him who his true father was. Because she could not bear to see him upset, his mother pointed to the gates and said that his father was the gatekeeper, who she would marry in an instant, if only they were of the same rank.

"Married or not, it is not fit that my father should suffer as a servant." And so the boy brought Truth into the house, gave him the best garments, and placed him at the front of the table and called him Master of the House. His mother was proud that her son had shown such great courage. Still, their son's curiosity was peaked. "Father how was it that you became blind?" he asked. Truth then told him of his brother's betrayal. The boy was immediately consumed with wanting to avenge his father,

TOP: The slaughtering of animals for the meat offerings of the Gods at Habu temple; **ABOVE:** Maat, the goddess of truth; **OPPOSITE:** Extract from the *Tale of the Two Brothers.*

un ȧn paif sen āa ḥer
His brother elder

χeperu mā ȧbu shemātu ȧu-f ḥer
became like panthers southern. He

ṭāt ṭemtu paif nui
made sharp his dagger,

ȧu-f ḥer ṭātu-f em ṭet-f un ȧn
he placed it in his hand.

paif sen āa āḥā en
His brother elder stood

ha pa sbai paif
behind the door of his

and he vowed to make it right. He clothed himself with weapons, gathered food and water, and then chose an ox to carry him over the mountains to the estate of Falsehood.

When he reached the outskirts of Falsehood's estate, he hailed a servant.

"Hello! I have a problem that you can help me with. I need to go into town for several days, but I cannot take this ox with me. Will you keep it here with your herd and tend it for me while I am gone?"

"I will," replied the herdsman. "But what will you give me for this service?"

"Everything that I carry," replied the boy. And so, he gave him the bread, water-skin, staff, good sandals, sword, and handed over the reins of the ox to the herdsman. There the boy's fine ox mingled with Falsehood's cattle.

Days later, Falsehood came to the pastures to choose an ox for a feast. When he saw how fine, healthy, and fat the boy's ox was, he pointed to it and commanded the servants to take it for slaughter.

"I'm sorry, my lord," said the herdsman. "I cannot give you that particular ox, for it belongs to another. Please choose another, for I cannot break a promise."

"Fie on your promise!" shouted Falsehood. "Give me that ox or I will have you beaten."

Reluctantly, the herdsman handed over the ox, and it was taken for slaughter. When Truth's son returned and asked what had happened to his ox, the herdsman apologized and explained what happened. He offered to let Truth's son take one of Falsehood's cattle as recompense.

"Nonsense!" exclaimed Truth's son. "Where is an ox like mine? That ox was so large that its tail could reach the delta if it stood in the South. Its horns were as wide as the Nile, and I must have one like it."

Astonished, the herdsman protested. "That is not at all what I remember your ox was like," he responded.

"Nevertheless, those are the facts, and I will take you to the court of the Nine gods," Truth's son replied.

So Falsehood and Truth's son journeyed to come before the Nine gods, and Truth's son laid before them how great and mighty was his ox, how huge, how fine its pelt was. The gods deliberated among themselves for a few moments before turning back to the boy.

"Surely there is some mistake, for we have never seen an ox of that size or nature."

"And where, O gods have you seen a knife with a blade made of rarest metal, with a handle of Lebanon cedar, with the finest leather with an inscription of a god? Judge therefore between the brothers Truth and Falsehood once again, for I am Truth's son, and I have come to avenge him."

The gods, who remembered everything, turned to Falsehood. "What shall we do then?" asked the gods.

"In Ra's name, if Truth still lives, then let me suffer his fate to which I once condemned him," he replied, thinking that Truth had been devoured by lions.

Truth's son added, "Yes, if Truth is alive, then let Falsehood suffer everything that my father suffered. Let him be beaten and mistreated, let him be blinded, and his property taken. Let him be made a servant."

The gods agreed, and a messenger was sent to look for Truth, who found him in the great lady's house in the mountains. He was brought to the court, where Falsehood realized with horror that his brother still lived. His sight was struck from him, and he was made into a servant.

Truth was given all of Falsehood's property, and was raised to his former rank. He could then marry the great love of his life. The gods restored his sight and renewed the youthfulness of both he and his wife. They named Truth's son "Loyalty," and gave him the lands of his mother. When his parents had passed into the west, Loyalty became the richest man in the Two Lands, save for the pharaoh.

OPPOSITE: Bas relief of an Egyptian herdsman and his ox.

THE BOOK OF THOTH

Once in the ancient days of Egypt lived a man named Setna, who was the greatest of all magicians, until his son, Se-Osiris was born and took his place as the wisest of all.

Setna was not like other men, who spent their time hunting, fishing, or fighting, for sport. Rather, Setna loved to spend his time reading books, studying ancient magic, and gathering the secret knowledge of magicians. His studies led him to decipher ancient writing on temple walls, and he was the quickest scribe. He knew hundreds of hieroglyphs, and none knew more than he. Because he knew writing, he learned spells that not even the priests could read.

One day, he was reading an ancient scroll in the halls of the great library. He chanced upon a story of a Pharaoh's son, Naneferkaptah, who was also a scribe and great magician, and who was even wiser than Setna, because he had read the Book of Thoth and learned the language of beasts and birds. Setna grew excited as he read, for he, too, wanted to possess the knowledge of the Book of Thoth. He learned that the book had been buried in the scribe's tomb in Memphis. Once he finished the scroll, he knew that he would never be satisfied until he had found it and learned all the magic and wisdom in it. But he knew he would need help in such and undertaking, so he took his brother and said, "Help me find the Book of Thoth, for I would rather die than live without its knowledge. It will be a perilous quest, but you are the only one I trust to go with me."

His brother, Anherru, agreed to travel with him and stay with him no matter what danger they faced. They made ready their horses and chariots and rode to Memphis. It was not very hard for Setna to find the tomb of Naneferkaptah, for he was exceedingly wise. They went to the central chamber where the scribe's body lay in death. It was still wrapped in its linens. Although the sight of a body might have scared others, what was truly frightening to behold were two ghostly figures standing on the stone sarcophagus. They were the Kas of a young woman and boy. Although Setna quivered in fear, he bowed reverently to them, for behind them, laying on the breast of Naneferkaptah, was the Book of Thoth. He spoke up.

"May Osiris keep you, Naneferkaptah, and whoever accompanies you in death. I am Setna,

OPPOSITE: The ibis-headed god Thoth.

the priest of Ptah, son of Rameses the Pharaoh, and I have searched for that very book that lies on your body. Please let me take it in peace and learn all its wisdom, for I have neither the heart nor the strength to take it by force or magic."

But the Ka of the woman replied, "Do not take the Book of Thoth. It will bring you more trouble than you can possibly imagine, and you will live to regret it. Listen to me and my tale, and I will explain. I am Ahura, the wife of Naneferkaptah, and this is not his Ka but the Ka of our son, Merab."

Then Setna and his brother settled themselves into the sand as Ahura told her tale.

"My beloved husband was like you—he searched the world over for magic, for knowledge, and for words of power. He wanted to learn every spell on the temple walls, within tombs, and within pyramids of kings. One day, he was studying a scroll to learn what ancient magic it contained, in the temple of one of the ancient gods. But a priest walked up and laughed at him mockingly. He said, 'You waste your time on worthless scrolls like that. There is another work far more important and magical called the Book of Thoth, which the god of wisdom wrote with his own hand with ink of his own blood. When you read its first page, you will learn how to control the heavens and the earth to do your bidding. When you read the second page, you will be able to control the mountains and seas and enchant the birds of the air and speak with them and also the beasts of the earth and reptiles of the sea. When you read the third page, your eyes will be opened, and you will know all the secrets of the gods and know how to read the hidden wisdom of the stars. I could tell you where that book is.'

"Naneferkaptah was, of course, enchanted by the idea. He replied, 'By all that is holy, tell me where it is. I will pay any price, do anything that you request, for I must have that book.'

"The priest said, 'All I ask is one hundred bars of silver and to have me buried like a king when I die.'

"Immediately, Naneferkaptah gave the priest the silver. When it had exchanged hands, the priest said, 'The Book of Thoth lies at the bottom of the Nile River at Koptos, locked within a series of boxes. The outer box is made of iron and within that a box of bronze; within that is a box of sycamore, then an ivory, then ebony box. Within the ebony box is a silver box, and finally within the silver is a box of solid gold. It is guarded by a serpent who cannot be slain, and its minions are smaller snakes and scorpions who surround the box on all sides.'

"Despite such a dire pronouncement, my husband leapt with joy and hurried back to our house to tell me what he had learned. But I warned him to forget the Book of Thoth, for I greatly feared some evil would come of this mad pursuit of power and magic. 'Please do not leave your family in search of this book, for I know that it will bring sorrow to us all.'

"But he did not listen. He hurried to the Pharaoh and asked for a royal boat to carry him, our son, and myself to Koptos. So, we sailed up the Nile until we came to that wretched town. The priests and the priestesses of Isis knew of our arrival and welcomed us to the Temple. Naneferkaptah sacrificed his best ox and a fine, fat goose, and the best wine. Then we feasted with the priests and priestesses that night and for the next four nights.

"But on the morning of the fifth day, my husband walked down to the river and waved his wand and spoke an enchantment over the waters. First, he created men from the mud of the river and made them work, digging in the sand at the bottom of the river until they had found the book. They toiled for five days and five nights until they found the iron box that contained the Book of Thoth. They raised it to the banks of the river, where it was still guarded by snakes and scorpions, and the great serpent that could not be slain. When the snakes and scorpions struck the mud men, they simply fell away into dust once more.

"So Naneferkaptah cried a great word of power, and all the lesser snakes and scorpions became still and could not move a single muscle.

"Finally, Naneferkaptah walked until he faced the huge serpent that could not die. It curled around the box until it saw my husband;

ABOVE: Ptah statuette; **OPPOSITE:** Statue of Ramses II.

then, it reared up, ready to strike. No charm or word of power could be used against it, so Naneferkaptah tried to kill it with a sword. He swung and struck off its head with one blow. Immediately, the head and body of the snake fused itself together again. Once more, Naneferkaptah struck off its head and threw it far away into the Nile, but once more, the head and body fused together, and it bared its fangs, ready to fight. Finally, Naneferkaptah swung his sword and sliced its head off, but before they could join together, he scrubbed sand on each part so that when the two pieces tried to come together, they simply slid off. The serpent thus lay helpless.

"Walking among the now-harmless snakes and scorpions, my husband opened the series of boxes—the iron, bronze, sycamore, ivory, ebony, silver, and finally, gold. Within was the Book of Thoth, and he rejoiced to find it. He opened it and read the first page, and immediately had power over the heavens and earth; he read the next page and could enchant the mountains and seas and gained knowledge of the speech of animals; he read the third page and divined the secrets of the gods and could read the stars.

"Immediately, he rejoiced at the power he now had. He commanded his workmen to take him back to Koptos, where I waited for him, neither eating nor drinking for fear of what might befall him. When my husband returned, he gave the book to me, and I read its pages as well and learned the knowledge he had. Then

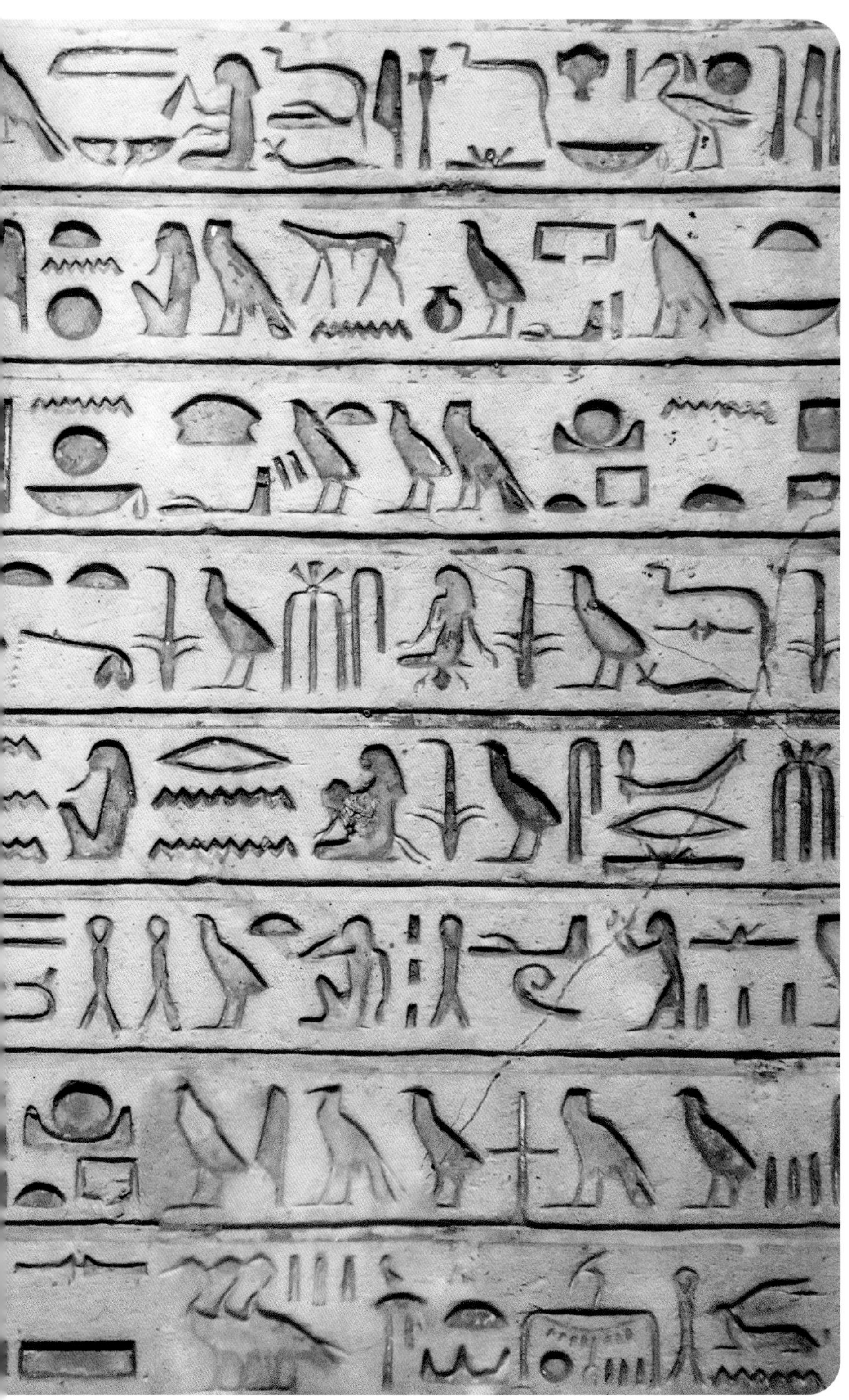

ABOVE: Hieroglyphics; **OPPOSITE:** The god Thoth as baboon.

Naneferkaptah took a piece of papyrus and wrote all the spells in the best ink. Then he placed the papyrus in a cup of beer so that the ink washed off into the liquid. He drank the beer so that the knowledge of the magic entered his very being. I cannot write and cannot remember all the spells, for they were many and difficult to learn.

"We left Koptos and set sail for Memphis. But we had barely begun our voyage when a terrible power seized our little son, and he was pulled into the river and sank to the bottom. Immediately, Naneferkaptah read from the Book of Thoth to raise Merab's body from the water, but not even the magic and power contained in the book could bring him back to life. Still, he could make his Ka speak and commanded it to tell him what had happened. The Ka of Merab said that Thoth had learned that his book had been stolen and his guards had been slain, so he had gone to Ra to ask for justice. Ra had replied that he would punish the thief, his wife, and child.

"We lamented long and hard for our child, for our hearts were broken at his death. We embalmed him and gave him all the necessary rites for his soul to pass on. When he was properly buried, we sailed back to Memphis to tell the Pharaoh all that had passed. But when we came to the spot where Merab had died, the power of Ra pulled me into the river, and I drowned as well. My husband had my body embalmed and buried me in the tomb beside our son.

"He left, once again, for Memphis. When the ship reached the city, the pharaoh himself came aboard to welcome him back. But all he found was Naneferkaptah lying dead, with the Book of Thoth on his breast. He was buried with all the rites as fit a son of Pharaoh. His body remains in this tomb, where my Ka and Merab's Ka watch over him for all time.

"Now you know all the evil that came from reading that wretched book," she said. "You ask for that book, but it is not yours to claim. I tell you, turn away from this place and never look back."

Now Setna had listened to the entire tale, and he was astonished to learn what had happened to the family, but his desire to have the Book of Thoth and all its secrets was so powerful that he declared, "Give me the book, or I will take it by force."

Then the Ka of Naneferkaptah rose from his body and stepped toward Setna. He said, "If you will not heed my wife's warning, then the Book of Thoth is yours. All you must do is win it in a game of draughts with me. It will be until fifty-two points. Each time you lose, you will sink a little bit into the ground, until your head is completely covered. Do you dare play?"

Setna replied, "I am ready."

A board was conjured from the air, and the game commenced.

Naneferkaptah won the first game, and so Setna sank into the ground to his ankles. When he also won the second game, Setna sank to his waist. The third game made Setna sink all the way to his chin.

Setna then cried out, "Brother! Run to Pharaoh and ask him for the amulet of Ptah, for only by that can I be saved, if you place it on my head before the last game is played and lost."

So Anherru ran with all his strength to Memphis to beg the sacred amulet from Pharaoh, where it was held in great reverence at the temple. The Pharaoh gave it, saying, "Go quickly, and rescue your brother."

So he sped back to Saqqara where his brother still played the dark game with the Ka of Naneferkaptah. Even as he stepped inside the tomb, Setna made his last move that would sink him forever out of sight. But Anherru ran to his brother and placed the amulet on his head. As soon as it touched Setna, he sprang from the ground, snatched The Book of Thoth, and they both ran as fast as they could out of the tomb. As they left, they heard the cries of the Ka, "You will bring back the Book of Thoth, and come begging to my tomb with a forked stick in your hand, and a fire-pan on your head!"

Then the tomb slammed shut behind them, as if it had never opened. When Setna told his father, the pharaoh, all that had passed, Rameses told him to return the book, for fear of the evil that might come to pass because of it. Setna did not heed this advice. He returned to his home and pored over the spells in the book, studying until the morning light broke over the horizon. He read from it often, and people sought him out for its wisdom.

One day, as he sat in the shade of the temple, he saw a maiden enter, accompanied by fifty-two girls. The maiden was more beautiful than any he had ever seen. She wore a headdress of gold and bright jewels that sparkled in the sun. She was called Tabubua, and she was a priestess of Bastet. As soon as he laid eyes on her, it was as if Hathor had cast a love spell over him. He forgot about everything, even his beloved book, in his desire for her. He wrote her a message, asking to allow him to share a bed of divine

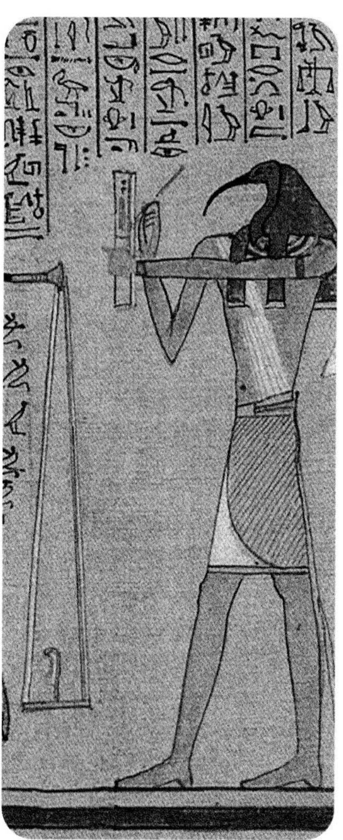

ABOVE: Thoth recording the judgment of the dead; **OPPOSITE:** Small statuette of ibis-headed god Thoth.

ecstasy with him. He forgot about his wife and his devotion to her. She replied that he could come as he pleased, but only to her palace in the desert in Bubastis, city of Bastet. He went to meet her there immediately, and she brought him to her chamber and served him wine from a golden cup. He announced his love and devotion to her and begged her to sleep with him.

She answered, "I will allow this, but I am no common woman to be used and discarded. If you want me, we must be wed. But as a daughter of Bastet, I suffer no rivals. Therefore, you must divorce your wife, and you must slay your children to ensure that they will not plot against me in their jealousy."

"It is done!" he cried. He took out his brush and ink and wrote that Tabubua would be his wife, that he would divorce his current wife, and his children would be slain and fed to the sacred cats of Bastet. When he had signed his name, Tabubua handed him the wine to drink, and she took off her garments, until nothing was left except a sheer dress that displayed all her loveliness.

From the window in her palace, Setna heard the cries of his children as they were slain. He turned to her and said, "My wife is cast aside, and my children have been given to you and your goddess. Come, let us lie together."

Then the priestess of Bastet walked toward him, more desirable with each step she took. Setna embraced her on their marriage bed, but as soon as he did, Tabubua let out an unholy shriek and changed; all the life energy fled her, until she was nothing more than a horrible, hideous corpse. Setna gasped in terror, and all at once, darkness enveloped him. When he awoke, he was naked, lying in the desert beside the road that led to Memphis. Everyone who passed laughed at him and mocked him.

When he reached his home, he found his wife and children alive and quite well. He was so happy to see them whole and healthy that he vowed to never stray again and to return the Book of Thoth to the tomb, for he knew that the sorcery of Tabubua was a warning of what might befall him. When he told the Pharaoh Rameses what he intended to do, he said, "Make haste then, and go in humility, with a forked stick in your hand and a fire-pan on your head."

Setna then returned to the tomb, exactly as the Pharaoh had advised. The tomb opened from within, and he found the Kas of Ahura and Merab, as they had been before. He laid the Book of Thoth on the body of their husband. When he did, the Ka of Naneferkaptah rose from his body and said, "Did I not say that you would return here? You have restored the Book of Thoth to its rightful place, but you are not free of my wrath, nor the wrath of the gods yet. If you do not do what I command, all that passed under Tabubua's sorcery will be made into reality."

"What must I do?" asked Setna, bowing low into the sand. "Only tell me, and I will do it immediately."

The Ka of Naneferkaptah answered, "It is but a small request. My body lies here, but the bodies of Ahura and Merab are in a separate tomb, at Koptos. Bring their bodies here, so that we may be reunited in death, until Osiris returns to reign on Earth forever. We will finally be able to be at peace."

Setna set off at once to ask the Pharaoh for his blessing to use the Royal boat to sail to Koptos. When he arrived, he went immediately to the temple of Isis and Horus, to make sacrifices to them, to bless him in his endeavor. Then he asked the priests where he could go to find the bodies of Ahura and Merab. Although they searched in the records of the temple, they

MAIN IMAGE: Limestone slab depicting Hapi.

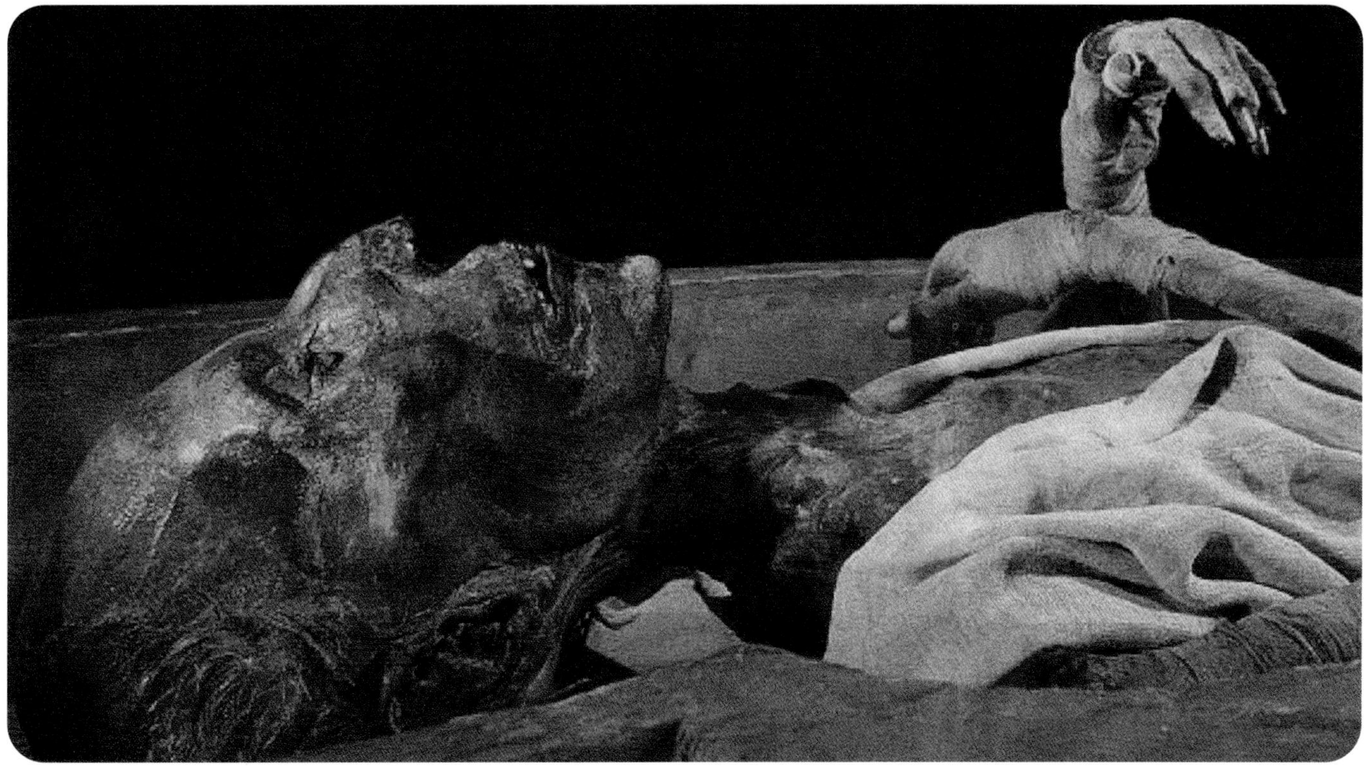

ABOVE: The exposed mummy of Ramses II; **OPPOSITE:** Egyptian relief carving of Thoth and hieroglypics.

could find no reference to their names. Setna left the temple filled with despair. He offered a huge reward to anyone who knew where they were buried, but none could help. However, an old man approached him, shuffling, and stooped with age. He said, "I know where Ahura and Merab are buried. Keep your reward, for you will soon have need of it." With a wave of his hand, the old man bade Setna to follow him.

Soon they came to a house on the very edge of the city. "They are buried beneath the foundation. You will have to tear down the house and dig beneath it."

And so Setna bought the house for a great deal of money from the owner. After, he paid laborers to tear down the house and dig into the very foundation. When they did so, they encountered rock and stone. This was the tomb of Ahura and Merab. They cut away the stone, and Setna found their bodies. With a cry of wonder and delight, the old man lifted his arms, then faded from sight. Setna realized then that it had been the Ka of Naneferkaptah in the guise of an old man.

Setna took the mummies of Ahura and Mera and bore them back to the Royal Boat with all the honors and rites that befitted royalty, as if they had been a queen and king of Egypt. When they reached Memphis, the Pharaoh himself led the funeral procession to Saqqara, and finally, Setna buried the bodies alongside Naneferkaptah, where the Book of Thoth was still on his breast.

After the funeral procession had dispersed, Setna spoke a magic spell over the tomb. The doors closed, leaving no trace of its existence. Then Setna spoke magic over the sand, and it heaped itself over the entrance, and soon, a sandstorm arose, nearly blinding them. After it passed, the tomb was so covered that it would be impossible to find it again. There the Book of Thoth remains, until the Day of Awakening, when Osiris shall return to rule forever.

THE CUNNING GENERAL

The pharaoh Tuthmosis III, was victorious in all his wars, winning to the north and east, expanding Egypt's boundaries, and adding much glory to his name.

ABOVE: Thuthmosis; **OPPOSITE:** Djehuty and his Mother Receiving Offerings, Tomb of Djehuty.

It came to his attention that an officer had more courage and ferocity in fighting than any other of his soldiers. This officer's name was Djehuty, and it seemed that he was blessed by the gods, for he always emerged victorious in fighting.

One day, the Prince of Joppa rose in rebellion against Egypt, slaying all the Egyptian soldiers, and announcing that his allegiance to the pharaoh was over. Joppa was a city in a very strategic position, which lay directly along the supply routes, and thus was a great worry to Tuthmosis. He and his forces would be trapped unless his counsellors could figure out a solution. They gathered in the royal tent to discuss the problem. Djehuty spoke up. "Great pharaoh, it is true that you possess a magical staff, which has been in your family's possession for generations. It is said that this staff is a powerful talisman, blessed by the gods, and that he who wields it is granted the power to become any person or thing, even becoming invisible."

"It is true, General," replied the Pharaoh. "But how will that help us now?"

"If you lend me that staff, and a force of two hundred men, I will conquer the city of Joppa and slay the prince," he replied. Tuthmosis agreed, only for the confidence of his general, for the staff had indeed belonged to his house for hundreds of years. So, carefully unwrapping the ancient relic, he gave it to his general. Djehuty bowed and departed and gathered two hundred of the pharaoh's troops. He then tasked a craftsman to prepare a large bag of animal skins, two pairs of shackles, cuffs, yokes, and several lengths of rope. When all was ready, they set out for the city of Joppa. The other soldiers in the pharaoh's army wondered why this group set out so oddly equipped. They sat on donkeys with large urns strapped to their backs. They marched swiftly to Joppa and reached it within three days. When the city was within sight, Djehuty ordered his men to make camp, and then he called on the magical staff to disguise him as a humble messenger. In this form he made his way into the city.

The Prince of Joppa was alarmed to see a group of Egyptian soldiers near his city. He expected the Egyptians to demand full and immediate surrender, but the humble

messenger bore a different letter. The prince cut the seal of the scroll and began to read. The message said, "Prince of Joppa, I am the General Djehuty, risen through the ranks and famed on the field of battle. I was once the military counselor to Tuthmosis of Egypt but am no longer. The Pharaoh raised me in his ranks, but he grew jealous of my skill on the battlefield. He would not listen to any of my strategies or counsel and so he resolved to fire me. I accepted my fate with honor, but he plotted to kill me with poison. Thus, I renounce my allegiance to the coward and traitor that is Tuthmosis and offer instead my services to you and the City of Joppa. As a token of my good faith, I will present you with the pharaoh's own magical talisman, in the form of a staff, which I stole from him by guile."

The Prince of Joppa was astonished at the letter and quickly commanded his scribe to pen a reply. The prince accepted the general's offer, and promised him all the land, titles, and wealth that he could provide. He handed the reply to the messenger who was Djehuty in disguise, who then bowed and made his way back to the encampment outside the city. The next morning the Prince of Joppa set out to meet with Djehuty. He took his personal bodyguards with him, for his was very eager to meet with the daring warrior-turned-ally and eager to receive the magical staff.

Djehuty welcomed the ruler and invited him into his tent to dine. Though the food was the humble fair of soldiers, the prince and general soon got along well. After a few hours, the prince brought up the magical staff. "Thank you for your generous offer of such a talisman," said the prince. "I am very anxious to see what wonders it can do."

"It is yours, my prince," replied Djehuty, sending a soldier to fetch it. When he had returned, the prince regarded it skeptically.

"Is that plain stick the magical staff you spoke of?" he asked.

"Yes, but to demonstrate its power, I must raise it above my head," said the General. And so, Djehuty raised the staff, and before the prince could even blink or cry for his

MAIN IMAGE, TOP: The Greek story of the Trojan Horse has many similariities to *The Cunning General* tale; **ABOVE:** General Djehuty's gold bracelet; **OPPOSITE:** Thusmosis; **TOP, RIGHT:** Taking Joppa; **TOP:** Golden bowl of Djehuty.

bodyguards, the general brought it down on his head with such force that the prince fell senseless to the ground. He then stuffed the unconscious prince into the large skin bag, shackling his hands and feet. He used the staff's power to turn himself into the shape and appearance of the Prince of Joppa. He then called for one of the bodyguards, who immediately came into the tent. He gestured to the skin bag. "I have overpowered and bound the treacherous Djehuty, whose true intent it was to slay me. I wager that the cowardly Egyptians have fled." They all exited the tent to find nary a single Egyptian soldier left.

The guards of Joppa were amazed by their ruler's cunning and strength. Djehuty pointed to the donkeys. "See those heavily laden donkeys? The general told me that they bear treasure from the northern cities. Take them into the city as my tribute. Tell the keeper of the gate that Djehuty is conquered and that he must stand ready to open the gates to receive the bounty of my vanquished foe."

And so, a procession set forth from the Egyptian encampment. Djehuty, still disguised, led the company, and the prince was still in a sack strapped to a donkey behind him. The guards followed as they led two hundred donkeys each bearing two large urns. When they arrived, the gatekeeper opened the gates to the city and let them all in—guards, Djehuty, donkeys, and all. As the gates closed behind them, Djehuty said, "Let us now open the jars which are filled with gold and treasure and rejoice in our victory." At his command, the two hundred jars were opened, and two hundred armed Egyptian warriors sprang out. Djehuty abandoned his disguise, slashed open the bag that held the true prince, and cried to the soldiers of Joppa, "Surrender now, or I will strike the head from your prince's body." At his words, the warriors fell to their knees and surrendered.

With the yokes, shackles, and rope, the soldiers of the Pharaoh bound their captives while Djehuty climbed to the tallest tower and raised the standard of Amun-Ra, the patron god of Egypt. The general sent a message to the camp of the Pharaoh and said, "Lord of the Two Lands, I have captured the Prince of Joppa, and all his soldiers are my prisoners. Let them pass into your house as slaves, and let Amun-Ra, your father, the god of gods, have glory forever."

The Pharaoh Tuthmosis praised the ingenuity of his cunning general and showered him with titles and lands and raised him to the status of a noble. Thus, Djehuty prospered and lived a very long life.

The Pharaoh Rameses was the most powerful ruler of Egypt and all its surrounding lands. Many lesser kings offered gifts to the Pharaoh in hopes of attracting his good favor.

THE PRINCESS AND THE DEMON

They offered all sorts of spectacular gifts, from precious stones, gold, lapis lazuli, incense, and beautiful carvings. Among those who wanted to present an offering to the pharaoh was the king of Bakhtan, a small kingdom. He wished to gain the support of the pharaoh because armies were constantly threatening his land. But he was a poor king, with no jewels or gold to offer. How could he compete with the other kings vying for the attention of the Pharaoh?

He struck upon an idea that he did have something of great value to offer the Lord of the Two Lands. He had twin daughters, who loved each other dearly. He thought that surely the pharaoh would fall in love with one of them. He could not bear to send both, as they were the light of his eyes and the pride of his heart, so he decided to send his eldest daughter to Egypt. When the sisters heard that they would be separated, they wept and were inconsolable. The eldest told her younger sister that if she ever needed help, to send a message. She then set forth with her royal accompaniment to the land in the south.

It was a very difficult journey. The party had to pass through mountains, wastelands of nothing but sand, and fierce bandits roamed the deserts, waiting for hapless victims to attack. The princess desperately wished for her sister and missed her homeland, but she set her chin straight and upright and had courage. Finally, the royal party made it to Egypt. The princess was shown to the best rooms of the city, filled with sweet perfumes and she was kept in comfort and safety. Eventually, she was summoned to the throne room of the Pharaoh, and as she walked through the endless corridors of the palace, she trembled with nervousness. However, when she looked at the Pharaoh, she instantly fell in love. Rameses commanded that she lift her veil and look at him directly. As soon as she did so, he was astonished to see her radiant beauty. Never his all his life had he seen such loveliness and the pharaoh swore that she would be his wife above all others. Thus, Ramses married the princess and made her queen, calling her Neferure, which means "Beauty of Ra."

ABOVE: The mummy mask of Khonsu; **OPPOSITE:** Khonsu the Expeller.

A year passed, and the happy couple lived in peace and contentment. During the Opet festival, a messenger pushed his way through the crowds and demanded an audience with the pharaoh. He was so insistent that he was brought before the king. He spoke strangely, his voice accented with the pattern of Bakhtan. Neferure gave him wine from her own cup and asked him to present his message.

"Oh Queen, it concerns your sister, Bentresh. Even now, it might be too late. The princess would not be consoled, and she wept for your loss. There could be no cure to her melancholy. Not long after you left, a wild demon from the mountains descended upon her and took hold of her body. She wailed and thrashed in the demon's grip. The king of Bakhtan summoned his wisest magicians and healers but none could help her. So, he sent me in desperation, hoping that the Pharaoh's physicians are better equipped and skilled in such matters."

The Pharaoh immediately summoned his best doctor, in his love for Neferure. The doctor's name was Tehuti-em-heb, and he was known as a master of the arts of medicine and magic. He set off for the kingdom in the north, not pausing any longer than necessary. He found Princess Bentresh writhing on her bed, still in the grip of the demon. He then burned sweet-smelling herbs to draw out the demon. He also raised his magic wand, in preparation for battle with the evil demon. The demon began to ooze from the poor princess and raged against the magician. All through the night, they fought fiercely, neither gaining the upper hand. But the demon exhausted Tehuti-em-heb so thoroughly that he was near death. He had to flee the room, and once again, the demon took possession of Bentresh.

Tehuti-em-heb stood before the king and told him that the power of the demon was so great that he could not defeat it. He could only hope to limit its evil influence, but he advised the king to send a message to the pharaoh, relating all that he had said. When the messenger reached Egypt, Queen Neferure despaired at the plight of her sister. She vowed to make a great sacrifice at the altar of the moon god, Khonsu. So, she and the pharaoh made their way to the sanctuary of Khonsu, son of Amun-Ra. They passed down the main road and entered the mighty temple. The pharaoh and his queen then purified themselves with holy water and put on clothes that had never been worn before. They passed into the interior of Khonsu's shrine. With a flourish, the pharaoh poured a libation offering at the altar and spoke the magical words and prayers to summon him. Then a great voice rose to greet him.

"Greetings Rameses and Neferure. Why do you seek me?"

Neferure replied, "Mighty god, will you please aid my sister, Bentresh, who suffers the affliction of a demon?"

"I will," replied Khonsu. "But first, you must do this one thing. Bring the image of myself as Khonsu the Contriver, so that I may instil the statue with my power. Then send that statue with your magician to battle the demon."

And so, the pharaoh commanded that Khonsu's statue in the form of a falcon be brought to the temple. The statue was found, and Khonsu imbued it with his power. The priests transported it through the mountains and wastelands to Bakhtan, then carried it into the room of Princess Bentresh. There, they burned incense and sprinkled holy water. Bentresh writhed in her bed, and her body was soaked with sweat as the demon was called forth. Rising from the statue was the ka of Khonsu, who challenged the demon to fight. The light of the moon penetrated the horrible darkness of the demon, and the demon shrieked in pain and rage as they fought. The cloud of darkness finally dissipated, until the demon revealed its true form as a hunched, hideous man.

"I am defeated," said the demon. "By the great Khonsu. Bakhtan is now yours, as I take my leave. I am your slave forever."

"Leave this land then and disturb it no more," commanded the god of the moon.

TOP : Statue Of Senenmut And Neferura; **ABOVE:** The Bentresh Stella or Bakhtan Stella, the Egyptian sandstone stela with an hieroglyphic text telling the story of Bentresh, daughter of the prince of Bakhtan; **OPPOSITE:** Ramesseum.

Thus, the demon fled at once, and Bentresh was restored to health. There were many celebrations, and the king of Bakhtan begged for the statue to be kept in his kingdom. For three years, the statue remained. However, when the time came for the statue to return to its rightful place in Egypt, the king of Bakhtan said, "Let it be known that Khonsu is the one who expelled the demon from my daughter and thus should be called 'Expeller of Demons.'"

The Egyptians lined up in a long procession to take the statue back to the Land of Two Kingdoms. The whole population of the country came out to watch. People brought gifts to the king of Bakhtan, who grew rich with the wealth they brought. And so Queen Neferure returned with her husband to Egypt, and never went a year without seeing her sister at least once. The statue of Khonsu was placed inside his shrine, and was named Khonsu the Expeller.

THE RATS OF MEMPHIS

The pharaoh Seti was a priest of Ptah, and rose to become the king. He did not forget the benevolence of his patron deity and moved his capital to Memphis, the cult center of Ptah.

He was a pious man, and the beginning of his reign was marked by many festivals and sacrifices. As pious as he was, though, he did not listen to his subjects, who were going hungry in the face of so many sacrifices, nor did he heed the words of his soldiers, who warned him of the approaching armies. The army of Assyria swept through the land and was so strong that none of the armies of the surrounding lands of Egypt could fight. Soon, all the generals and leaders of the surrounding lands sent sacrifices and tributes to the king of Assyria. Only Egypt remained out of his grasp. Because of the Pharaoh's many sacrifices to Ptah the Egyptian army became demoralized and hungry: they surrendered and would not fight. When Seti heard of this, he wept in despair, for he knew that his mistreatment of his people had led to this downfall. He walked to the temple of Ptah and laid face-down in the dust and prayed to his god. He prayed all day, all night, and all the following day. Finally, he fell into a deep sleep from his exhaustion. As he slept, Seti dreamed of Ptah who began to speak to him.

"Do not be afraid," said Ptah. "You have always been my faithful servant. I will not depart from you. Know by my hand, that this crisis will be averted."

"But Lord," said Seti. "Egypt is defenseless. My armies have fled from me. The hordes of the king of Assyria are coming ever closer."

"Take up the Blue Crown of War," answered Ptah. "Gather your guards. Ride against the Assyrians. You will be triumphant."

Seti awoke in the temple, his face still pressed against the granite floor. He smiled, knowing that what Ptah had said was true. His courage thus rallied, he called for his guards to ready themselves and their horses for battle. He clothed himself in royal robes of the warrior and fixed the Blue Crown on his head. The number of men who followed him were less than two hundred, yet they followed him all the same. Seti climbed into his chariot and began to ride toward the Assyrians. Upon seeing their king thus clothed, his face shining with courage, everyone who saw him joined their pharaoh. As he rode through the streets of Memphis, every laborer, shopkeeper, farmer, and merchant

ABOVE: Statuette of Ptah; **OPPOSITE, MAIN IMAGE:** Temple frieze of the Assyrian hordes...with rats.

joined him with any weapon they could find. They, too, wanted to defend their land against the invaders. Soon the forces of the Assyrians reached the walls of the city. Thousands of them surrounded the city and they settled in for the night, not attacking but simply waiting for the clear light of dawn. That night, Seti paced in his tent, wondering if he had made a ghastly error. Was he unwise to trust the words of a dream? Was he risking his entire kingdom? Only time would tell.

As light broke over the sky, the Assyrians still did not attack. Rather, shouts of worry rose from the enemy camp. Seti thus climbed into his chariot to see the state of the Assyrian army. He ordered the city gate to be opened and he went to explore the situation. He came upon an amazing sight. The Assyrian army had awoken to find their weapons completely destroyed. The straps of their armor were broken; the strings to their bows were chewed through, and the reins of their horses were broken as well. All was useless. Immediately, Seti attacked with his small army. The Assyrians had no choice but to flee or fight without weapons. Choosing life, many fled, although a few brave ones stood their ground, and were slain. Of those who survived, some were taken as slaves. The king of Assyria had already fled, as he could not rule without an army. Later that day, everyone rejoiced at the good fortune of Seti. The Egyptians were saved, and there was great triumph through their camp. Seti sat content in his tent, giving thanks to Ptah. But he wanted to know how it was that the army's weapons and equipment had broken down. He commanded his guards to bring a slave from the Assyrian camp. His guards then brought a captured Assyrian, and he fell before the Pharaoh, begging for his life. Seti ordered the Assyrian to tell him what had happened in his camp. The servant said, "O Great Pharaoh, merciful as you are wise, we all thought that victory was in our hands. We knew of your pitiful forces and knew that you had not a chance to resist the might of the Assyrian king."

Seti motioned for the slave to continue.

"We all lay down in our tents for the night. But then, in the middle of the night, when the moon was highest in the sky, a strange rustling sound met our ears. From the brush, the fields, the marshes, and all the canals, came forth rats. Rats in such numbers as you would not believe, of all shapes and sizes. They did not care that there were men trying to trample them underfoot. They infested every tent, every cot, chewing and nibbling whatever they could get their teeth into. They gnawed on bowstrings, on every armor strap, on every chariot tackle. They left nothing but scraps of leather, useless for anything except to be thrown out. We had no way to defend ourselves, nothing."

The slave finished and bowed before the Pharaoh. Seti spared the slave's life and sent him away. He and his army packed up and returned to their beloved city of Memphis, where crowds greeted him with shouts of joy and acclamation. After a time, Seti went to the temple of Ptah to give thanks again for the army of rats that had saved him, his kingdom, and all the people in it. He swore that he would be a better ruler, to listen to his people, and to give them what they needed.

ABOVE: The Blue Crown of War; **OPPOSITE:** Pyramid of Djoser at Saqqara, Memphis.

THE SECRETS OF THOTH

Long, long ago, there lived a great pharaoh by the name of Khufu, who was called "The Living Horus." His father had just passed into the land of the west, and so Khufu held a large feast in his honor.

Everyone gathered in his large palace in Heliopolis, the City of the Sun. Khufu's feast was splendid with musicians and dancers, and many tales were told. Khufu commanded each of his three sons to tell a story to entertain their guests.

The first was Prince Khafre. He told a story of a marvel that happened long ago, during the reign of King Nebka. It was a tale of a priest of Ptah and his adulterous wife. The priest called on the names of Ra, Ptah, and Sobek. When the prince invoked Sobek, a fierce crocodile emerged from the Nile, no less than fourteen feet in length, and caught the cheating wife and her consort and dragged them into the river. Thus, with magic did the priest take revenge.

When he was done, everyone in the court applauded, for the story was well told, full of magic and wonder. The next brother rose from the table. The Prince Baufra told the story of the King Sneferu and how he had suffered from incurable sadness. His scribe was summoned to cure him. He told of how the trusted scribe commanded that a magnificent boat be prepared, crewed by only the most beautiful of maidens and dressed in the finest clothes and jewelry. When one of the maidens lost a headpiece, she was despondent and would not row until the magician-scribe called on the name of Hapi, the Nile god. He parted the waters with magic, retrieved the lost headpiece, and made the waters form into a whole once again.

Everyone was enchanted with the tale, which they said was even better than the last. Finally, it was the third prince's turn. Prince Horbaef stood up and said, "Thank you, brothers, for your fine tales, which are glorious fictions of the past."

This earned the prince glares from his other brothers. "Who can say if they are true or false?" they replied. "There is no one left alive who witnessed the marvels."

"Indeed, but my story is true, for it takes place not in the past but right here, right now, in Egypt," replied Prince Horbaef. Everyone held their breath as they waited for the prince to continue. He said, "There lives a man far

ABOVE: Statuette of Khufu; **OPPOSITE:** Thoth.

away to the south whose power in magic is so great that he can raise the dead to life. He can tame lions and all sorts of wild creatures. He lacks for nothing, even though he lives in a desert. He consumes no less than a thousand loaves of bread per day and drinks one hundred flasks of beer. He physically satisfies the ladies of his extensive harem, even though he is one hundred and ten years old. But more than this, he possesses the secrets of Thoth. He has the knowledge needed to complete the greatest pyramid of all time—which you desire to build, Father."

The two other brothers cried out in protest at these ridiculous claims. "We demand proof!"

The Pharaoh Khufu was a wise pharaoh, and he did not respond immediately. However, his two sons were correct. "The Princes Khafre and Baufra stand right. As you have boasted so greatly, you will equip an expedition to find this man and bring him back to my palace, so that we may see this wonderworker. Do not dare return without him."

Prince Horbaef bowed low and ignored the jeers of his brothers. The entire court was silent with wonder at the charge.

With his own money, the prince found servants, a ship, and a crew. They sailed up the Nile to the south, and the ship seemed to pass the very limits of civilization. Finally, they reached the desert that was the home of the magician.

When Prince Horbaef reached the dwelling of the magician's sumptuous house, he was brought before an old man being massaged by beautiful women dressed in fine clothes and jewelry. However, the old man did not rise or acknowledge the prince in any way, even though it was obvious from his clothes and hairstyle that he was royalty.

The prince said, "I have traveled a long way and a long time to find the one called Djedi, the great magician. I am on a mission commanded by my father, the great King Khufu."

However, the old man still did not respond or even look at the prince. The prince grew nervous and said, "I am commanded to bring you to the king, or else I will be stripped of my titles, royal status, and forbidden to return. Are you the wise and venerable Djedi?"

Finally, the old man stirred and waved his servants away. He replied, "I am he. But I am a person of most refined tastes and luxurious comforts, and the idea of traveling on a long voyage down the Nile displeases me. I am one hundred and ten years old, and my time grows short upon the earth. I'd rather not waste it on the whims of a king. He is but one in a long line of kings, who come and go, but there is only one Djedi."

The prince was shocked at his words, not only at his refusal to come but also at the disrespect to King Khufu. He tried once more, and in an effort to persuade the old man, he said, "If you come with me, all your comforts will be maintained, and you will also be richly rewarded by the king upon our arrival."

With a show of great reluctance, the magician agreed. The next day, his servants brought all his magical books and equipment to the royal boat. Djedi was carried to the royal vessel in a litter far more splendid than even the prince's. When they were on board, the magician aimed his staff at his palace, and with the whisper of a word of power, the mansion vanished, leaving only sand. Djedi then waved his hands, and a wind emerged, and quickly filled the sails so that the wind propelled them northward. It took them less than a quarter of the time to reach the capital than had the prince's initial voyage.

When they arrived, his father and brothers were deep in discussion about important matters of state.

"Did I not tell you to not come to the palace again, unless you produced the magician?" demanded Khufu. "Or have you come to beg for mercy?"

"I sought him out, and I have found the

ABOVE: Cartouche name of Nebka; **OPPOSITE:** Depiction of Khufu.

magician Djedi, and he is on his way to the palace," replied the youngest prince. At his words, the palace doors opened, and the small, wizened figure of Djedi made his way into the court of the Khufu. He walked slowly past the scribes and other administrators until he stood before the pharaoh. He inclined his head in the smallest of bows.

"I have been told that you are the greatest magician in the world," said the Pharaoh. "Yet I have never heard your name before. Why is that?"

When the magician spoke, his voice was so ancient that it creaked like the opening of a sarcophagus. "Only they on whom I call can know my name, O Pharaoh. I called to your son, who spoke of me to you, and he came to fetch me to bring me to your presence."

"My son boasted, perhaps too greatly, of you," said the pharaoh. "He claimed that you can raise the dead to life. Is this true?"

"It is," replied Djedi.

"Then prove it," commanded the Pharaoh. "For I will not believe it until I see it with my own eyes."

So Djedi commanded that a duck be brought from the marshes. It was beheaded before the entire court, and its body was placed at the west end of the hall, and its head was placed at the east. Djedi stood between the two parts of the slain bird and raised his staff. He called on Osiris, the lord of the dead, and on Isis, the goddess of magic. At once, the two pieces flew through the air and came to land at Djedi's feet, where they fused together once more. The magician clapped his hands, and the duck flapped its wings and squawked. It had been raised from the dead.

The Pharaoh was nearly delirious with rapture. "So, it is true," he said. "But what of your wisdom? My son has said that you know the secrets of Thoth, which I need to complete the greatest pyramid of all. Is this so?"

The wizened old man smiled and said, "Indeed, it is for that very purpose that I called your son to me and was brought before you. But I tell you that the secrets that you need are here within the very walls of this city, concealed in a stone chest."

"Then let us retrieve it at once!" cried the Pharaoh.

"Unfortunately, your Majesty, this cannot be so, for it is beyond your power, and even mine, to lay hands on the chest. The gods, in all their wisdom, have decreed that only the eldest of three sons of Rud-Didet can bring it to you."

"And who is Rud-Didet?" demanded Khufu.

"Rud-Didet is the wife of Ra-User, the High Priest of the sun-god Ra, and the Lord of Sakhebu. She lives in Leontopolis. However, Ra-User is not the true father of the three sons. Ra himself is, and he has decreed that the children shall reign over Egypt."

Pharaoh Khufu was deeply troubled, for it meant that the favor of the gods was leaving him. Djedi continued, "But do not be too dismayed, for Ra has also decreed that the eldest will not ascend the throne until both your son and grandson have ruled after you and passed into the land of the west. The sons of Ra are not yet born."

The pharaoh listened to the magician's words and contemplated them for several moments. Then he leaned forward on his throne and said, "Give this magician the best apartment reserved for royal guests. Make sure that his servants and women of his harem are well taken care of, and bring him one thousand loaves of bread, one hundred jars of beer, and one hundred strings of onions, and an ox each day."

The pharaoh's servants quickly did all as their king commanded. Everyone, including the pharaoh's three sons, left the court, and Khufu was left alone to contemplate the troubling news that Djedi had given him.

It came to pass that Rud-Didet became

TOP: Head of Khufu; **ABOVE:** Statue of Khafre; **OPPOSITE:** A fresco, depicting ducks and fish, from the Tomb of Nebamun, Thebes.

pregnant and bore three healthy sons. A great feast was held in Leontopolis to celebrate the event. Ra, the children's true father, commanded the goddesses Isis, Nebhat, Meskhent, and Hakt to disguise themselves as dancing girls to attend the feast. They were to be escorted by Khnum, the god of fertility, who would disguise himself as their servant. When they arrived, the feast had already started. The goddess took tambourines, cymbals, and flutes, and played them for Ra-User. They also danced for the guests, and everyone was enchanted by them, at how well they played and danced. As they sang and danced, they named the sons User-ref, Sahu-ra, and Kaku. They danced their way to the door of Ra-User, asking him to rejoice at this great fortune. In his delight, Ra-User presented the goddesses with a generous amount of barley as payment for their dancing and entertainment, not knowing their divine nature. The god Khnum placed the barley on his head and followed the women into the night.

When they were out of sight of the inhabitants of the city, the goddesses resumed their divine forms. Isis said, "I think we should also bestow upon the children our blessing in the form of a gift." The others agreed, and they made two crowns by magic—the White Crown of Upper Egypt and the Red Crown of Lower Egypt. They gave them to Khnum, who, in his guise as a servant, returned to the house of Ra-User with the crowns hidden in a sack of barley.

When he knocked on the door and Ra-User answered, Khnum said, "Greetings Lord, thank you for your generous gift of barley, but I am too weak to bear the burden of such a heavy sack. The dancing women instructed me to return it to you."

"I understand, and there is no shame upon you. However, I cannot take back what was given as a reward. Place the barley in some cellar or other. There it will be safe until the dancers return once again to grace us with their presence." So, Khnum hid the sack in a cellar of Ra-User's own house, and all the divinities left Leontopolis.

TOP LEFT: The Khufu ship, an intact full-size vessel that was sealed into a pit in the Giza pyramid complex, at the foot of the Great Pyramid of Giza, around 2500 BC. **MAIN IMAGE:** Temple of Khnum.

Time passed, and Rud-Didet one day was calculating the accounts of the house, and she enquired of her chief maid if all was accounted for in the house.

"Yes Mistress," replied the servant. "However, an extra sack of barley was found in a cellar."

"Hmm, we do need barley to make more beer," replied Rud-Didet. "Very well. Use the extra barley for brewing."

The maid hurried away to open the cellar to retrieve the sack of barley. However, when she entered the room, the air was filled with the noise and sounds of chariots, singing, talking, loud instruments, such as one might hear at the court of Pharaoh. The frightened servant fled the room and ran to tell her mistress all that happened.

Rud-Didet returned with her to the cellar and found that the servant had spoken truely. When they opened the door, once again sounds of feasting, celebration, and loud recitations of the titles of Pharaoh filled the room.

Rud-Didet immediately knew that it was an omen. She opened the sack of barley and found the two crowns. She made the servant swear to tell no one of the crowns, and placed them both in a wooden chest. This was placed inside a stone chest, which was finally placed inside a sarcophagus for safekeeping. Each chest was locked with many locks, and now, the sounds coming from the crowns was muffled enough that no one could hear them. There was little chance of their discovery, even by accident.

One day, Rud-Didet had to punish the maid for carelessness. The servant was so angry that she decided to go to the present Pharaoh and tell him all about the two hidden crowns. She packed her belongings and set out. She had not gone very far, when a terrible thirst overcame her. She made her way down to the river's edge, where she knelt to drink. Suddenly, a huge crocodile rose from the waters and seized the poor girl in its jaws and dragged her into the water to eat her. When Rud-Didet knew of the servant's fate, she knew that her three children were protected by the gods and destined to rule Egypt.

When they were older, the gods told them the secret necessary for Khufu to complete his greatest pyramid. They were summoned to court, where they revealed what the gods had shown them. Thus, Khufu was able to complete his pyramid and the peaceful succession of kings was ensured.

TOP, LEFT: Nile God Hapi;. **TOP, RIGHT:** Stela showing a male adorer standing before two Ibises of Thoth; **OPPOSITE:** The Great Pyramid of Khufu.

INDEX

CREDITS

The majority of the images in this book are in the public domain, but in all cases are courtesy of: **The Metropolitan Museum of Art**, New York City; **Shutterstock**; **Wikipedia**; and **Wikimedia Commons**. Contact Moseley Road Inc. for errors or omissions.